LAND, SEA & TIME

Book Two

LAND, SEA & TIME

Book Two

EDITORS

Edward A. Jones

Shannon M. Lewis

Pat Byrne

Boyd W. Chubbs

Clyde Rose

BREAKWATER

BREAKWATER
100 Water Street
P.O. Box 2188
St. John's, NF
A1C 6E6

Series motif by Boyd W. Chubbs, featuring Avalon *an original typeface by Boyd W. Chubbs.*

National Library of Canada Cataloguing in Publication Data

Main entry under title:

Land, sea & time

Includes indexes.
ISBN 1-55081-160-6 (v. 1).—ISBN 1-55081-175-4 (v. 2).—
ISBN 1-55081-177-0 (v. 3)

1. Canadian literature (English) — Newfoundland. 2. Canada literature (English) — 20th century. 3. Art, Modern — 20th century — Newfoundland. I. Jones, Edward, 1939-

NX513.A3N452000   C810.8'09718   C00-950054-5

Copyright © 2001 Breakwater Books Ltd.

ALL RIGHTS RESERVED. No part of this work covered by the copyright hereon may be reproduced or used in any form or by any means—graphic, electronic or mechanical—without the prior written permission of the publisher. Any request for photocopying, recording, taping or storing in an information retrieval system of any part of this book shall be directed in writing to the Canadian Reprography Collective, 6 Adelaide Street East, Suite 900, Toronto, Ontario, M5C 1H6. This applies to classroom usage as well.

Every reasonable effort has been made to find copyright holders for material contained in this book. The publishers would be pleased to have any errors or omissions brought to their attention. Credits appear on pages 297-304.

Breakwater wishes to thank the Department of Education whose cooperation on this project is much appreciated. In particular we wish to express our indebtedness to Eldred Barnes, Language Arts Consultant, all the pilot teachers and the school boards in Newfoundland and Labrador who worked with us on this educational venture. Best wishes to you all.

We acknowledge the financial support of the Government of Canada through the Book Publishing Industry Development Program (BPIDP) for our publishing activities.

Land, Sea & Time is a three-volume collection of a variety of Newfoundland and Labrador texts.

Text is defined as any language event, whether oral, written, or visual. In this sense, a conversation, a poem, a poster, a story, a photograph, a tribute, a music video, a television program, a radio documentary, and a multi-media production, for example, are all texts.

The series, *Land, Sea & Time, Book One, Book Two,* and *Book Three* offers a blend of previously neglected voices, new voices, and those often found in anthologies. Together, these books give readers an opportunity to explore the literary and cultural heritage of Newfoundland and Labrador.

The cover art for this book is a photograph by Ray Fennelly of a sculptural work created by Emily Flowers, an artist from Hopedale, Labrador. The title of the work is "My Dog." It is a mixed media involving a caribou hair sculpture of an Inuit with a dog silhouetted against a painting of a Labrador blue sky with a full moon. This work is reproduced with the kind permission of the "Birches Gallery" in Goose Bay.

Table of Contents

Away to the North: A Landscape is Singing	Boyd Chubbs	10
Away to the North	Boyd Chubbs	10
Excerpts: *Journals* "Sixth Voyage"	George Cartwright	12
George Cartwright - circa 1790 from Labrador Journals	George Cartwright	12
High on the Mountain of Old Mokami	G. Mitchell & B. Chaulk	13
Excerpts: Labrador Footprints	Winston White	14
Inuit woman with toddler in sealskin packing-parka	Them Days	17
Jeremiah the Bandmaster. "He wraps himself in his big trumpet."	Them Days	17
Powerhouse – Churchill Falls (Labrador)	CFLC Ltd.	20
Inukuluk Designs	Susie Igloliorte	21
Detail from Grenfell parka	Grenfell Handicrafts	21
Child's duffle coat	Nellie Winter	22
My ancestor was a shaman	Shirley Moorehouse	22
To See Things and to Understand	Lydia Campbell	23
The Land God Gave to Cain	Byrne, Byrne & Rose	24
Boarding School in Muddy Bay	Millicent (Blake) Loder	25
Where They Built Their Lives: An Exhibition of Mats	Lois Saunders	28
Curator's Statement	Gerald Squires	28
François	Lois Saunders	29
Hebron	Lois Saunders	29
Trouty	Lois Saunders	30
Brigus	Lois Saunders	30
Battle Harbour	Lois Saunders	31
Bottle Cove	Lois Saunders	31
Towers and Monuments	John Steffler	32
Fog, This Time	Scott Strong	33
St. John's shrouded in fog	Dennis Minty	33
The Soul of a Newfoundlander	Cyril Poole	34
Profile: Jean-Claude Roy	Editors	42
Beaumont Hamel	Jean-Claude Roy	43
French's Cove, Bay Roberts	Jean-Claude Roy	43
The Fruits of Toil	Norman Duncan	44
Illustration	Boyd Chubbs	51
Excerpts: *What Happened Was…*	Chris Brookes	52
Miners	Michael Crummey	55
Saltwater Joys	Wayne Chaulk	56
Winter view of Bonne Bay	BBL Archives	57
Buddy and the Other Fellers	Mark Vaughan-Jackson	58
d'Lard Liftin'	Buddy Wasisname	59
Strip-mined	Christopher Pratt	60
Rodway's Point	Lois Saunders	61
King's Point Pottery	L. Yates & D. Hayashida	62
Whale and wave bowl	Kings Point Pottery	62
Shell plate	King's Point Pottery	63
Whale and waves tableware	King's Point Pottery	63
Above the Harbour	Carmelita McGrath	64

The Voice of Dinah	*Kathleen Winter*	65
An old fishing stage	*BBL Archives*	66
Aquaforte	*Lois Saunders*	67
Artist's Statement	*Jerry Evans*	68
Know Me, Know You	*Jerry Evans*	69
Traditional Spiritualism	*Michael Joe*	70
Untitled	*Kathleen Winter*	70
Call Me an Indian: The Calvin White Story	*Chris O'Neill-Yates*	73
Humour: Forms and Functions	*Herbert Lench Pottle*	77
Excerpts: *The Life and Times of Ted Russell*	*Elizabeth Russell Miller*	85
Jethro Noddy	*Ted Russell*	90
King David	*Ted Russell*	91
Edward Russell	*George Story*	93
Special DADication	*Kevin Tobin*	94
Cartoon	*Kevin Tobin*	94
The Outdoor Motor	*Arthur Scammell*	95
"Hauled up and rotting…"	*BBL Archives*	96
Uncle Mark White's Rat	*Bruce Stagg*	97
The Poor We Have With Us Always	*Ray Guy*	102
This Dear and Fine Country	*Ray Guy*	105
Chimney Cove	*BBL Archives*	105
A Fairy Tale	*Ed Smith*	106
Mosey	*Donald Gale*	108
Mosey	*Lloyd Pretty*	109
Recipe	*Gordon Rodgers*	111
The Badger Drive	*John V. Devine*	112
Sharpening a traditional bucksaw	*A. Barker*	113
Newfoundland Outport Furniture	*Walter Peddle*	114
Labrador travelling box	*Brian Ricks*	115
Keels dish dresser	*Brian Ricks*	115
Artist's Statement: Paterson Woodworking	*Mike Paterson*	116
Paterson Woodworking showroom	*Brian Ricks*	116
Rocking chair	*Brian Ricks*	117
Carved washstand	*Brian Ricks*	117
Bucket, Grub box / Lunch bucket, piggin	*Brian Ricks*	117
A River Runs Through Her	*Al Pittman*	118
The Phantom Iceberg	*Adrian Fowler*	119
Iceberg	*Nellie Strowbridge*	120
Appeal to Parnassus	*Irving Fogwill*	121
Required Reading	*David Benson*	122
Exploits	*Lois Saunders*	123
Mining	*Christopher Pratt*	124
The Money Crowd	*JoAnne Soper-Cook*	125
Illustration	*Boyd Chubbs*	129
The Time That Passes	*Agnes Walsh*	130
Marriage	*Hilda Chaulk-Murray*	131
Wedding photo, 1940	*BBL Archives*	135
Harbour Le Cou	*Traditional*	136

Two Dresses from St. Pierre	*Ruth Lawrence*	137
A Harmless Deception	*Anastasia English*	138
Interview with Grant Boland	*Shannon M. Lewis*	148
September	*Grant Boland*	149
The Price of Bread	*Gregory Power*	152
The *Caribou* Disaster	*Cassie Brown*	156
S. S. *Caribou* and Captain Ben Tavenor	*PANL*	157
Illustration	*Boyd Chubbs*	160
S. S. *Eagle*: The Secret Mission 1944-45	*Harold Squires*	161
Captain Kirk Surveys the Seal Hunt	*Joan Strong*	163
Newfoundland Sealing Disaster	*Enos Watts*	165
Excerpt: *But Who Cares Now?*	*Douglas House*	166
Ocean Ranger monument and plaque	*Lisa LeDrew*	168
When Orchards Green	*Genevieve Lehr*	170
Your Last Goodbye	*Bruce Moss*	171
Final remnant of the *Ocean Ranger*	*Evening Telegram*	172
Those Thirsty Critters	*Gilbert Lynch*	173
Bogwood	*Gregory Power*	175
Address to Convocation	*Edythe Ryan Goodridge*	176
An Interview with Mike Massie	*Matthew Fox*	178
Snowy Owl	*Mike Massie*	179
In My Dream, We were Together as One	*Mike Massie*	183
Wise to Who From Within	*Mike Massie*	183
Middle Son	*Patrick O'Flaherty*	186
The Old *Royal Readers*	*A. C. Hunter*	191
Inglewood's Childhood Beach	*S. R. (Bert) Cooper*	195
Little Orly	*Bryan Hennessey*	196
Illustration	*Boyd Chubbs*	200
Excerpt: *Up Off Our Knees*	*Chris O'Neill-Yates*	201
Branch	*Lois Saunders*	203
Proverbs and Sayings	*P. K. Devine*	204
Big Davey's Maxims	*Florence P. Miller*	206
Excerpts: *The Vinland Sagas*	*Magnus Magnusson*	207
Helge & Anne Stine Ingstad	*BBL Archives*	211
Helge Marcus Ingstad	*George Story*	212
Anne Stine Ingstad	*George Story*	213
Interior of Viking longhouse	*Govt. of NF*	214
Excerpt: *Eiriksdottir*	*Joan Clark*	215
Gaia off L'Anse aux Meadows	*BBL Archives*	220
River Man	*Valerie Legge*	221
The First Good Friday	*Michael Harrington*	222
Didymus on Saturday	*David L. Elliott*	223
Illustration	*Boyd Chubbs*	224
The Listeners	*Irving Fogwill*	225
Illustration	*Boyd Chubbs*	229
Artist's Statement	*Elena Popova*	230
Cry, My Chest Hurts	*Elena Popova*	231
The Oyster	*Peter Walsh*	232

Black Coral	Clyde Rose	233
Canadien Cultural Games	Tim Ronan	236
Hockey Night in Canada	Vernon Mooers	239
December hockey	Ian Wiseman	240
St. John's	Lois Saunders	240
Should Pro Athletes Be Unionized?	Don Power	241
Hockey Then…And Now…	Kevin Tobin	242
Pictures	Bernice Morgan	243
Illustration	Boyd Chubbs	246
Excerpt: *Waiting for Time*	Bernice Morgan	247
Excerpt: Playing Around With Time	Bruce Porter	249
Sesame and Lilies: Tattered Treasure	James Wade	253
Old Bonaventure	Lois Saunders	255
Dunville	Lois Saunders	255
Artist's Statement	Cary S. James	256
Sterling silver ring	Cary S. James	256
Chrome tourmaline brooch	Cary S. James	257
Sterling silver brooch	Cary S. James	257
Will of Peter Weston	R. J. Fitzpatrick	258
Winter scene, western Newfoundland	BBL Archives	259
Commentary on the Will of Sir James Pearl	R. J. Fitzpatrick	260
Will of John James, Trinity	trans. Shannon Lewis	261
Her Mark	Michael Crummey	263
"Bounded above by the sky…"	BBL Archives	263
Artist's Statement	Anne Meredith Barry	264
Coastal Journey #2: Past the Dog Islands	Anne Meredith Barry	265
Ghostly Yarns of Ishmael Drake	Tom Dawe	266
Afraid in the Dark!	Ron Pollett	270
Dark woods and winter gales	BBL Archives	273
The Ghost of the Murdered Cook	A. Lannon & M. McCarthy	274
The Loss of the *Marion*	Bud Davidge	276
The Savage Cove Devil	Ellen Learning	278
The Savage Cove Devil	Neil Lethbridge	278
The Savage Cove Devil	Samson Learning	279
St. Mary's Keys	Capt. George Whiteley	280
Lobster pots	BBL Archives	282
Fair Marjorie's Ghost	Kenneth Peacock	283
Excerpt: *The Miners of Wabana*	Gail Weir	284
The Miner, Bell Island Newfoundland	Bell Island Murals Assoc.	287
Save Our Ghosts	John Steffler	288
"and now they're driven away"	BBL Archives	289
Our New Flag	Govt. Nf & Lab	290
Newfoundland Flag	Govt. Nf & Lab	290
Labrador Flag	Govt. Nf & Lab	291
Labrador Flag	Govt. Nf & Lab	291
Ode to Newfoundland	Sir Cavendish Boyle	292
Ode to Labrador	H. Paddon & S. Montague	293

Away to the North: A Landscape is Singing

Boyd Chubbs

The Past is always with me.
It breathes through every stone and cliff; is illuminated
in the soft, wild moss; is seen across the heavy swells
of sea; heard in the pitch and tone of thunder and lashing
wind; is found in the low and slow murmur through the ground,
the ancestral sound and story.

And carried in the song and glory of birds, it settles
through my heart and head, anchoring me with the
liberating power of a true, eternal home.

This land, this Labrador, brings the breath of its long age
to rest in my soul; engages all I do and insures my labours.
This place is my Holy Land.

Inuit Language

Sivullivinivut uvannenginnatut.

Anitsataujuk ilonnainut ujakKanut innanullu;
Kaumagutauluk aKittuni piggapijanni;
takutsaujuk inglulialunni;
tusatsaujuk ikummalammi kallumilu anuggaumijanimmilu;
napvatausok nunaup atani ivuluvvalaningani, sivullita uKausingit
piusingillu.

Natsataujuk tutsianginnut ananauninginnulu Kupanuat, natsivuk
ommatikkut niaKukkulu, tunggavittalunga apvitannisamma
pitsatunitsanganik, mitsiKattumik, isuKanggitumik angiggasaganik.

Una nunak, Labrador, aninniminik itsasuanitamik tuniggutiKavak
minggui siKullugu tarnigani; tigullalvuk ilonnainik piusikkanik
sulijotillugillu suliagijakka.
Una nunak itjunaigivage.

Innu Language

Neme utat nantem nikunuenten nin.
Nete ut nenemikan kassinu ashinit mak
Nete estashekat utshiti nete ut uasteu ne
enushkast uapitsheuska muk; kie kassinu nete
Nuken nete uinupekut; kasinnu nete petakanu
Nete ut nanamisut tshetutau mak ne niutiki
Kie tshipa mishken nete minaush pietakuak e
nutik netu assit mak ne tshiashinut kaeitit mak
utipatshamunaua.

Mak nete ispanu nete nikamunt mak nete
ispatentakushit peneshishat nete isteu nete
enteit mak nistakuant. Kie ne ispish
Shutshian e tapian. Nete ntshisk nitshit.

Ume assi, nitasinat, kie mue kheipish iniuimikak
tshikeisteu ute nteiti kie kassinu tshekuau
ispish tutaman mak itusian.
Umue assi ekun tshiatuauentiman assi.

Away to the North by Boyd Chubbs

Excerpts from
George Cartwright, *Journals* "Sixth Voyage"

1786
August
Wednesday 23
Wind fresh
N. Moderate

The land hereabouts looks well to the eye, being clear of wood; the hills rise gradually, but not high, exhibit great verdure, and an appearance of more fertility than I have ever seen on any other part of the coast. In the valley where Noble & Pinion's fishery is carried on is a garden in which every thing grows more luxuriantly than I ever saw before in this country; and I also observed great plenty of scarlet strawberries growing among the grass. Curlews are now abundant and fat; I killed one. The fishery has proved very indifferent here this season.
A very fine day throughout.

Monday 28
S. S. W. fresh

The boats being returned, and Captain Packenham having finished his business at this place, we went to sea at eight this morning, and at one o'clock came to an anchor in Forteau Bay. I went on shore to Mr. Durrell's house, where I staid the night; he is an agent to a Jersey company. Several planters live here who, dividing their winter business between this place and the opposite part of Newfoundland, do tolerably well for themselves.

George Cartwright, circa 1790. Taken from George Cartwright's Labrador Journals.

High on the Mountain of Old Mokami

Lyrics: Byron Chaulk   Music: Gerald Mitchell

O-ver look-ing the wa-ters of Lake Mel-ville so grand, One of the big-gest in all this great land. Proud-ly we watch as it flows to the sea, From high on the moun-tain of Old Mo-ka-mi. The beau-ti-ful fo-rest where the wi-ld life roam, where none but the free can ev-er call home. Old mo-ther na-ture lets an-y one see, From high on the moun-tain of Old Mo-ka-mi.

Our mighty rivers are all of the best,
They flow from the North, the South and the West,
Their great dancing waters so lovely to see,
From high on the mountain of Old Mokami.

The tall Mealy Mountains off to the Southwest,
Where the caribou feed and the ptarmigan nest,
All these and more great wonders to see,
From high on the mountain of Old Mokami.

They can talk of their cities, their riches untold,
All the things that they bought with their silver and gold,
All the gold that they have couldn't buy what I see,
From high on the mountain of Old Mokami.
From high on the mountain of Old Mokami.

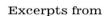

Excerpts from
Labrador Footprints
Winston White

"Labrador Footprints" is an eight-part series on the people, history and culture of Labrador. It was published in the "Digest" page of the *Sunday Telegram*, February 2-March 2, 1997.

Part One, *Living on the Land*

As another of Labrador's untold riches is uncovered with the discovery of the Voisey's Bay nickel, copper and cobalt deposit, I thought it would be timely to relate some of the history of the people who have called the region "home."

The first people of the area are known as Inuit [Ee-noo-weet], which one time were referred to by white people as Eskimo. The other original people are Innu [Ee-noo], who have previously been called Naskaupi [Nas-cop-ee] and Montagnais [Mon-tan-yea].

Inuit and Innu footprints have been on the Labrador land for a long, long time. Local people and archeologists are constantly finding signatures of our cultures which date from modern times to five to six thousand years ago or likely even longer. It is not absolutely clear at this time which of the two was first to arrive in Labrador, but traces in the land through old remains indicate that a people whom archeologists have tagged as Maritime Archaic, and whom they catagorize as Innu or Indian lived in the area around 6,000 years ago.

Our cultures lived and gathered food from the land and sea in the bays and around the islands of this northern frontier. Voisey's Bay or Tessiujatsoak, in Inuktitut meaning "a land-locked harbor place," was one of those bays which attracted our foreparents. Here they could find Arctic char, brook trout, Atlantic salmon and codfish. They would also count on the ducks, geese, their eggs, beluga whales, caribou, beaver, porcupine, ptarmigan, black bears and polar bears for food and clothing. They trained dogs to haul and transport them in their daily living. The land in the area produced wild berries and edible plants, timber for snowshoes, canoes, kayak frames and paddles, hunting spears and frames for "tupiks" (tents and tepees) and firewood.

It all sounds like a land of bountiful game and a life of easy living.

On the contrary.

Often fish and game were scarce or even a total failure, which made life full of challenges and harsh realities.

Out of the short summers, long, bitterly cold winters, and ever-changing weather with vicious winds, snowstorms and cold, damp weather from the North Atlantic Ocean evolved human beings of such physical and emotional stamina that would make the highest priced professional sport stars of today look like a kindergarten class.

The muscle, strength, and quick, accurate thinking required of an Inuk hunter sitting, legs flat and in a straight-out position, in a buoyant kayak ready to throw a five-pound harpoon along with a coil of sealskin line into a bobbing seal target the size of a turnip, over a distance of one hundred feet or more and strike it dead-on, illustrates the kind of physical and mental condition our ancestors developed through the course of daily life.

The Innu or Naskaupi Indian moved around the area and across the "barren lands" of the Labrador and Ungava region in small family bands of varying sizes ranging from several to twenty or thirty people. Travelling on foot, in only skin moccasins, or on snowshoes in winter, and by hand-crafted canoes in summer, they would camp in one area for weeks at a time and then move distances up to thirty to fifty miles or even further, depending on the time of year and the whereabouts of animals or birds they might be counting on.

Inuit also moved from area to area in small family groups following the food and seasons. Their extended journeys inland up onto the Labrador tundra again were a result of their search for caribou and usually lasted just several weeks. These travels included long and hazardous trips to and from northern Labrador or the shores of Ungava Bay.

Part Two, *Legends of the Bay*

Voisey's Bay is roughly thirty miles southwest of Nain. Using parameters used by local people, the bay is considered to be about twenty miles long and in places it's up to four miles across. There are five major rivers or brooks dumping into the bay, and another dozen or so small watercourses can be found along its shores. What we call "brooks" in Labrador seem to be rivers to people from other parts of the province. The landscape is magnificent with rolling hills partly covered with mosses, lichens, alders, spruce trees, juniper trees and the odd birch. Once you reach four hundred feet or so above sea level the hilltops are treeless.

Sandy beaches, windswept islands, rivers and waterfalls are dwarfed by the Toma Hill or Makhavinekh Mountain which tops out at 1,969 feet above the blue waters of the bay. From a deep water and modern shipping perspective Voisey's Bay doesn't have what it takes for a good seaport. The inner part of the bay has a lot of shoals and sandy deltas dumped by the rivers flowing into the bay. The approaches to the bay from the outer coastline are also shoal infested. For this reason, Anaktalak Bay to the north has been selected as the place to put the port for handling the Diamond Fields' mineral discovery and its future operations. The next major bay to the north is called Anaktalik Bay.

Part Three, *North to Labrador*

In 1911, a young St. John's man gave up law for a life on the land....

Part Four, *A Tale of Two Cultures*

Mom described how her father would take her on his hunting trips in the summer. She was about five years old and her dad would hunt for seals, ducks and gather eggs from nesting birds among the islands in the area by kayak. Kayaks in those days, like everything else, were hand made from wooden and bone framing lashed with caribou babish and covered with hand sewn sealskin. Judy would settle herself on her tummy and feet to the rear of the craft. She said it would become dark inside the kayak when

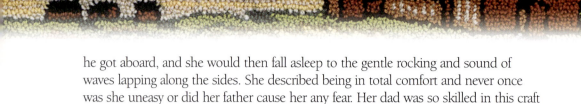

he got aboard, and she would then fall asleep to the gentle rocking and sound of waves lapping along the sides. She described being in total comfort and never once was she uneasy or did her father cause her any fear. Her dad was so skilled in this craft and environment that she felt absolutely safe.

Mom said she would be awakened by the gentle nudge of the kayak against the shore, and daylight would spread into the space around her as her dad got out of the craft. Emerging from her space inside, she would always find a seal, birds or other food secured onto the deck of the kayak. The entire family would be on the beach to welcome them, prepare the skinning and distribution of the game, which just an hour or two prior was swimming or living freely on the land and sea.

Mom was just a small woman, but the challenges she faced and took on never seemed too big. She raised thirteen of us, made all our skin clothing. Using her ulu (Inuit cutting blade shaped like a half moon set on a tee handle and pronounced ouloo) to cut patterns, needles, and sinew from caribou for thread she tailored our jackets, pants, boots and mitts from seal and caribou skins. Just like many mothers in those days, her day started before dawn and often ended not much before midnight.

Her work was not solely inside her home looking after children. She could hunt, fish and manage her own trap line. She would call birds like ducks, geese or raise the curiosity of loons to come within a sure shot range of her .22 rifle and make the shot count. She carried and combined the best of her culture and way of life with the best of the white way of doing things. Mom didn't have the opportunity to attend school, so dad taught her how to read and write. Judy also spoke three languages, her own Inuktitut, English which Dad taught her and Innu Eimun (Indian) which she learned through her twenty-five years in Voisey's Bay.

She even made boots for our dogs to wear in spring to protect their sensitive watersoaked paws from the sharp ice and frozen snow of early morning travel. Mom handled and drove her own teams. I will always remember travelling on them with her as a boy. Those dogs could tell where ice was thin or non-existent under a layer of snow. A good leader could always take you right to your door even when you could not see a hand in front of your face. Even the fanciest of snowmobiles designed today cannot tell us where the ice is bad or withstand the extreme drifting conditions without the engine failing. There is no record of a dog team ever failing unless forced under poor direction by the driver.

Like everyone in her time, Mom smoked. Tailor-made cigarettes were rare, so everyone rolled smokes by hand. Mom was so good that she could roll them with one hand. At seventy-six she developed lung cancer but she still enjoyed a cigarette right up to a few hours before she died, Jan. 29, 1979, in the hospital at Goose Bay.

Family friends made her casket from Labrador spruce plank, draped the inside with nice linen and I put one of her ulus by her side. I then chartered a single-engine Otter airplane on skis and chose Capt. Ian Massie to fly us to Nain. Massie was born in Hebron and the first Labrador man ever to become a bush pilot. Mom had great admiration for his achievement. He circled Nain three times and the old Otter gently touched down on the Nain harbour ice. We buried her in Nain where her journey had started.

Inuit woman with toddler in sealskin packing-parka.

Jeremiah the Bandmaster. "He wraps himself in his big trumpet."

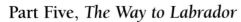

Part Five, *The Way to Labrador*

On Dec. 30, 1928, the 150 or so people living in Nain were treated to another invention from the outside world. U.S. Navy Commander Donald B. MacMillan wrote in his log for that day. "Great excitement upon our arrival in Nain. The whole village was out, including the dogs. We drove up over the snowbanks and came to a stop at the Moravian Mission. Since this is the first automobile which they had ever seen, naturally such would cause some excitement."

MacMillan had just driven 20 miles over ice from his scientific station in Anaktalak Bay. He was in a Model T Ford motor car which he had converted into a snowmobile! He had noted the day before, "the [snowmobile] worked beautifully to the credit of Bert and Henry Ford."

Part Seven, *Bound for the Coast*

"It started with a sweat bath," recalled Max. "Michel constructed the bath by making a circular framework of spruce saplings which he covered with blankets. A hole was left in the top but covered with a single blanket which could be removed by a person outside on direction from a person inside. Stones were heated and placed in the bath around the rim of the enclosure. Only men were given the privilege of the bath. We stripped and entered one at a time taking a kettle of water. Inside water was poured on the hot stones creating steam. When the heat became unbearable the person outside was directed to remove the top blanket which allowed steam to escape."

After a short cooling off period each person dressed and went to the feast tent. The feast tent was again for men only. A drum was suspended from a tripod in the tent which the older men beat in time to chant with a single drum stick. These drums had only one side covered with caribou leather. "The songs or chants, in so far as I could follow, concerned stories of travel and hunts, but one I could follow quite well extolled the virtues of reaching the status of an elderly man. A literal translation of the title would be to respect a man with greying hair as the chant went on to say that such a man had acquired knowledge which is useful to younger men."

During these feasts, great quantities of food were brought into the tent by the women. Waterfowl, fish, dried caribou and bone lard. Sitting on the fir bough covered floor the men began. "We ate to repletion, fell asleep where we were, woke and ate again. During the whole period, food was always before us and when the feast ended I think the camp was destitute," Max discovered. "The dried meat and lard which was easy to carry and which could have probably sustained us to Seven Islands had disappeared. They are so competent in their environment that security in the form of a more than adequate food supply is a challenge they must meet by liquidating security and facing tomorrow's situation as it arises," Max learned.

Following the feast they had no white man's food at all, not even tea or flour, and likely of more concern, no tobacco. Yet everyone was cheerful and happy. The next day the whole camp was dismantled and in seven canoes they set off up the George River for the Labrador plateau. It was now early June.

Part Eight, *Northern Living*

In 1925 Dad was offering vacations to "Northern Labrador, the magnetic north." He wrote up Labrador as: "Not chiefly a wilderness of ice and snow, but virgin hunting ground, whose Inuit, Indians, dog teams, fisheries and healthy, vibrant climate call you to a vacation of health, pleasure and interest. Sportsmen can here meet the primeval in its truest sense and recuperate their energy in the vivifying air and intense silences of the north. Come now before the big game of the north join the buffalo, the passenger pigeon of America, the Great Auk, the Beothuk Indians and the caribou of Newfoundland in the halls of yesterday."

    Dad continued writing through the '40s, noting the changes in Voisey's. A rare breed of energetic, versatile and skillfully clever people were passing on.

    The autumn weather of 1950 was good. As usual by September he was ready for the winter. One of the things Dad did each day of his life was observe signs of approaching weather. He knew well those rare perfect days found in northern Labrador for travelling. On Oct. 23 he suddenly suffered a stroke and the next day on Oct 24, he died.

    Hammond was there and wrote, "It was one of those sun-brilliant frosty days. With just enough young ice on salt water to scar a punt's plank. The willows were golden against brown-red bare alder branches, spruces lively green below grey hills stippled scarlet with dying berry bushes. A robin's egg sky and sharp air to wine the spirit. The last words I heard him say were: 'A wonderful day. For anyone with somewhere to go.'"

    "We laid him out in the little store, between flour and biscuit bags and bolts of bright print, under frying pans and kettles hanging from the beams. We made his coffin in the kitchen and hauled him over the land by dog team after the snows came and buried him in Nain." He had just turned seventy-two that September.

    The challenges, dedication and accomplishments of the people in this series has not been hitherto well known. The author's hope is that readers have gained a fresh insight on life in earlier times in Labrador and the contribution made by these sons and daughters of our province.

Powerhouse, Churchill Falls (Labrador) Corporation Limited

Inukuluk Designs
Susie Igloliorte

I was the first one to make the inukuluk design at Hopedale. When my daughter was only two-and-a-half years old, I made the design on her little parka. The design I made was two little children taking up water from the well we used to have. How I come to get the inukuluk design done, was because I wanted something different from the others. That was the first one in Hopedale, and that was in 1945.

Katie Hettasch, in Nain, was making inukuluk designs quite a while before I done them on the little parka. It was the same year, but I didn't know she was making them, and she didn't know that I was making them. Well, we done it about the same time. That was in 1945. Katie was making them on cloths, tablecloths, in the early 1940's. She didn't do them on parkas, not them times.

Maybe we got the idea from Cartwright. I was up to Cartwright, in the hospital, and while I was there I used to do sewing for Mrs. Keddie. That was in 1939. She was having embroidery done on cloth, but not on duffel.

Inukuluks we makes on duffel, that only came around 1956, and

Detail from Grenfell parka.

that was started by me at Hopedale. I came to Happy Valley in the 1960's. Mrs. Bursell told me that she was told that the figures wasn't able to be worked on duffel. Mrs. Bursell was a Newfoundland woman. She wanted me to make two little parkas for her sister's children, and that was how she come to know I was able to make inukuluk designs on duffel. When they saw that I made them, everyone started making them.

Before we used the inukuluk designs, we just put braid around the tail of the parkas. We put the flowered trim, amameotaks, around the hoods. Some used to put ivory tassels around the tail. Those were the only decorations that I saw. There was some flowers embroidered on parkas before the inukuluk figures, but not too many, and that was only for the outsiders, not for ourselves.

If people want to use our designs, I guess that's okay. We take ideas from other people.

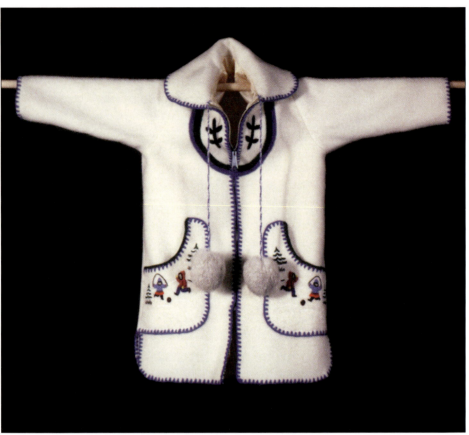

Child's duffle coat by Nellie Winter.

My ancestor was a shaman, textile by Shirley Moorehouse.

To See Things and to Understand
Lydia Campbell

If you wish to know who I am, I am old Lydia Campbell, formerly Lydia Brooks, then Blake, after Blake now Campbell. So, you see, ups and downs has been my life all through, and now I am what I am. Praise the Lord.

When I remember first to see things and to understand, I thought this was the only place in the world, and that my parents and sisters were the best in the world. Then our good father used to take me on his knee and tell me his home was a better country, only it was hard to live there after his good old father died…and he had to come out to this country to try his fortune. Then, of course, they had to take wives of the natives of this country. There were very few white men here, much less women. Going ashore they found my dear, good mother and carried her off, and so it came to pass that I was one of the youngsters of them. We lived up in the riverhead, at a long bay and no one near us—more than seventy miles from anybody.

We would enjoy ourselves pretty well. There was my sister Hanna to be talking and reading with me, father and mother and an old Englishman by the name of Robert Best. Our dear Bible and a common prayer to teach us in, nothing but a family Bible and a common prayer to teach us. So we learned a little in that way.

I remember so well the day my mother died. Father met us at the door as we came from seeing our rabbit snares, with a book in his hand and told us she was dying. We all went in and kneeled down near our good mother breathing her last. By the time father was done reading and praying she was gone. Oh what did I do! Where to go! Only five of us and far from any habitation; but the Lord was with us.

When I was about twenty, I think, (I never kept account of the times or how they went) I was teaching the children of a large family, the Blakes, that I got married into. I could not write then, but I could read and teach them to read and sing hymns and to pray oft as my dear father teacht me. There were no ministers nor schoolteachers them times in this country.

Now my sister Hanna is over eighty years old and she is smart still. I have known her fighting with a wolverine, a strong animal of the size of a good sized dog. She had neither gun nor axe, but a little trout stick, yet she killed it after a long battle. It was very wicked. I wish there were more Hannas in the world for braveness.

My day's work begins before daylight, rising to make a fire, say my prayers, wash lamps, get on breakfast, sweep the house, after then I am ready with our Bible and hymn books and prayer books on the table. So, after breakfast, I, old Lydia, seventy-five years old, puts on my outdoor clothes, takes my game bag and axe and matches, and off I goes over ice and snow, two miles or more, gets maybe three rabbits out of twenty or more snares. You may say, well done old woman, but such is life in Esquimaux Bay among a few, while some is naked and half starving for want of a little exercise.

The other day I was walking in the woods with my snowshoes on all alone looking up at the trees. At the spruce and birches looking so high and stately. I saw in the sunshine such a pretty sight above the highest trees, a flock of the beautiful white partridge, how pretty it looked and the snow glistening and the ice and the trees, and me…poor mortal…drinking in all the beautiful scenery, who will soon be out of sight but not lost, ah no, only going the way all the people as gone before.

The Land God Gave to Cain

Pat Byrne, Joe Byrne and Clyde Rose

Long before the white man came to haul the shining cod, When the wild and stately caribou traversed the snow clad sod, The native man he walked these hills and he fished the silvery lakes, Content with what the land would yield not one bit more would take

But soon the word it was put out from every country
To find the northern passage from sea to shining sea.
The first to come were trappers then the men of God who preached
That they would return a hundredfold an equal share to each.

For years the men of Newfoundland those fishermen so poor,
Went down each year in springtime for to fish on the Labrador.
But soon the fish they were all gone with the fur it was the same.
And the native suffered silently in the land God gave to Cain.

The years went by and as time passed the companies moved in.
For ore and wood and hydro power the struggle did begin.
But the working men on both sides tried to live their lives the same.
And the native suffered silently in the land God gave to Cain.

Now it's for the future both sides do share a fear.
The old ways they are passing like the caribou and hare.
And now they all are wondering if it was all in vain.
And the native suffers silently in the land God gave to Cain.

Personal Account of Attending Boarding School in Muddy Bay
Millicent (Blake) Loder

I recall evenings at home when we were little children gathered around the warm stove talking about the great things we would do when we grew up. I was always going to "find babies." Suddenly, Ma would speak up, "First of all, all you children got to go to school and get all the learning you can, eh John?" and Pa would say, "Yes," and that was it for their decisions were final.

I started school in Rigolet where there was a small one-room school and where, each year, some young person came from Newfoundland to teach. In the fall when the rest of my family went to our winter home in Double Mer, I was left behind in care of friends so that I could attend school. Their daughter Eva and I became fast friends and rabid competitors for first place. I loved school from day one.

I was heart-broken the final year at the Rigolet school when I was beaten by my friend, by a few marks. Taking my second prize (a skipping rope) home, I threw it on the floor and burst into tears and would not be comforted even when Ma told me how pleased she was with the good marks I got. During the summer months my wound quickly healed. I was very happy when my parents told me that they had made arrangements for me to attend boarding school at Muddy Bay, a place not far from Cartwright and a school owned and operated by the Grenfell Mission Association.

Ma was busy the last few weeks of the summer getting me ready for school. She made my older sister's clothes over to fit me, made skin boots and duffels for the winter, helped me to knit long woolen stockings, and all the while telling me, "Always be a good girl. Don't forget to say your prayers morning and evening. Be respectful to your elders. Listen to the mistresses, and try to let us know how you are getting along."

The day finally came, early in September, where the *Strathcona* steamed into Rigolet Harbour, and I, dressed in my Sunday best and very proud, was rowed aboard, after saying good-bye to my family. I was the only child on board and was placed in the dispensary of the boat, with a warning not to touch anything. The half-door was barred for safety and I found myself alone.

As the houses of Rigolet faded in the distance, I became very homesick and stood at the door crying and miserable until, finally, Dr. Grenfell came in. He sat me on his knee and started leafing through a magazine, telling me about the things and places pictured there. Finally he came to a picture of a grand lady and he said to me, "If you'll be a good girl and work hard and get all the education you can, you'll be a lady like that someday." I have never forgotten the words he said to me and, like all children who knew him, I loved him dearly.

Finally we arrived at Muddy Bay. The school building looked monstrous to me. As the *Strathcona* drew up to the wharf, the children and staff of the school poured down on the wharf to greet us. I was taken by someone up to the school building and handed over to the head mistress. She just looked at me without smiling or making me welcome by offering me a cup of tea. Calling one of the working girls to her she said, "Take her upstairs and show her where she is going to sleep, check her head, give her a bath and put some decent clothes on her." I was devastated.

This being my first time away from home I suffered severe homesickness for quite some time. Gradually I made friends with the other children, but life at the school was very strange at first. There were so many rules and regulations to get used to. You must "never go into the staff rooms, knock on the door if you want anything, ask permission to go outdoors and to come in, eat everything on your plate, make your bed before leaving your room, button the clothes of the smaller ones, take your cod oil without fussing" and so on.

But the hardest thing to hear was that there was no one to put their arms about you when you were feeling bad and no one to tell you how pleased they were when you did well. No one understood how you could miss your family and home so much, but would tell you how lucky you were that you were in a place where you could get better food and nicer clothes. No one understood that, for children, there is nothing that can compensate for the love and understanding and the feeling of security that you have in a close-knit family.

I soon learned to adjust, as children do, and my happiest hours were spent in the classroom. I could read quite well by then and was hooked on books. There was a small library and often I hid away behind a chair or in a dark corner and would read anything I could lay my hands on. Once I was caught and wasn't allowed to have a book for a week.

Early in the school year, our teacher told us that someone had offered a prize of a five dollar gold piece each for the girl and boy who got the best marks at the end of the year. I intended to work hard for it.

In that first winter I became a Brownie and then a Guide and at ten years old was considered old enough to be responsible for playing with and minding the little ones. We all had our chores to do. Some peeled and prepared vegetables (when there were any), others scrubbed the wooden bedroom floors, cleaned, filled and trimmed the lamps, and it was considered a privilege to be allowed to tidy and dust the staff rooms or to mend their clothes and darn their socks and perhaps iron some of their clothing. They had such nice things—clothes with lace on them, pretty beads and flowered hand mirrors.

Sunday was a special day. There was no studying and we spent the day reading, playing and having services, each of us saying aloud the Bible text we had been set to learn that week. Then for an extra special treat each Sunday, as we filed out of the dining room after eating our supper, we were given a candy. We all looked forward to Sunday, especially for the candy.

The winter flew by and we had our school examinations. When our grades were handed out, I was very proud to find that I had won the five dollar gold piece for the girls, and John Heard was just as proud to win the boys' prize. Our money was locked in a drawer in the office for next year.

Most of us returned to our homes for the summer holidays. A short trip of the old *S. S. Kyle* brought me to Rigolet and oh, was it good to be home with a loving family.

When I returned to school for the second year a brother and sister accompanied me. They too suffered the pangs of homesickness, but I was now an old hand at the school and, hopefully, made things a little easier for them.

I think it was early in the fall when there was an outbreak of scarlet fever at the school, and those of us who were affected were all isolated in one room. Once the fever stage had passed we had great fun. That year there was a nurse with us and she must have had her hands full. As soon as she left the room we were out of bed, dashing about and throwing things out of the window to the children below, who were always there when they weren't in class. They in turn would try to throw things up to us until we were all caught and were forced back to bed.

Long before Christmas we were all well and back in the classroom in time for all the excitement and talk that precedes the visit of Santa. Although I can recall Christmases earlier at home, even to what was in my stocking, I cannot recall the details of those two Christmases at Muddy Bay. Maybe it was because we had too many items to remember. The thing I remember best was the holiday time when we were free to be out sliding and playing, and best of all, there was time for reading in the library.

One cold Sunday evening in February we were all in the dining room eating our supper and sneaking peeps at the candy we would get when we filed out, when one of the working girls came in and said something to the mistress. She always stood by the food table watching us while we ate, and she said to us, "Children, get up immediately and file quietly out into the hall and go straight out the front door." We did as we were told, though we all felt like grabbing our candy as we passed by the table. As we passed the stairway, there was smoke coming down and we could hear the crackling of the fire. Outside the door someone told us to go out on the harbour and then up to Bird's Eye cottage and wait there. We could see the school burning from the window. I had found my brother and sister and we all tried to help the little ones. It was very cold and the snow was deep and we had to leave without our coats and parkas.

In Cartwright the people saw the glow of fire in the sky and hastily made ready their dog teams. They came for us with komatik boxes and whatever blankets and wraps they could find. Soon we were wrapped in blankets and on our way to Cartwright. It was only a short drive but it was very cold. The manager of the Hudson's Bay store had opened the store, built a warm fire, and had hot cocoa and biscuits ready when we arrived. It was so good to be in a warm place again.

It wasn't long before the kind people of Cartwright came and took us into their homes and fed and comforted us and gave us what clothing they could spare. I wondered where my brother and sister could be, for by now we were separated.

Next morning we learned that our school had burned to the ground and that one little girl, who had been sick in her bed upstairs, had just escaped when one of our teachers had managed to get her out by handing her to people standing below the roof of the porch. Then he was forced to jump himself and broke his ankle or knee, I don't recall which. It is tragic to note that the same little girl lost her life when a new and safer school dormitory, built at Cartwright, was destroyed by fire some time later.

The laundry building near the school was left standing, so it was decided that those of us who were in the sixth grade would finish our school year. The laundry was turned into a classroom and a bunkhouse, formerly used by the Bird's Eye people, was now our dwelling quarters. The Hudson's Bay gave us ledgers for scribblers and sent us pencils and wooden crates for desks.

As soon as we returned to Muddy Bay, I went poking through the ashes with a stick to see if I could find my five dollar gold piece but I never did.

The people along the coast gradually learned of the fire and came to get their children. When Pa came to get my brother and sister, I didn't mind at all because I loved going to school and wanted to get my grade six. Pa said if I stayed and got my grade six, perhaps I could go on to St. Anthony and get as high as grade eight.

We had a lovely time getting our grade six. There were six of us, five girls and one boy. We all passed our grade six and I got more for my five dollar gold piece than money could ever buy.

Artist's Statement
Where They Built Their Lives: An Exhibition of Mats, 1997
Lois Saunders

At their backs the cliffs, wild, desolate, unforgiving, majestic. Ahead of them the sea, equally wild and unforgiving, bounteous. A fresh water supply, scraps of reasonably flat land, a place.

My work is a celebration of those men and women whose creative tenacity built their lives along this rocky coast. Self-evident is their pride—and mine.

Curator's Statement
Gerald Squires

Lois and I spoke only occasionally about the work during the creation of this exhibition. I felt my job was to keep out of the creative procedure and keep the reins only on the exhibition as a whole—sizes, shapes, verticals, and horizontals, textures—the look and feel of the show. I left my thoughts at a safe distance and tended to the mundane.

Back in the early 1970's Lois was working at the CBC and I was establishing myself and my family at the Ferryland Lighthouse. One day we were having a beer at the old Press Club when she asked me, "Do you think my work is any good?" I resounded with an affirmative "YES!" She then asked me, "But do you believe in it?" I answered her with a quiet hesitating "yes." "That's all I wanted to know," she said, "that's all I wanted to know."

The work in this show is strong and deliberate. It's been a pleasure to play a part in her voice, which for me, now as a listener, is a resounding "YES."

François by Lois Saunders.

Hebron by Lois Saunders.

Trouty by Lois Saunders.

Brigus by Lois Saunders.

Battle Harbour by Lois Saunders.

Bottle Cove by Lois Saunders.

Towers and Monuments
John Steffler

three hundred years
and what's *there* to show?

earthquakes are not the problem, but the sea
always quakes more than the earth ever has
and we live on its edge

balancing
boats on the waves
homes on the shrugging rock

the framing we build spans shore and grey horizon
every day, but the sea slides after us
erasing what we've done

the towers, the monuments you miss are *there*
in the space between ocean and heaven,
we trace them, conjure them out of the bustling air
in our songs and stories, we hold them
wild again on the crest of the running instant
and let them go,
back to our dead and the faint days

with nothing to show

Fog, This Time
Scott Strong

The light inside this pearl is a liquid silver-gray that washes away gross distinctions and leaves only the imagination to find edges, crevices, any demarcation of extent. Buildings assume an attitude of thoughtfulness, their clapboards and stones sweating with acquired moisture.

Somewhere beyond the bounds of the land, twined in the gritty North Atlantic, two great engines are meshing currents and this is their exhaust. The fetid Gulf stream is yielding its heat to the frigid swath of the Labrador and the confluence has taken the coast. This pearl.

You could lose yourself in this light, evaporate. You could find yourself absorbed, wandering past the houses that march down to the water. At the dockside you could marvel at the tons of ready, floating steel, rocking, biding their time. You could almost believe that the world ended at the harried fringes of your vision, that only you inhabit this tenuous environment.

That tanker is dog-ribbed from years of pounding through waves that would suck the breath from your lungs, bridgedeck abristle with a hedgehog array of antennae, no one visible on deck, engine pulsing shoreleave. The bowl of the harbour holds it softly, an immense glacially-formed parabola that sends sound in ricochet its entire length, amplifies lovers' whispers, tells secrets. Don't speak.

Don't even breathe. This place would steal the thoughts in your head, if you were so bold to have any. This is home. I have trod its clever landscape for too many years to trade it for a mess of potage or a Brylcream smile. I was born here, and I'll die here, and that's just the way it is.

Some places are inhabited; some inhabit the souls of those who live there, inform their choices, sing in their muscles, flow in their words, power their hearts. "You're not from here" is not an accusation, just an observation. You don't know.

Could anyone ever be from anywhere else?

St. John's shrouded in fog by Dennis Minty.

The Soul of a Newfoundlander
Cyril Poole

Newfoundlanders are a peculiar people, a fact noted by many native and foreign observers. Indeed a large number of writers, including Moses Harvey and Joseph Hatton, Julian Moreton, George Allan England, J. R. Smallwood and Farley Mowat, have gone so far as to refer to us as a race. None of these writers, of course, used the term 'race' in its scientific sense. But it is revealing that they thought it natural to use the strongest term expressive of distinctness. It is stronger than "tribe" or "people." That we are so distinct as to make the use of 'race' natural and easy is an observation also supported by Newfoundlanders abroad, who see us both from within and from outside. I take it for a fact, then, that we are a singular people or as our saying goes 'queer sticks.' And we are all queer sticks, all bent the same way; for despite differences of origin, dialect and religion we are all children of the sea. That is what Pratt conveyed in "Erosion."

> It took the sea an hour one night.
> An hour of storm to place
> The sculpture of these granite seams
> Upon a woman's face.

No more imaginative title will ever be found for a study of the Newfoundland soul than Mowat's *This Rock Within the Sea*. Regarding the sea as our "ultimate existence." Mowat views us as "eminently successful survivors of an evolutionary winnowing process that few modern races have undergone." That winnowing process was fishing from the great waters. As Al Pittman so aptly put it, the sea was "at once their sustenance and deprivation, their life and their death."

A full explanation of our peculiarity would have to take several factors into account. Like all peoples we are partly children of our ancestors and of their history. Most of our traits are traceable to England's West Country and to Ireland. But there can be no doubt that they have been molded and magnified by our life on this island and in particular by the way we have earned our daily bread, as described in the lines of R. A. Parsons' major poem "Salute to Port de Grave": "for labours tend / To mark the labourers...."

One of the striking traits of Newfoundlanders is our sense of fatalism. It has seeped into the very marrow of our bones. It found expression in our newspapers and literature, in a thousand sermons, and more significantly, in the very language of our people. There is, of course, a strain of fatalism in many peoples and certainly in some of our ancestors. But in Newfoundland it is so pronounced that in explaining it we must look for a peculiar cause. That factor is, I believe, centuries of dependence on the stormy North Atlantic. In his characterization of North Atlantic fishermen in *Grey Seas Under*, Farley Mowat caught the essence of this fatalism.

> They believe that man must not attempt to overmaster the primordial and elemental forces and break them to his hand. They believe that he who would survive must learn to be a part of the wind and water, rock and soil, nor ever stand in braggarts' opposition to these things.

Contrasts between the tiller of the soil and the fisherman on the troubled waters of the North Atlantic shed much light on the Newfoundlander's fatalism. The contrast has been drawn by several observers. The writer who probed into our relation with the sea as brilliantly as it has ever been done was Norman Duncan. Born in Ontario in 1871, Duncan made several visits to Newfoundland and Labrador between 1900 and 1906. His keen observations of the fisherman's life and philosophy were published in several works, including *The Way of the Sea* (1903); *Dr. Luke of Labrador* (1904) and *Dr. Grenfell's Parish* (1905). The brilliance of Duncan's insights into the sea-touched character of the Newfoundlander has not been surpassed; not by George Allan England's *Vikings of the Ice* (republished in 1969 under the title *The Greatest Hunt in the World*), or even by Pratt's magnificent "Rachel." Duncan was particularly perceptive on the contrast between the farmer and the fisherman. Those who settle as farmers even in the remotest wilderness do so with the hope of taming it. As Duncan noted in *The Way of the Sea*:

> Now the wilderness, savage and remote, yields to the strength of men. A generation strips it...a generation tames it and tills it, a generation passes into the evening shadows as into rest in a garden, and thereafter the children of that place possess it in peace and plenty, through succeeding generations, without end, and shall to the end of the world.

To till the soil is to enclose it against the beasts of the forest; to spread lime where there is acid; to fertilize when it is deficient; to irrigate against a drought and to ditch against the flood. In a word to till is to thwart laws of nature or at least to bend them to one's will.

But the fisherman can do none of these things. It is not given to him to still the waters. In language imitative of the rhythmic pounding of the seas on our rugged shores Duncan captured the contrast between land and sea:

> But the sea is tameless: as it was in the beginning, it is now and shall be mighty, savage, dread, infinitely treacherous...yielding only that which is wrested from it, snarling, raging, snatching lives, spoiling souls of their graces....The deep is not...subdued: the toiler of the sea...is born to conflict, ceaseless and deadly and, in the dawn of all the days, he puts forth anew to wage it.

As Duncan observed of an old Black Harbour skipper, "He did not know that in other lands the earth yields generously to the men who sow the seed." When the young boy Jack is told that some men in other places have never even seen the sea, he asks: "Sure, not a hundred haven't?" Told "More than that," he mutters, "'tis hard t' believe, zur, terrible hard."

That we who have for so long faced the sea bear its marks upon our countenance is a fact noted by other writers. As in "Rachel" and "Florizel," Pratt understood the powers of the sea, "a stark and wild inebriate," to sculpture granite seams in a face set against it. Writing in 1937, J. R. Smallwood also drew imaginative conclusions from the fact of our struggle with the untameable sea, and alluded to the theme almost four decades later in his *I Chose Canada*. Observing that Canadian farmers had "coaxed millions of acres into smiling green meadows and prosperous fields," he contrasted this achievement with that of Newfoundlanders: "at the end of the first four hundred years of toil, they had no productive meadows.... For during those four centuries, their cultivation was of the unquiet, infuriate North Atlantic… and all the toil and danger had not won an acre for them....” Farley Mowat mused over the same contrast both in *Grey Seas Under* and in *This Rock Within the Sea*. On the theme of the tameless, untillable sea he quotes a wise old fisherman, "Ah, me son, we don't be *takin'* nothin' from the sea. We has to sneak up on what we wants, and wiggle it away." The land can be tamed to man's purposes, but we cannot enclose and cultivate the seas. We are capelin fishermen casting our nets on wild, exposed beaches, casting between the breakers ready always to dash for safety, ever looking over our shoulders for the yet more furious comber rolling in unobserved or poised to dash us against the rocks. He who casts his net must sneak up and wiggle his catch away.

But to till the soil, to enclose the land and year by year to improve it is to "over master the primordial and elemental forces" of land and sky. This was the advantage and the promise given in the dawn of the days to the first farmers.

> And the Lord God planted a garden eastward in Eden; and there he put the man whom he had formed. And a river went out of Eden to water the garden. And the Lord God took the man, and put him into the garden of Eden to dress it and keep it.

As a tiller of the soil, Adam had the power to appropriate and to possess it. But the fisherman cannot possess the sea. For him the stilling of the waters is a miracle.

> And there arose a great storm of wind, and the waves beat into the ship, so that it was now full. And they say unto him, Master, caress thou not that we perish? And he arose, and rebuked the wind, and said unto the sea, Peace, be still. And the wind ceased, and there was a great calm.

Is it any wonder that Peter was a man of little faith? And is it not fitting, nonetheless, that history has been kinder to him than to Adam?

The tiller of the soil "passes into the evening shadows as into rest." He turns his face homeward toward the setting of the sun with a sense of ownership. Having mixed his labours with the soil, he has a firm hope that on the morrow it will bear fruit, for himself and for "succeeding generations, without end." As Duncan noted in *The Way of the Sea*: "The tiller of the soil sows in peace, and in a yellow hazy peace he reaps; he passes his hand over a field, and, lo, in good season he gathers a harvest, for the earth rejoices to serve him."

If labours mark the labourers, Adam gained a sense of mastery over the great primordial forces and a consequent sense of inner freedom and control over his own destiny. Perhaps that is why he so quickly decided to take matters into his own hands and was banished from the garden. As a tiller of the soil, Adam was not simply a toiler, but a creator. And the more he created, the more his sense of control dominated his thinkings. But this sense of control and creativity does not come naturally to those who wrest their living from the ocean depths. The fisherman is not soon possessed of that pride and *hubris* which led to Adam's fall. The sea cannot be cultivated, nor can it be enclosed and brought into one's possession. In it there is no seed time and no assured harvest, and no part of it can be passed on to the next and succeeding generations. Man leaves no mark of his labours upon the sea. In the Old Testament language of Duncan's *The Way of the Sea*, the sea "groweth not old with the men who toil from its coasts. Generation upon the heels of generation…go forth in hope against it, continuing for a space, and returning

spent to the dust." Recently I saw in a book of Irish photography a striking pastoral scene. An elderly man is standing on a hill, looking out over his farm in the fertile valley below. His dwelling is old, his land enclosed by fences of weathered stone: on his right hand is an ancient tree, and in front of him, shrubs yearly renewing themselves. For the hundredth time and perhaps for the thousandth the land had yielded its harvest, the grain or hay already raked into neat stacks on the harvest-brown field. It is the evening of the old farmer's day. And how telling the caption: "Generations."

As an encloser and possessor, the tiller of the soil can rest in the evening and behold the work of his hands and of his father's hands; and cast his eye over his children's inheritance. But it is not given to the fisherman to feel this deep sense of possession. No work of his hands can be passed on to his children. True he can build a new boat for next year. But, unlike the enduring hedges of stone and the tilled fields, that too is impermanent. It will soon spring a leak or go with the wind to feed what Pratt called "the primal hungers of a reef" ("The Ground Swell"), or, like Uncle Nick Top's *Shining Light*, fall prey to the teeth of an ice-pack. Thus it is interesting to contrast pastoral hymns with hymns of the sea. It is not accidental that pastoral hymns are hymns of thanksgiving. Thus:

> Come ye thankful people, come
> Raise the song of harvest-home:
> All is safely gathered in,
> Ere the winter storms begin.

or:

> By Him the rolling seasons
> In fruitful order move;
> Sing to the Lord of harvest
> A song of happy love.

But while the tiller of the soil lifts up his voice in praise for the bounties of his land, the fisherman, like Peter on Galilee, must pray for his very survival. "O hear us when we cry to Thee / For those in peril on the sea." Where the farmer sows in the appointed season, the fisherman must await a time. And when the time comes there is no assurance that the fish will be running. "And Simon answering said unto him, Master, we have toiled all night, and have taken nothing." Simon's nets were filled only by a miracle. As Duncan so aptly put it in *Dr. Grenfell's Parish*, the fishery "is a great lottery of hope and fortune." It is not surprising, then, that the awaiting upon events which we cannot control, and the daily facing of primordial forces which we dare not defy, have coloured our outlook with the dark hues of fatalism.

It is surprising on first view that while the stormy North Atlantic was sculpturing into our souls dark caverns of fatalism, it was turning us into fighters, warrior Vikings on the sea. Fatalism, however, is not a conviction that our dory will fail to make it, but a sense that it is beyond one's control whether she makes it or not. Fatalism permits of struggle and battle even though the outcome rests with the gods.

However difficult it is to reconcile this with our fatalism, we came to look upon the fishery, whether on the Grand Banks or the Labrador, whether at the Funks or at the Front, as a battle to be waged. The undertones of battle in our life on the sea have seized the imagination of a variety of observers. One of the first writers to note this was J. B. Jukes, an English geologist engaged by the Newfoundland government in 1839, whose curiosity led him to the ice in the *Topaz* in March 1840. One day when he had left the *Topaz* in a punt to participate in the kill he was revolted by the sight of slaughter and blood, and was seized with a desire to return immediately to the ship. But he was caught up in the battle cry. As he put it, "the hunting spirit which makes almost every man an animal of prey, and delight in the produce of his gun or bow, kept me in the punt till the late hour of the afternoon." The same feature of the hunt was noted by Moses Harvey and Joseph Hatton in their *Newfoundland, The Oldest British Colony* (1883), the seal hunt depicted as "an army going out to do battle for those who remain at home," while the hunters come back "like returning conquerors." And in his *The Way of the Sea* Norman Duncan noted that "cod and salmon and seal-fat are the spoils of grim battles."

George Allan England, an American observer, best captured the spirit of battle in the seal fishery. His *Vikings of the Ice* is by far the best account of the seal hunt. On first sighting seals, he observed, "confusion burst like a shell." "Keen with blood lust, all who could go on ice began heaving on their gear. Such a shouting, such a leaping to arms, such a buckling-on of sheath knives, steels, belts; such a grabbing of tow ropes and murderous gaffs you could never imagine." Young Cyril, a lad of sixteen, led the warriors over the side of the ship. "He led the leaping, yelling crowd that jumped to the loose-broken pans; that scrambled…to solid floes, and…ran like mad demons, yelling, across that fantastic confusion." Back on ship at night Uncle Edgar Tucker, under strong persuasion, cleared his throat and rhymed off seven verses of "Willy March," the first of which ran:

> De home of his childhood, in Nothren Bay.
> He quit it fer pleasure, much more 'an fer pay
> On de icefields he ventured, most yout'ful an' brave,
> Whereon he sought death, but his life could not save.

Of the writers who reported a spirit of battle in our approach to the sea, and in particular to the seal fishery, Farley Mowat is the last I shall mention. In his *Wake of the Great Sealers*, he reports a sealer's own explanation as to why men went to the ice in the face of danger and for uncertain gain. "Oft-times I asks myself why we was so foolish. Perhaps it was like going off to the wars. Certainly there was risk enough and blood enough. It seemed like you weren't a proper man at all unless you'd gone to the ice…."

Is it possible that our battle with what R. A. Parsons in "Salute to Port de Grave" calls our "beloved enemy the sea" has, paradoxically, induced in us resignation on the land, passivity in social and community affairs? It is not hard to imagine that while tillers of the soil naturally develop a positive and creative spirit, those who must go down to do battle with the sea are likely to become more negative and passive as citizens. What does the character of Pratt's Rachel reveal? Her practiced eye on ominous clouds coming out of the dark west, the widow, having already lost father and husband to the sea's rage, waits alone through the long hours of her young son's first—and last—night at sea "her long thin fingers intertwined / And resting on her lap." Passively waiting on the will of forces beyond her control, was not Rachel one of us? And is it possible that this passive and stoic philosophy is reflected in our social and political attitudes? Certainly active efforts to plan communities and to establish for that purpose town councils were few indeed

until the years immediately following Confederation. And when town councils did spring up were they not the artificial creations of a "centralist" government? The question I am suggesting for future treatment by poet and novelist is whether our battles with the sea have not, surprisingly, turned us into mystics and stoics on the land.

Certainly more than one writer has raised the thought. In an article written in 1937 J. R. Smallwood put it as clearly as any. "Perhaps," he wrote, "the very nature of our struggle, of our methods of wresting a living from Nature, has helped to unfit us for creative and constructive effort."

> It is a fact that for centuries we have lived by *killing* cod and other fish; by *killing* seals in the water or on the ice, and animals on the land; by *killing* birds, and *cutting down trees*. Has all this developed in us a trait of destructiveness or narcotised what ought actually to be an instinct of creativeness?

Richard Gwyn in his study of Smallwood quotes this striking passage concluding that our "struggle for survival exhausted ambition and creativity." I believe, however, that it was not struggle as such that marked us; but the kind of struggle, a tearing down, a "killing," in contrast to the farmer's building up, growing and cultivating; the snatching of our daily food from a hostile environment. In expressing puzzlement as to why Newfoundlanders, a people "given to storytelling, warmly appreciative of song and verse, the turn of a phrase," had not produced more creative writers, Ebbitt Cutler, editor of the *Greatest Hunt in the World*, also quotes Smallwood's passage, and concludes that killing "as a substitute for creativeness is certainly relevant."

And why was it true, as J. R. Smallwood observed in *I Chose Canada*, that after four hundred years we had "precious few substantial houses?" Is it possible that our poverty alone cannot explain this? Did lack of means prevent us from erecting buildings on more secure foundations, did lack of money prevent us from taking elementary steps to keep window curtains from spreading like sails on a windy night: and why were our fish-flakes always about to collapse on their rickety legs? Approached from seaward our fishing villages, our dwellings, flakes and stages, and even our roads, present an air of impermanence. Like the fishing stations of Black Jo, Fichot Islands and Pillar Bight, they seem to have been erected for a season, the expectation of imminent abandonment built into their flimsy structures. As one's boat approaches Cook's Harbour, Shoe Cove or Stocking Harbour the impression deepens that the name 'fishing station' would most accurately describe the scene before him. He might suddenly be struck by the fact, and think it not unnatural, that in Newfoundland these outports, these clusters of houses, are not referred to as villages by local people. I am suggesting that the explanation of this atmosphere of impermanence lies less in our economics than in our souls. For it is not far-fetched to suggest that a life-long battler on the sea, a fish killer, will be a less than enthusiastic planner, creator and builder ashore.

For it may be that the fisherman's dwelling does not serve the same purposes as the farmer's. He does not envisage generations inheriting his dwelling as they inherit the durable homes, the stone hedges and the tilled soil: his house is a roof over his head. His time is the time of his own life and of his children's while they are young. For him past time does not flow over into the future as it must do for the settled farmer. Time is

not arrested in the hills or in his home's firm foundations, or in the stone hedges and ancient trees; it is an ever-rolling stream. Unlike the farmer he lacks a deep sense of the permanence of things. That is why I felt it not untrue to suggest, in another place, that a Newfoundlander is "a person who dwells between the beginning and the end, who has one eye fixed on history and the other on eschatology."

Turning now to a last question about the sea and our souls, it has been suggested that our encounters with ocean storms, as representations of primordial laws admitting of no alteration and of no tampering by man, has profoundly affected our religious sensibilities. On the purely intellectual level, perhaps one would be surprised to find belief in any extraneous forces among people to whom nature presents her face as a cosmos of iron-clad law. Yet it is on a deeper level natural that a North Atlantic fishing people should find a place for powers and agencies outside nature itself. For whereas the great forces of nature, the rampaging flood, the raging tempest, the over-powering Alps, viewed with detachment from afar, that is from a safe vantage point, appeal to the artist in us, and are called sublime; seen in terms of their effects, as threats to our very existence, they evoke in us fear and dread. And that is why we so naturally personify them, why capricious and malignant forces are but the other side of nature. As Thomas Crewe of Finger Cove observed, "the wind is the hand o' the Lard, without pity and wonderful for strength." The people of Ragged Harbour on the night of the great storm "wondered what the Lord God Almighty intended." It was only natural, then, that Billy Luff became converted on the very night "when the vibrant voice [of the minister] was lifted above a gusty night wind and the roar of the Black Rock breakers." Thus where the laws of nature threaten man, it is natural that he should personify them.

How far beneath the surface of our sea hymns is the terrible, personified side of nature? The tiller of the soil affirms his being led into green pastures, beside the still waters. But what the night wind carries from the lips of the mariner is always a question, and the question is never answered until the anchor is cast and the sail furled. "Oh hear us when we cry to Thee." To the Newfoundlander the stilling of the waters of Galilee is the most surprising and most satisfying of miracles.

Are the gods of the sea less to be loved than propitiated and sometimes defied? May they not be harsher than pastoral gods? Is this what Duncan meant by the statement that the untamable ocean robs "souls of their graces," and by this striking passage from The Way of the Sea?

> When they (fishermen from the bleak coast) roam afar—as from bleak places, where no yellow fields, no broad, waving acres, yielding bounteously, make love manifest to the children of men...when they roam afar, it may be, the gods they fetch back are terrible gods.

Perhaps our religion reflects more the might of the seas than the fertility of the land. Certainly in Ragged Harbour and Twist Tickle souls are stirred less by the promise of green pastures than by the majesty of the restless wave. And "a great whirlwind shall be raised up from the coasts of the earth. The Lord hath his way in the whirlwind and in the storm." In Ragged Harbour, "some men have fashioned a god of rock and tempest and the sea's rage—a gigantic, frowning shape, throned in a mist, whereunder black waters curl and hiss, and are cold and without end."

Perhaps we personify the terrible by a psychological law, some law of our nature as iron-clad and unalterable as the laws of sea and the wind. For when threatening forces are personified the battle becomes personal and the hope for victory a little more realistic. The sailor's belief in jinkers illustrates this law of our nature. In his book *Forty-Eight Days Adrift* Captain Job Barbour discusses the jinker. A jinker, as this seasoned mariner wrote, "is a member of a ship's crew who is believed always to bring bad luck." "Of one thing I am certain," Barbour says, "and that is that all sailors and fishermen believe in the malign influence of the jinker and fear him." Barbour himself professes to be willing to leave the question of the truth of this belief to readers, but in telling how five years before he shipped a jinker on the *Sea Bird* and was immediately battered by a hurricane he confesses: "Of course, I was responsible in the eyes of the crew for having taken the jinker on board and I punished myself and kept clear of their accusing looks by holding the wheel for eleven consecutive hours." Was Barbour driven to this measure by fear of the crew only? On a ship the jinker soon becomes responsible for the demons of the storm, and can be dismissed from his duties, sent below for the duration of the voyage, his powers nullified: or, in the extremity, he can be cast into the midst of the sea. "But the Lord sent out a great wind into the sea, and there was a mighty tempest...so that the ship was like to be broken." Then the sailors were afraid and said everyone to his fellow, "Come let us cast lots, that we may know for whose cause this evil is upon us." And they cast lots and "took up Jonah, and cast him forth into the sea: and the sea ceased from her raging."

We have not only jinkers, but ghosts. Why are there more ghosts per harbour and cove in Newfoundland than anywhere else in North America? Is it unnatural that a people as bound and confined by the laws of nature as they were confined on the close of navigation should envisage a place for beings subject to none of these limitations? Or, far from being unnatural, is it inevitable that such a people would make room for free spirits as the Epicureans left spaces for their gods in a universe that was otherwise but matter in motion? Perhaps these are questions to which the dark sides of our souls will yield no answer. In any case we delight—even when our nerves tingle—in the sight of ghosts and spirits breaking all of the laws that so confine us and so often take on the countenance of enemies. So much the worse for the laws of nature when a ghost at one and the same time can be seen in Julie's Harbour and boarding a boat at anchor in Hussey's Cove: when wingless it can defy gravitation, or appear as a ball of fire on the crest of a wave. Do ghosts take upon themselves our impotence as the scapegoat took our sins into the desert?

The carved and rugged headlands of this sea-worn rock witness to the might and fury of the tempest. The marks it has made on our souls are as deep, and perhaps as abiding, as the seams in the granite cliff. As my little tribute to that son of Newfoundland whose words so beautifully caught the voice of the sea. I end with these lines from Pratt.

> Tell me thy secret, O Sea,
> The mystery sealed in thy breast:
> Come, breathe it in whispers to me,
> A child of thy fevered unrest.

Profile:

Jean-Claude Roy

Editors

Jean-Claude Roy, a French-born artist, has spent many years of his artistic life in Newfoundland.

He has been deeply inspired by the rugged grandeur of Newfoundland and his numerous paintings of this place reflect his love of his "second home."

One peculiar feature of his work is the image of a "black sun." His rationale for painting the sun black stems, he says, from the notion that when one looks at the sun directly, one is blinded by its brilliance. Thus the black sun appears in many of his works.

As an artist, he is fond of creating contrasting images of Newfoundland and southwest France, where he lives when he is not in Newfoundland. One can compare, for example, the rugged beauty of a coastal headland peppered with boulders thrown up by the sea to the tranquil beauty of a field filled with sunflowers in southern France. But there in the top right-hand corner of each painting is the identifiable mark of this unique artist, the black sun.

Beaumont Hamel, oil on canvas, 36" x 48" by Jean-Claude Roy.

French's Cove, Bay Roberts, oil on canvas, 36" x 48" by Jean-Claude Roy.

The Fruits of Toil
Norman Duncan

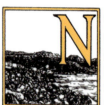Now the wilderness, savage and remote, yields to the strength of men. A generation strips it of tree and rock, a generation tames it and tills it, a generation passes into the evening shadows as into rest in a garden, and thereafter the children of that place possess it in peace and plenty, through succeeding generations, without end, and shall to the end of the world. But the sea is tameless: as it was in the beginning, it is now, and shall ever be—mighty, savage, dread, infinitely treacherous and hateful, yielding only that which is wrested from it, snarling, raging, snatching lives, spoiling souls of their graces. The tiller of the soil sows in peace, and in a yellow, hazy peace he reaps; he passes his hand over a field, and, lo, in good season he gathers a harvest, for the earth rejoices to serve him. The deep is not thus subdued; the toiler of the sea—the Newfoundlander of the upper shore—is born to conflict, ceaseless and deadly, and, in the dawn of all the days, he puts forth anew to wage it, as his father did, and his father's father, and as his children must, and his children's children, to the last of them; nor from day to day can he foresee the issue, nor from season to season foretell the worth of the spoil, which is what chance allows. Thus laboriously, precariously, he slips through life: he follows hope through the toilsome years; and past summers are a black regret and bitterness to him, but summers to come are all rosy with new promise.

Long ago, when young Luke Dart, the Boot Bay trader, was ambitious for Shore patronage, he said to Solomon Stride, of Ragged Harbour, a punt fisherman: "Solomon, b'y, an you be willin', I'll trust you with twine for a cod-trap. An you trade with me, b'y, I'll trade with you, come good times or bad." Solomon was young and lusty, a mighty youth in bone and seasoned muscle, lunged like a blast furnace, courageous and finely sanguine. Said he: "An you trust me with twine for a trap, skipper, I'll deal fair by you, come good times or bad. I'll pay for un, skipper, with the first fish I cotches." Said Luke Dart: "When I trust, b'y, I trust. You pays for un when you can." It was a compact, so, at the end of the season, Solomon built a cottage under the Man-o'-War, Broad Cove way, and married a maid of the place. In five months of that winter he made the trap, every net of it, leader and all, with his own hands, that he might know that the work was good, to the last knot and splice. In the spring, he put up the stage and the flake, and made the skiff; which done, he waited for a sign of fish. When the tempered days came, he hung the net on the horse, where it could be seen from the threshold of the cottage. In the evenings he sat with Priscilla on the bench at the door, and dreamed great dreams, while the red sun went down in the sea, and the shadows crept out of the wilderness.

"Woman, dear," said this young Solomon Stride, with a slap of his great thigh, "'twill be a gran' season for fish this year."

"Sure, b'y," said Priscilla, tenderly; "'twill be a gran' season for fish."

"Ay," Solomon sighed, "'twill that—this year."

The gloaming shadows gathered over the harbour water, and hung, sullenly, between the great rocks, rising all roundabout.

"'Tis handy t' three hundred an' fifty dollars I owes Luke Dart for the twine," mused Solomon.

"'Tis a hape o' money t' owe," said Priscilla.

"Hut!" growled Solomon, deep in his chest. "'Tis like nothin'."

"'Tis not much," said Priscilla, smiling, "when you has a trap."

Dusk and a clammy mist chased the glory from the hills; the rocks turned black, and a wind, black and cold, swept out of the wilderness and ran to sea.

"Us'll pay un all up this year," said Solomon. "Oh," he added, loftily, "'twill be easy. 'Tis t' be a gran' season!"

"Sure!" said she, echoing his confidence.

Night filled the cloudy heavens overhead. It drove the flush of pink in upon the sun, and, following fast and overwhelmingly, thrust the flaring red and gold over the rim of the sea; and it was dark.

"Us'll pay un for a trap, dear," chuckled Solomon, "an' have enough left over t' buy a—"

"Oh," she cried, with an ecstatic gasp, "a sewin' machane!"

"Iss," he roared. "Sure, girl!"

But, in the beginning of that season, when the first fish ran in for the capelin and the nets were set out, the ice was still hanging off shore, drifting vagrantly with the wind; and there came a gale in the night, springing from the northeast—a great, vicious wind, which gathered the ice in a pack and drove it swiftly in upon the land. Solomon Stride put off in a punt, in a sea tossing and white, to loose the trap from its moorings. Three times, while the pack swept nearer, crunching and horribly groaning, as though lashed to cruel speed by the gale, the wind beat him back through the tickle; and, upon the fourth essay, when his strength was breaking, the ice ran over the place where the trap was, and chased the punt into the harbour, frothing upon its flank. When, three days thereafter, a west wind carried the ice to sea, Solomon dragged the trap from the bottom. Great holes were bruised in the nets, head rope and span line were ground to pulp, the anchors were lost. Thirty-seven days and nights it took to make the nets whole again, and in that time the great spring run of cod passed by. So in the next spring, Solomon was deeper in the debt of sympathetic Luke Dart—for the new twine and for the winter's food he had eaten; but, of an evening, when he sat on the bench with Priscilla, he looked through the gloaming shadows gathered over the harbour water and hanging between the great rocks, to the golden summer approaching, and dreamed gloriously of the fish he would catch in his trap.

"Priscilla, dear," said Solomon Stride, slapping his iron thigh, "they be a fine sign o' fish down the coast. 'Twill be a gran' season, I'm thinkin'."

"Sure, b'y," Priscilla agreed; "'twill be a gran' cotch o' fish you'll have this year."

Dusk and the mist touched the hills, and, in the dreamful silence, their glory faded; the rocks turned black, and the wind from the wilderness ruffled the water beyond the flake.

"Us'll pay Luke Dart this year, I tells you," said Solomon, like a boastful boy. "Us'll pay un twice over."

"'Twill be fine t' have the machane," said she, with shining eyes.

"An' the calico t' use un on," said he.

And so, while the night spread overhead, these two simple folk feasted upon all the sweets of life; and all that they desired they possessed, as fast as fancy could form wishes, just as though the bench were a bit of magic furniture, to bring dreams true—

until the night, advancing, thrust the red and gold of the sunset clouds over the rim of the sea, and it was dark.

"Leave us goa in," said Priscilla.

"This year," said Solomon, rising, "I be goain' t' cotch three hundred quintals o' fish. Sure, I be—this year."

"'Twill be fine," said she.

It chanced in that year that the fish failed utterly; hence, in the winter following, Ragged Harbour fell upon days of distress, and three old women and one old man starved to death—and five children, of whom one was the infant son of Solomon Stride. Neither in that season, nor in any one of the thirteen years romping after, did this man catch three hundred quintals of cod in his trap. In pure might of body—in plenitude and quality of strength—in the full, eager power of brawn—he was great as the men of any time, a towering glory to the whole race, here hidden; but he could not catch three hundred quintals of cod. In spirit—in patience, hope, courage, and the fine will for toil—he was great; but, good season or bad, he could not catch three hundred quintals of cod. He met night, cold, fog, wind, and the fury of waves, in their craft, in their swift assault, in their slow, crushing descent; but all the cod he could wrest from the sea, being given into the hands of Luke Dart, an honest man, yielded only sufficient provision for food and clothing for himself and Priscilla—only enough to keep their bodies warm and still the crying of their stomachs. Thus, while the nets of the trap rotted, and Solomon came near to middle age, the debt swung from seven hundred dollars to seven, and back to seventy-three, which it was on an evening in spring, when he sat with Priscilla on the sunken bench at the door, and dreamed great dreams, as he watched the shadows gather over the harbour water and sullenly hang between the great rocks, rising all roundabout.

"I wonder, b'y," said Priscilla, "if 'twill be a good season—this year."

"Oh, sure!" exclaimed Solomon. "Sure!"

"D'ye think it, b'y?" wistfully.

"Woman," said he, impressively, "us'ill cotch a hape o' fish in the trap this year. They be millions o' fish t' the say," he went on excitedly; "millions o' fish t' the say. They be there, woman. 'Tis oan'y for us t' take un out. I be goain' t' wark hard this year."

"You be a great warker, Solomon," said she; "my, but you be!"

Priscilla smiled, and Solomon smiled; and it was as though all the labour and peril of the season were past, and the stage were full to the roof with salt cod. In the happiness of this dream they smiled again, and turned their eyes to the hills, from which the glory of purple and yellow was departing to make way for the misty dusk.

"Skipper Luke Dart says t' me," said Solomon, "that 'tis the luxuries that keeps folk poor."

Priscilla said nothing at all.

"They be nine dollars agin me in seven years for crame o' tartar," said Solomon. "Think o' that!"

"My," said she, "but 'tis a lot! But we be used to un now, Solomon, an' we can't get along without un."

"Sure," said he, "'tis good we're not poor like some folk."

Night drove the flush of pink in upon the sun and followed the red and gold of the horizon over the rim of the sea.

"'Tis growin' cold," said she.

"Leave us goa in," said he.

In thirty years after that time, Solomon Stride put to sea ten thousand times. Ten thousand times he passed through the tickle rocks to the free, heaving deep for salmon and cod, thereto compelled by the inland waste, which contributes nothing to the sustenance of the men of that coast. Hunger, lurking in the shadows of days to come, inexorably drove him into the chances of the conflict. Perforce he matched himself ten thousand times against the restless might of the sea, immeasurable and unrestrained, surviving the gamut of its moods because he was great in strength, fearlessness, and cunning. He weathered four hundred gales, from the gray gusts which come down between Quid Nunc and the Man-o'-War, leaping upon the fleet, to the summer tempests, swift and black, and the first blizzards of winter. He was wrecked off the Mull, off the Three Poor Sisters, on the Pancake Rock, and again off the Mull. Seven times he was swept to sea by the offshore wind. Eighteen times he was frozen to the seat of his punt; and of these, eight times his feet were frozen, and thrice his festered right hand. All this he suffered, and more, of which I may set down six separate periods of starvation, in which thirty-eight men, women, and children died—all this, with all the toil, cold, despair, loneliness, hunger, peril, and disappointment therein contained. And so he came down to old age—with a bent back, shrunken arms, and filmy eyes—old Solomon Stride, now prey for the young sea. But, of an evening in spring, he sat with Priscilla on the sunken bench at the door, and talked hopefully of the fish he would catch from his punt.

"Priscilla, dear," said he, rubbing his hand over his weazened thigh, "I be thinkin' us punt fishermen'll have a—"

Priscilla was not attending; she was looking into the shadows above the harbour water, dreaming deeply of a mystery of the Book, which had long puzzled her; so, in silence, Solomon, too, watched the shadows rise and sullenly hang between the great rocks.

"Solomon, b'y," she whispered, "I wonder what the seven thunders uttered."

"'Tis quare, that—what the seven thunders uttered," said Solomon. "My, woman, but 'tis!"

"'An' he set his right foot upon the sea,'" she repeated, staring over the greying water to the clouds which flamed gloriously at the edge of the world, "'an' his left foot on the earth—'"

"'An' cried with a loud voice,'" said he, whispering in awe, "'as when a lion roareth; an' when he had cried, *seven thunders uttered their voices*.'"

"'Seven thunders uttered their voices,'" said she; "'an' when the seven thunders had uttered their voices, I was about to write, an' I heard a voice from heaven sayin' unto me, Seal up those things which the seven thunders uttered, an' write them not.'"

The wind from the wilderness, cold and black, covered the hills with mist: the dusk fell, and the glory faded from the heights.

"Oh, Solomon," she said, clasping her hands, "I wonder what the seven thunders uttered! Think you, b'y, 'twas the kind o' sins that can't be forgiven?"

"'Tis the seven mysteries!"

"I wonder what they be," said she.

"Sh-h-h, dear," he said, patting her grey head; "thinkin' on they things'll capsize you an you don't look out."

The night had driven all the colour from the sky: it had descended upon the red and gold of the cloudy west, and covered them. It was cold and dark.

"'An' seven thunders uttered their voices,'" she said, dreamily.

"Sh-h-h, dear!" said he. "Leave us goa in."

Twenty-one years longer old Solomon Stride fished out of Ragged Harbour. He put to sea five thousand times more, weathered two hundred more gales, survived five more famines—all in the toil for salmon and cod. He was a punt fisherman again, was old Solomon; for the nets of the trap had rotted, had been renewed six times, strand by strand, and had rotted at last beyond repair. What with the weather he dared not pit his failing strength against, the return of fish to Luke Dart fell off from year to year; but, as Solomon said to Luke, "livin' expenses kep' up wonderful," notwithstanding.

"I be so used t' luxuries," he went on, running his hand through his long grey hair, "that 'twould be hard t' come down t' common livin'. Sure, 'tis sugar I wants t' me tea—not black-strap. 'Tis what I l'arned," he added, proudly, "when I were a trap fisherman."

"'Tis all right, Solomon," said Luke. "Many's the quintal o' fish you traded with me."

"Sure," Solomon chuckled; "'twould take a year t' count un."

In course of time it came to the end of Solomon's last season—those days of it when, as the folk of the coast say, the sea is hungry for lives—and the man was eighty-one years old, and the debt to Luke Dart had crept up to $230.80. The offshore wind, rising suddenly, with a blizzard in its train, caught him alone on the Grappling Hook grounds. He was old, very old—old and feeble and dull: the cold numbed him; the snow blinded him; the wind made sport of the strength of his arms. He was carried out to sea, rowing doggedly, thinking all the time that he was drawing near the harbour tickle; for it did not occur to him then that the last of eight hundred gales could be too great for him. He was carried out from the sea, where the strength of his youth had been spent, to the Deep, which had been a mystery to him all his days. That night he passed on a pan of ice, where he burned his boat, splinter by splinter, to keep warm. At dawn he lay down to die. The snow ceased, the wind changed: the ice was carried to Ragged Harbour. Eleazar Manuel spied the body of Solomon from the lookout, and put out and brought him in—revived him and took him home to Priscilla. Through the winter the old man doddered about the harbour, dying of consumption. When the tempered days came—the days of balmy sunshine and cold evening winds—he came quickly to the pass of glittering visions, which, for such as die of the lung trouble, come at the end of life.

In the spring, when the *Lucky Star*, three days out from Boot Bay, put into Ragged Harbour to trade for the first catch, old Skipper Luke Dart was aboard, making his last voyage to the Shore; for he was very old, and longed once more to see the rocks of all that coast before he made ready to die. When he came ashore, Eleazar Manuel told him that Solomon Stride lay dying at home; so the skipper went to the cottage under the Man-O'-War to say good-bye to his old customer and friend—and there found him, propped up in bed, staring at the sea.

"Skipper Luke," Solomon quavered, in deep excitement, "be you just come in, b'y?"

"Iss—but an hour gone."

"What be the big craft hangin' off shoare? Eh—what be she, b'y?"

There had been no craft in sight when the Lucky Star beat in. "Were she a fore-an'-after, Solomon?" said Luke, evasively.

"Sure, noa, b'y!" cried Solomon. "She were a square-rigged craft, with all sail set—a great, gran' craft—a quare craft, b'y—like she were made o' glass, canvas an' hull an' all; an' she had shinin' ropes, an' she were shinin' all over. Sure, they be a star t' the tip o' her bowsprits b'y, an' a star t' the peak o' her mainmast—seven stars they be, in all. Oh, she were a gran' sight!"

"Hem-m!" said Luke, stroking his beard. "She've not come in yet."

"A gran' craft!" said Solomon.

"'Tis accordin'," said Luke, "t' whether you be sot on oak bottoms or glass ones."

"She were bound down north t' the Labrador," Solomon went on quickly, "an' when she made the Grapplin' Hook grounds she come about an headed for the tickle, with her sails squared. Sure she ran right over the Pancake, b'y, like he weren't there at all, an'— How's the wind, b'y?"

"Dead off shore from the tickle."

Solomon stared at Luke. "She were coming' straight in agin the wind," he said, hoarsely. "Maybe, skipper," he went on, with a little laugh, "she do be the ship for souls. They be many things strong men knows nothin' about. What think you?"

"Ay—maybe; maybe she be."

"Maybe—maybe—she do be invisible t' mortal eyes. Maybe, skipper, you hasn't seed her; maybe 'tis that my eyes do be opened t' such sights. Maybe she've turned in—for me."

The men turned their faces to the window again, and gazed long and intently at the sea, which a storm cloud had turned black. Solomon dozed for a moment, and when he awoke, Luke Dart was still staring dreamily out to sea.

"Skipper Luke," said Solomon, with a smile as of one in an enviable situation, "'tis fine t' have nothin' agin you on the books when you comes t' die."

"Sure, b'y," said Luke, hesitating not at all, though he knew to a cent what was on the books against Solomon's name, "'tis fine t' be free o' debt."

"Ah," said Solomon, the smile broadening gloriously, "'tis fine, I tells you! 'Twas the three hundred quintal I cotched last season that paid un all up. 'Twas a gran' cotch—last year. Ah," he sighed, "'twas a gran' cotch o' fish."

"Iss—you be free o' debt now, b'y."

"What be the balance t' my credit, skipper? Sure I forget."

"Hem-m," the skipper coughed, pausing to form a guess which might be within Solomon's dream; then he ventured: "Fifty dollars?"

"Iss," said Solomon, "fifty an' moare, skipper. Sure, you has forgot the eighty cents."

"Fifty-eighty," said the skipper, positively. "'Tis that. I call un t' mind now. 'Tis fiftyeighty—iss, sure. Did you get a receipt for un, Solomon?"

"I doan't mind me now."

"Um-m-m—well," said the skipper, "I'll send un t' the woman the night—an order on the *Lucky Star*."

"Fifty-eighty for the woman!" said Solomon. "'Twill kape her off the Gov'ment for three years, an she be savin'. 'Tis fine—that!"

When the skipper had gone, Priscilla crept in, and sat at the head of the bed, holding Solomon's hand; and they were silent for a long time, while the evening approached.

"I be goain' t' die the night, dear," said Solomon at last.

"Iss, b'y," she answered; "you be goain' t' die."

Solomon was feverish now; and, thereafter, when he talked, his utterance was thick and fast.

"'Tis not hard," said Solomon. "Sh-h-h," he whispered, as though about to impart a secret. "The ship that's hangin' off shoare, waitin' for me soul, do be a fine craft—with shinin' canvas an' ropes. Sh-h! She do be 'tother side o' Mad Mull now—waitin'."

Priscilla trembled, for Solomon had come to the time of visions—when the words of the dying are the words of prophets, and contain revelations. What of the utterings of the seven thunders?

"Sure the Lard he've blessed us, Priscilla," said Solomon, rational again. "Goodness an' marcy has followed us all the days o' our lives. Our cup runneth over."

"Praise the Lard," said Priscilla.

"Sure," Solomon went on, smiling like a little child, "we've had but eleven famines, an' we've had the means o' grace pretty regular, which is what they hasn't t' Round 'Arbour. We've had one little baby for a little while. Iss—one de-ear little baby, Priscilla; an' there's them that's hat none o' their own, at all. Sure we've had enough t' eat when they wasn't a famine—an' bakin' powder, an' raisins, an' all they things, an' sugar, an' rale good tea. An' you had a merino dress, an' I had a suit o' rale tweed—come straight from England. We hasn't seed a railroad train, dear, but we've seed a steamer, an' we've heard tell o' the quare things they be t' St. John's. Ah, the Lard he've favoured us above our deserts: He've been good t' us, Priscilla. But, oh, you hasn't had the sewin' machane, an' you hasn't had the peach-stone t' plant in the garden. 'Tis my fault, dear—'tis not the Lard's. I should 'a' got you the peach-stone from St. John's, you did want un so much—oh, so much! 'Tis that I be sorry for, now, dear; but 'tis all over, an' I can't help it. It wouldn't 'a' growed anyway, I know it wouldn't; but you thought it would, an' I wisht I'd got un for you."

"'Tis nothin', Solomon," she sobbed. "Sure, I was joakin' all the time. 'Twouldn't 'a' growed."

"Ah," he cried, radiant, "was you joakin'?"

"Sure," she said.

"We've not been poor, Priscilla," said he, continuing, "an' they be many folk that's poor. I be past me labour now," he went on, talking with rising effort, for it was at the sinking of the sun, "an' 'tis time for me t' die. 'Tis time—for I be past me labour."

Priscilla held his hand a long time after that—a long, silent time, in which the soul of the man struggled to release itself, until it was held but by a thread.

"Solomon!"

The old man seemed not to hear.

"Solomon, b'y!" she cried.

"Iss?" faintly.

She leaned over him to whisper in his ear, "Does you see the gates o' heaven?" she said. "Oh, does you?"

"Sure, dear; heaven do be—"

Solomon had not strength enough to complete the sentence.

"B'y! B'y!"

He opened his eyes and turned them to her face. There was the gleam of a tender smile in them.

"The seven thunders," she said. "The utterin's of the seven thunders—what was they, b'y?"

"'An' the seven thunders uttered their voices,'" he mumbled, "'an'—'"

She waited, rigid, listening, to hear the rest; but no words came to her ears.

"Does you hear me, b'y?" she said.

"'An' seven—thunders—uttered their voices,'" he gasped, "'an' the seven thunders—said—said'"

The light failed; all the light and golden glory went out of the sky, for the first cloud of a tempest had curtained the sun.

"'An' said—'" she prompted.

"'An' uttered—an' said—an' said—'"

"Oh, what?" she moaned.

Now, in that night, when the body of old Solomon Stride, a worn-out hulk, aged and wrecked in the toil of the deep, fell into the hands of Death, the sea, like a lusty youth, raged furiously in those parts. The ribs of many schooners, slimy and rotten, and the white bones of men in the offshore depths, know of its strength in that hour—of its black, hard wrath, in gust and wave and breaker. Eternal in might and malignance is the sea! It groweth not old with the men who toil from its coasts. Generation upon the heels of generation, infinitely arising, go forth in hope against it, continuing for a space, and returning spent to the dust. They age and crumble and vanish, each in its turn, and the wretchedness of the first is the wretchedness of the last. Ay, the sea has measured the strength of the dust in old graves, and, in this day, contends with the sons of dust, whose sons will follow to the fight for an hundred generations, and thereafter, until harvests may be gathered from rocks. As it is written, the life of a man is a shadow, swiftly passing, and the days of his strength are less; but the sea shall endure in the might of youth to the wreck of the world.

Excerpts from

"What Happened Was… The Story of the Newfoundland Cod Moratorium"

Chris Brookes

This documentary was produced one year after the July 2, 1992 announcement of the cod moratorium in Newfoundland.

Sam Lee, Petty Harbour fisherman
Chris Brookes, documentary producer
Anita Best, traditional singer
Wavey Brace, Chance Cove fisherman's wife

Sam Lee:

It was the right thing to do. They had to close it. I knew it had to be something like that done to save the fishery. And now coming into it this year, well it's only this summer now and then the fall, then we're back at it again. Hopefully the fish comes back.

Chris Brookes:

Maybe part of the problem was we could never really see it. Out there where two huge ocean currents meet and dance together: from the south, the Gulf Stream, warm; from the north, the Labrador Current, very cold. Above the surface, their dance looks like this, like fog. Underwater, the dance is much more rare and beautiful, but only the fish know what it looks like. For centuries, millions upon millions upon millions of them have come to breed and feed and dance with it. That's why for five hundred years the Newfoundland cod fishery was the greatest fishery in the world.

Anita Best [singing]:

So catch a-hold this one, catch a-hold that one, / Swing around this one, swing around she, / Dance around this one, dance around that one, / Diddle dum this one, diddle dum dee.

Chris Brookes:

The trouble is you can lose your way in the fog; the landscape you know can slip away—like the memory of what used to be.

Anita Best:

My name is Anita Best and I'm a traditional singer. I mostly sing traditional Newfoundland songs. This is a song that relates to the Newfoundland situation now since the fishing moratorium. You no longer can catch any codfish. And since there were a lot of people employed in catching that codfish and they made their living off it, the federal government came up with a compensation program. That's what they call "the package". [singing] *They called a moratorium, they left us high and dry, / They took our small communities and left us FPI, / They give us compensation, they hope to buy our soul, / Their fancy fisheries package just another kind of dole. / Now which side are you on, which side are you on?*

Sam Lee:

What is a fisherman? Some people says he's a fool. Everybody that's fishing says they're fools. You know, when you get up every day and you don't know, every day is just different. When I get up in the morning I don't know what it's going to be. I might go out to my trap, it may be full of fish; it may be empty, it may be gone. The ropes could bust clear of the grapelins and then tides take it away, a whale could take it away and there's so many different things, you know. That's one thing about fishing, it gets in your blood. When you're really fishing you're not really your own boss anymore. The fish dictate then how hard you work. If the fish is there, you work, you don't feel it, you don't see it, you just do it. But if there's nothing there, that's when it's hard work. That's when you feel every muscle in your body aching 'cause you're hauling on ropes and you know, you're probably taking a five or six hundred pound anchor and trying to haul it up by hand you know because you got to move it a bit. Then you feel it. But if there's any fish, you take that in one hand and go on with it, don't even think about it, you know.... No such thing as bad backs.... You straighten yourself up, hold onto your hips and bend yourself straight and go at it again. It's a good life. I wouldn't change it.

Anita Best [singing]:

There's lots of fish in Bonavist' Harbour, lots of fishing in around here, / Boys and girls are fishing together, forty-five from Carbonear.

Wavey Brace:

My name's Wavey Brace. My husband Albert is a fisherman and we live in Chance Cove, Trinity Bay. First when the moratorium came I was literally afraid for my husband. I was really scared. Excuse me, I get a little emotional, but I was afraid for his emotional health. He'd get up morning after morning and look out that window with tears in his eyes. What am I going to do? I'm going to go out of my mind, how are we going to live? That was before the package was brought forward, and even after that didn't take away from the fact that there was still nothing to do. He got to the point where his nerves were so on edge you couldn't look at him sideways. And I knew what was wrong, but I had to try and stay strong. I never let him see me cry. Never. I walked away because I figured that if he saw me cry it would kill him.

Sam Lee:

It's not just work, it's not just money. It's not just, you know—hell, I don't doubt but I could be a lot better off if I didn't have to go into the fishery, you know what I mean. But like, when I'm fishing my heart and soul is into what I'm doing. But for me to go anywhere else and get a job, I don't know. God, as soon as the sun is shining you'd want to be out and your mind would be on the water, what you would be doing—not what you're doing....

Anita Best [singing]:

Your heart would break all for their sake if you were standing by / To see them drowning one by one and no relief being nigh / Struggling with the boisterous waves, all in their youth and bloom / At length they sank to rise no more, all on the eighth of June.

Sam Lee:

...I don't know what to be thinking. I dreads the thoughts of selling it. If I sells it, then what do I do? I got nothing, right. And I know it's just as well to have nothing as have it up there lying up, because it's not doing me any good. But then it's like I'm quitting, like I'm giving up on it. I don't want to give up on it. Not yet. It's a big thing, you know, just to give up on it. When there is hope, there's always hope, not much of it, but my mind-frame now is telling me that the fish is not caught—it's gone, it's moved somewhere, right. And in time it'll come back to us. It's just, you can't even imagine now never having a cod again.

Miners

Michael Crummey

When they were forced to leave off fishing
they left everything they knew
strode tall and awkwardly young
into a mining town
green as the green salt water
they'd walked away from and started digging,
spading zinc and iron ore
and a little copper and gold
out of the earth's ocean,
coming up for air after
a ten-hour shift like whales
surfacing into light,
blowing dust out of their nostrils,
spitting out tiny shards of rock

Some of them lived in the darkness and damp
of the earth for forty-odd years
but never learned to love it,
never accepted it as theirs and welcome;
they'd seen enough friends swept under
a sudden flow of stone to fear for themselves,
waited uncomfortably for it each day
like a bill they half-expected in the mail

The fishing they remembered as something
like perfect freedom—
A man can bargain with the sea, they'd say
believe in it,
a cast-net is an honest prayer
a statement of faith you live by;
but they never understood the earth
or its ruthlessness
and never forgave it either

Even after the mine closed down
it stayed with them
this anger, the fear—
The earth collects on all its debts
they'd say, and resigned themselves to that;
sooner or later, the earth collects

Saltwater Joys
Wayne Chaulk

I was born down by the water it's here I'm gonna stay.
I've searched for all the reasons why I should go away,
But I haven't got the thirst for all those modern day toys,
So I'll just take my chances with those saltwater joys.

Following a little brook as it trickles to the shore,
In the autumn when the trees are flamin' red,
Kicking leaves that fall around me, watching sunsets paint the hills,
It's all I'll ever need to feel at home.

This island that we cling to has been handed down with pride
By folks who fought to live here takin' hardships all in stride.
So I'll compliment her beauty hold on to my goodbyes
And I'll stay and take my chances with those saltwater joys.

How can I leave those mornin's with the sunrise on the cove,
And the gulls like flies surroundin' Clayton's wharf,
Platter's Island wrapped in rainbow in the evening after fog.
The ocean smells are perfume to my soul.

Some go to where the buildings reach to meet the clouds,
Where warm and gentle people turn to swarmin' faceless crowds.
So I'll do without their riches, glamour, and the noise,
And I stay and take my chances with those saltwater joys.

Winter view of Bonne Bay

Buddy and the Other Fellers Keep on Trucking

Mark Vaughan-Jackson

Never let it be said that Buddy Wasisname and the Other Fellers do things ass-backwards. At least, not without a very good reason.

For much of this year, the musical and comedic talents of Kevin Blackmore, Wayne Chaulk and Ray Johnson—known to all and sundry as Buddy Wasisname and the Other Fellers—have been hard at work touring the country. After being in the musical game for so long, the trio have adopted a methodical, logical approach.

They tour the country in easy-to-swallow, seventeen-day chunks, then return home to recuperate, be with their families and work on new material.

The cycle begins again as the new material is then road-tested extensively. The fruits of their labours can be found on *d'Lard Liftin'*, their ninth album.

"We were lucky," said Chaulk. "(For) our last tour, the product was finished and we had it couriered to Saskatoon. When we arrived, it had just arrived, so we had it for our 12-show tour. We sold a load. You can imagine all the homesick Newfoundlanders who are dying for a little piece of home. And they're the first to buy it."

That continued throughout their tour.

"We had it on tour before our sales office had it to distribute it in the stores."

Touring first, then releasing an album may run against standard practice in the industry, but that's the way Buddy & Co. work.

"Live is paramount. Live shows is where we start and then our recordings are subsequently taken from live shows, normally," said Blackmore, the alter ego of Buddy Wasisname.

"We usually test out songs live on the stage before we go and record them, so we have some idea whether or not the fans are going to like them. We've always worked it that way and hopefully it keeps our audience."

Perhaps the best reason why they release an album in support of a tour, instead of touring in support of an album, is that it sharpens the material, ensuring the effort of the recording process isn't misplaced.

"We've had songs that we thought were gold. We practised them, we rehearsed them and then we played for the audience—and we were very disappointed with the reaction. And we dropped them," Chaulk said.

"So what you're hearing on this recording is the best of the last tour."

This measured, audience-driven approach to the recording process is much in line with the band's approach to the music industry—though Kevin Blackmore makes a face when he hears the word "industry."

From the onset in the 1980's, Buddy Wasisname and the Other Fellers have taken great pains to do their own thing. They still live in rural Newfoundland and base their entire professional lives around the time they spend at home. They prefer the independence of working with a Gander-based production company, Third Wave Productions, rather than courting a mainland mega-label.

Each of the three is responsible for a different facet of the band's professional side: Johnson handles publicity, Chaulk the finances and Blackmore the bookings.

It's a truly independent existence that suits the trio just fine, thank you very much.

The choice is a consequence of the trio's simple desire to be masters of their own destiny. They note that the music industry is notorious for wrestling control away from the artists it signs.

While some people may want the major record deal route to the "top" of the business, Buddy Wasisname and the Other Fellers do not.

"Anybody who wants to ride this roller coaster immediately to the top finds that the slippery slide on the other side is very fast and rapid, and it's a really flat bottom," Blackmore said.

"However, if anybody wants to take this on a ride which can last the rest of their life, that's possible too."

Views on self-management and the fortunes of the music industry reflect the serious side of the band's members, a side not often shown on stage, where Buddy and the Other Fellers display a knack for comedy that's brought the house down across the country.

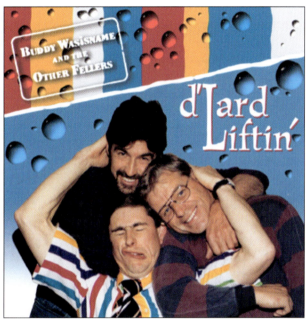
CD/cassette cover for d'Lard Liftin' by Buddy Wasisname and the Other Fellers.

"As time passes, we're getting the question asked us, 'How long are you going to keep doing this?'" Chaulk said, his tone showing exactly what he thinks of that particular question.

"The common response to this question is that we're going to continue. We're going to take this beyond right into the next life. And when the rest of you come over, the place will be sold out, the advertising will be all done and there'll be a seat waiting for you, right? Just have your twenty dollars ready."

Strip-mined
Christopher Pratt

Newfoundland has always been strip-mined in every sense: by the glaciers, which caused the absence of soil nearly everywhere; by paper companies; and by the domestic use of forests. It was strip-mined of its marine resources—take it, take it all out, don't even bother to put anything back.

This snatch-and-run reflex is very characteristic of Newfoundlanders because survival here is so marginal. You get your hands on something and hide it like a dog hiding a bone. Do it before somebody learns you have it and takes it from you.

People make money in Newfoundland and buy real estate in Florida. They don't trust anything here. That's another removal without replacement. We also lose an immense number of able people. That's true of Nova Scotia too, but the farther you are from a sponge such as New York or California, the more you are going to lose.

It's very difficult to convince Newfoundlanders to relinquish something today on the grounds that it may multiply tomorrow. In Churchill Falls, we learned what Confederation was going to be all about. The way our Churchill Falls energy was sold in Quebec taught us about the total disregard for equality and fairness in the Canadian political system; it has to do with numbers, as any democracy does.

We didn't even have the option of selling our electricity to New York. We had to sell it to Quebec. But if Quebec had had an immense resource and Newfoundland sat between this resource and its logical market, there wouldn't have been a question about transmission lines across Newfoundland. We would have just said, "Yes, sir, thank you, sir," and been grateful to get jobs putting up wire poles, which would have marched right across us without any questions whatsoever.

To me, this was an illustration that in Canada, the strong would not be fair to the weak. That the weak would remain weak and that the strong would rule. And that is the way Canada is run. Newfoundland is the weakest. We are thrown bones and told, "Bury this, bury that." But at what point is weakness cowardice, and at what point is it simply a result of having been crushed and humiliated by a succession of people from outside?

The presence of American bases emasculated us. About 30,000 Newfoundland girls married American servicemen, who had money in their pockets, who could buy liquors and cars, who had their own teeth. That meant there were as many Newfoundland guys who had to stand there and watch it happen.

The British maintained a colonial rule here, yet in 1932, we voluntarily surrendered our own administration and asked the British to come back and run us. The world's history of this century is a story of populations seceding from major confederations, of Pakistanis trying to get out of India, of Quebec trying to get out of Canada. But Newfoundland looked around to join someone else. Such humiliating behaviour is not supposed to happen in the 20th century.

Humiliation has a backlash. Newfoundlanders give an impression of meekness and sweetness to people who come here from outside, but they don't exhibit it to each other. If you have something that an average Newfoundlander doesn't have, it's a source of bitterness. If you sail your boat into one of the small communities and you have the Stars and Stripes on the back of it, everybody there is as sweet as can be. But if you have St. John's, Newfoundland, written on it, then it's automatically assumed you have robbed fishermen for three generations. A lot of animosity is directed against those who might be getting ahead of other people. And generations of our politicians have preyed upon it, cleverly using this sense of bitterness to their own advantage.

Rodway's Point by Lois Saunders.

Artist's Statement
King's Point Pottery
Linda Yates and David Hayashida

The sea gave birth to Newfoundland. Its waves shaped cove and headland, barachois and cape. The natural bounty of its waters beckoned settlers from distant lands. Their dependency on, and respect for the sea helped to shape the culture that is uniquely theirs. For centuries, Newfoundlanders and Labradorians have engaged in a complex dance with nature. Living here on the island portion of the province provides us with endless inspiration between the eagles and the whales. Our pottery reflects our passion for this land and her many inhabitants. These days the most famous "visitors" here in King's Point are the wild and wonderful whales of summer, so it will come as no surprise that we are best known for our "whales and waves" pots. Pottery is a way of life and our pots get their life from the extraordinary environment of Newfoundland and Labrador.

Whale and wave bowl by King's Point Pottery.

Potting is a "dirty" job and here at King's Point Pottery we're lucky enough to be able to do it every day. The best part of being a potter is the rolling-up-your-sleeves, mud everywhere, physically immediate process. However, running a successful pottery production depends on half of our twelve hour days being spent on business issues.

If you enjoy clay and are thinking of becoming a full time professional in the craft business, remember to be prepared for the business challenges like paying your daily bills. Not being prepared for business issues will lead you away from the original reason for becoming a potter, the "hands-on" creative challenge.

The creative challenge for the potter lies in manipulating both the two and three dimensional forms, while respecting function. The potter must therefore blend the skills of a painter, a sculptor, and a designer. As clay artists producing functional dinnerware we relish that challenge. We enjoy the creative interplay between form and function in our King's Point studio. Our personal satisfaction comes from the belief that finely crafted objects permit the moment-to-moment art of living.

Shell plate by King's Point Pottery.

Whale and waves tableware by King's Point Pottery.

Above the Harbour
Carmelita McGrath

now I live above the harbour
beyond the reach of sea,
I watch the chilly ships
in and out,
orange ships of steel: squint
and imagine those other ships—
those which brought great-grandmother
following her destiny
to the stair that needed scrubbing
not far from here.

now we have straightened our backs
from the stairs; we lounge
on couches by picture windows,
writing books
or cheques
trying to imagine
poverty worse than our own
while our ancestors haunt the harbour:
they walk the water
on auburn, blue-eyed evenings.

The Voice of Dinah
Kathleen Winter

John D. Ryan, publisher of Newfoundland's first newspaper *The Royal Gazette*, was one of the many United Empire Loyalists who brought slaves with them to Canada. His will is one of the few documents that mentions the presence of slaves in Newfoundland. While slavery was abolished in the British Empire in 1834, Ryan's will granted his own slave freedom after his death, which did not occur until 1847. The actual fate of this slave and of her two children is not known, but one document indicates she may have died before Ryan did. Church of England parish records for 1816 report a Dinah "a Negro, buried at age 39." The name of Ryan's slave was Dinah. The following is a letter she might have written if her circumstances had allowed it.

My name is Dinah. I am tall and beautiful. I keep my glossy hair in a coil at my neck. Today I am folding beautiful bed clothes made of fine material. The light coming through the bedroom window of my master, John Ryan, and Mistress Amelia has in it the whiteness of snow. I am black, and I am a slave. Ryan brought me to Newfoundland when I was thirty, and my children, Cornelius and Rachel, were small. Though there are only a few other Negro slaves in this place, my status is no more special than that of a slave in America. I clean, I scrub, I sew and I cook. But no matter what kind of work I do, I am not free when it is finished. This is hard for you to understand, nearing the year 2000, but for me, it is a fact of life, I am owned by my master. I am used to this, but when I look at my children and think how he owns them too, I feel an anguish no words can express. Only when on Thursdays I go down to the waterfront to purchase special things for the household, am I able to imagine freedom. The shipments of silks, fur tippets and gowns, limes and rum, and the foodstuffs—these I am allowed to handle because I purchase them for my master and mistress. I love the contours of these things, the smell of the wharf, the bustle of the people. Between the structure of the many shops, I see the ocean's horizon, that silver strip that melts, bleeds, into the sky.

For me that horizon is a place of mystery and yes, of freedom. I imagine myself reaching towards it. I picture Cornelius and Rachel able to fly, and flying straight into that silky place, to lands far away. Where they would be free children of God like any white girl, any pink boy. It is 1811 now—I have been in St. John's nearly six years. For nearly twenty years now, slavery has been abolished in England. That is so much longer than the lifetime of my children. Sometimes I feel ashamed that I could not have borne them into freedom, in some other place.

I know that my master has given me my freedom in his last will and testament. I know too that in it he has proclaimed that my children should be retained in his family's service or bonded out to service in another rich family until they reach the age of twenty-one. I think of those days, and begin to dream of where we will go. The three of us...I imagine us flying, the euphoria of the liberty is so great. But then I remember that if they are younger than the age of twenty-one, they will not be free to come with me, even though our master is dead. Then I feel sorrow and a suffocating anger. You who are living in the future will know all about the life of my master because he is an important man in this place—but about my fate, and that of Cornelius and Rachel, you will not be so certain. Which street I walked down on that last day of bondage, you will have to guess. I may die before my master does, and death will be my first freedom. The records which so carefully document my master's every move, will at the most, record only fragments of my fate. The mysteries into which I walk, found in history's obscure side streets, will hide me from you. This hidden life, this privacy, is perhaps the only freedom this life will afford me. What you do not know about me becomes the only power I have over you.

An old fishing stage

Aquaforte by Lois Saunders.

Artist's Statement
Jerry Evans

Like many artists I don't remember a time when I was not drawing or painting. In art school and during the early years of my career I explored varying imagery but it was not until the mid-eighties that I formed an intense focus on the social, cultural and spiritual issues of First Nations. It was at that time I confirmed my Mi'kmaq heritage, an issue which had been buried in my family for generations. Since then my quest has been to reclaim a part of my history which was obscured by a blanket of secrecy, denial and even shame.

Working in the media of painting and lithography, I am exploring native imagery and symbols gathered from research and studies at Memorial University. Traditional native icons such as feathers, quill patterns, dream catchers, hieroglyphs and archival photographs are an integral part of my work. Nineteenth century photographs and language symbols in particular provide a bridge to the past. I am looking to reinterpret these symbols by adjusting their relationship to each other and thereby presenting them in a light that causes a previously unsolicited response. While stretching the meaning of these symbols I am also experimenting with the medium of printmaking by using techniques like printing directly onto birch bark.

During the last several years my focus has been on printmaking and I have established a degree of proficiency in this medium that has enabled me to work with artists like Christopher Pratt, Anne Meredith Barry, Gerald Squires and Scott Goudie, to mention a few. While printmaking has served my objectives well and will continue to be an integral part of my work, I am drawn more and more into the realm of three dimensional expression. Incorporating further research I will continue the multimedia work and sculpture I have already begun, incorporating traditional craft techniques and skills like carving, beadwork and weaving as well as skills like hide tanning and canoe building. Further research and apprenticeships with native craftspeople will enable me to play a part in preserving methods of craftsmanship that are now threatened.

I am pleased by the degree of recognition my work is beginning to enjoy and I have recently been offered solo exhibits in Newfoundland, Ontario and Ireland. In order to fill the demand of these exhibits I am concentrating on building a larger, more varied body of work including further lithographs, paintings, sculptures and multimedia pieces. I am acquiring a solid foundation in traditional skills and plan to stretch their domain, while keeping intact their spiritual and cultural integrity. I feel compelled not only to celebrate but to dissect and explore my native heritage, how it relates to the European culture and how the two cultures, of which I am a part, interact and affect each other. My aim will remain to nurture a better understanding of aboriginal cultures and peoples both for myself and those experiencing my work.

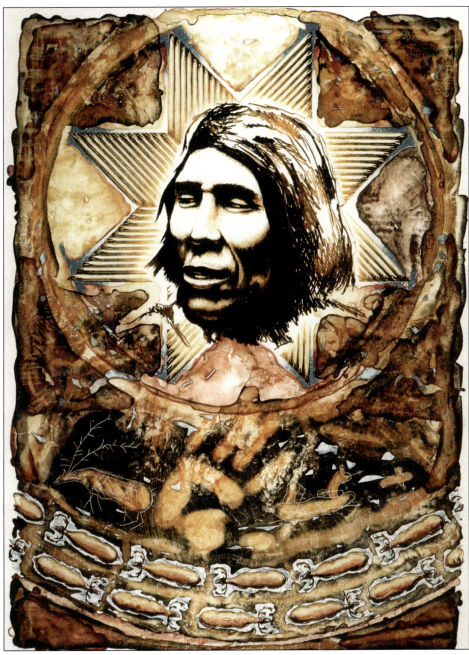

Know Me, Know You, 9 colour lithograph, 22" x 30", edition 25, by Jerry Evans.

Traditional Spiritualism
Michael Joe

Prior to the arrival of Europeans to our homeland, the Mi'kmaq Nation was a nation that was rich with customs, traditions and native spirituality.

In 1610 Grand Chief Membertou was the first Mi'kmaq to receive Christian baptism. Over the years there have been many arguments by our people as to whether this forced move away from our own spiritual beliefs was good or bad. On one side we hear from those people who have totally accepted Catholicism. They argue that this new way of life, whether forced on them or not, was good for our nation and good for our people. Our language was almost lost and our own spiritual beliefs were outlawed. In some communities, like Escasoni, Nova Scotia, the songs and language of our people were spoken freely in church, encouraged by the parish priest. In Miawpukek, Newfoundland, we were unfortunate enough to have a priest who did not believe in our people and in our spirituality. That priest referred to our language as "the devil's language." This has made our Mi'kmaq community dramatically different. Our people are basically, in terms of spirituality, a very confused community. We neither fully believe in the teachings of the Catholic Church nor do we know enough about our own spirituality to be able to come to grips with ourselves as a Mi'kmaq people.

Untitled by Kathleen Winter

Growing up in Miawpukek I saw very little spirituality, at least in the sense of what the Catholic Church taught us about spirituality. But as I grew older, I looked back and realized the difference in my grandfather and the people around me. What they practised was not necessarily being good Christians as the Catholic Church recognized. They were being good Mi'kmaq people, with their own spirituality that comes from their heart and soul, as passed down to them by their forefathers.

The Sweat Lodge Ceremony is a ceremony that is very humble and starts with Mother Earth. Trees have to be cut down to be used as poles for the Sweat Lodge. Cutting down these trees reminds us that we are cutting one more tree from Mother Earth. We have to give thanks for what we have taken, and appreciate what we have

here as a people. Each time we cut down a tree we leave an offering of tobacco, to give thanks for the good things that the Creator gave us.

The Sweat Lodge teaches us how to have respect for the women in our community and in the world. The Sweat Lodge teaches us that when we say mean and nasty things about one woman, we are saying them about all women, including our mothers. The Sweat Lodge teaches us to respect patience, endurance and speaking our minds freely. The rocks that we bring into the Sweat Lodge come from Mother Earth. We put those rocks into the fire to make them hot for our ceremonies. Those rocks have to give up their life so that we can have our ceremonies; therefore we must give thanks to the rocks. The water that we put on the rocks is made by the Great Spirit and put on this earth for our use. When we bring water into the Sweat Lodge our teachings say we must respect the water because it is a life-giving substance from the Creator. We teach our young people to respect this sacred liquid—it is a gift not to be abused.

Our Sweat Lodge also teaches our people to have respect: for the land and for each other—respect for our mothers, fathers and grandparents, and for all people, not just our own people. The Sweat Lodge Ceremony teaches us to respect other people's religion, and the different attitudes and personalities of other people. The Sweat Lodge teaches us to remember when we start our day that we can see the things around us, that we can rise from our place of rest and walk, and that we can witness the sunrise and sunset. It teaches us how to reach out and touch the people around us. The Sweat Lodge teaches us to appreciate people that love us and those whom we love. These are gifts from the Creator and we have to teach our young people to respect these things because they are truly one of the great wonders of the Creator, and they should not be abused in any way.

When we enter the Sweat Lodge we make offerings of tobacco to the four directions: East, West, North and South. The first offering is to the East—the Kitbou—the eagle. The Kitbou is the protector of all our children. The Kitbou is a sacred bird, respected and honoured by our people. It is said by our elders to be the only bird that has touched the face of God. It is appropriate that the eagle is the first offering.

The second offering, to the South, is to the Grandmothers, the protectors of all our women, even our unborn. Grandmothers are also the protectors of all our people who have gone to the spirit world. The Grandmothers are from the South, where the Sacred Pipe comes from. We ask the Grandmothers not only to keep our women strong and united but also to make the males in our nation strong with courage so they will show the proper respect to our women. We ask the Grandmothers to teach us not to abuse our women, physically, mentally or verbally. We ask them for the courage, strength and understanding to be able to withstand any bad teaching that has been taught to our people over the years.

The third offering is to the West, which is the Spirit World. The Spirit World is where our people go when they leave this earth. Once they are in the Spirit World they become our helpers, helping us to survive as a strong Mi'kmaq people on this earth. They have to continue to do their jobs as spirit helpers and as guides. We ask that they be accepted into the Spirit World with dignity, kindness and respect. We ask that they be given honoured places so that they can fulfill their roles in the Spirit World.

The fourth offering is to the North, to the Great White Bear, protector of the North. The Great White Bear is the giver of strength, courage, wisdom and understanding. We ask that the spirit of the Great White Bear visit our lodge. The Great White Bear teaches us not only to be strong in the physical sense, but also in spiritual strength, the inner strength we need to survive the many things that come our way in day to day life. We ask the Great White Bear to give us strength, courage, understanding, and wisdom to withstand the influence of bad things and be influenced only by good things.

The Talking Stick Ceremony is not Mi'kmaq; it has been adopted by a lot of our people, including myself. I like the Talking Stick Ceremony simply because it teaches not only our young people, but all our people, to have respect for the person who is speaking. The Talking Stick (or sometimes an eagle feather) is passed from person to person, and only the person holding it may speak—all others must listen. It teaches people patience and respect. It teaches people how to listen.

Our Sacred Pipe is sometimes referred to as the Peace Pipe. It is sacred, and is used in the Sweat Lodge Ceremonies. The Peace Pipe is broken into two pieces, symbolizing a man and a woman. When these pieces are joined, to symbolize unity, it becomes a sacred part of the ceremony. The Peace Pipe also demands respect. It gives me peace within myself to be able to accept who I am and where I live. My role as a pipe carrier gives me inner peace and allows me to be at one with my Creator.

These are the things that the Europeans and Catholicism took away from us: things that had laid hidden for so long.

Our ceremonies teach us to have dignity and pride in ourselves as Mi'kmaq people. We have pride in the fact that we practise a different way of living. The Catholic Church never taught us—and never can teach us—this way of life. These ways are the ways that lie in the hearts of all aboriginal people and of all our elders.

Conne River, like a lot of other aboriginal communities, is slowly but surely returning to traditional spiritualism. I am sure that in our community there will always be a place for the Catholic Church because there will always be people who will not totally accept traditional spiritualism. But now our people have the alternative of being able to practise traditional spiritualism. It is important not to have disrespect for other peoples' beliefs, but to have respect for your own. Our people have many times doubted the strength, courage, and respect of our people, and that should never be.

The more our young people become involved in our way of life the better are our chances of survival in this world. We have to teach our young people that it is not enough to be educated in the white man's world. We also have to be educated in our own way of life. The survival of our people depends on that education in order for us to survive as Mi'kmaq people.

Call Me An Indian: The Calvin White Story
Chris O'Neill-Yates

Prologue:

Gordon White (the youngest son of Calvin White):

You give a man a pool stick and he thinks he's God. This is one of the many morals my father would teach me as we played pool in my basement. I watched him in his rituals, preparing a stick, placing the cue ball just so for the break, muttering to himself, almost chanting as he circled the table like a hawk. He seemed to ignore me. I thought he was showing off. Now I don't think so.

You can see the showoffs in any bar. They take themselves too seriously, curse if they miss or if they lose. I don't think that most of them are aware of the power they play with. My father was. As he shot, several people would watch him, some rooting for him, some against him, others wanting to challenge him. But he was the focus.

To me, my father didn't carry a cue stick. He carried a magical staff and with it he could control the laws of nature, physics, mathematics, kinetics, geometry. He could also control people. He seemed to slip into a transcendental state, a form of meditation and motion, as he moved with a grace I never thought he had. How could he not seem like a god?

I never really thought of my father as a spiritual man. I know better now. Pool is just a game. My father and I haven't played in quite some time. I look forward to our next game. Who wins is irrelevant. He will always be the master. I'm young, I'm still learning. To me, my father is not a hustler or pool shark. I call my father a shaman, and he has handed down his staff to me.

From *Call Me An Indian: The Calvin White Story*:

Calvin White:

It was an embarrassment to be an Indian, I mean, you know, we're talking about the fifties and sixties when entertainment in the movies was at its peak and Indians were naked people who ran around wagon trains and provided opportunity for John Wayne to shoot them. So that's the last thing in the world that you wanted to be publically.

It was a kind of an attitude that exists in people who feel that they're superior to other people. I recall as a boy we'd walk down to the Flat Bay River and some lady would row [my Mom and I] across the river, and we'd walk to St. George's clinic, and my mom would probably be about seven or eight months pregnant. And we'd go in the clinic and nobody in there would offer her a chair. And they'd hold the door for each other to go into the doctor to make sure that she didn't get in between. They felt that they should be priority. Well, when she would finally get an opportunity to go inside the door and get into the doctor, she would be the focus of entertainment for

the rest of the people who were in there. She could be from the Cape. No, she don't wear enough red, so she's not from the Cape. Maybe she's from Mattis's Point. No, she's not from Mattis's Point because she don't have her hair in rollers. Well, she gotta be from Flat Bay. And these are the kind of things that they would talk about. It was to provide entertainment for them because they looked down so much on the people from these three particular surrounding areas. They would ignore an eight year-old boy who'd be standing up against the wall. That was me.

Judy White (daughter of Calvin White):

My name is Judy White. I'm Calvin White's daughter. My first memory of the word jackatar was when a visitor came in the community and referred to people as being jackatars. And my grandmother, being the kind of woman that she was, didn't challenge them at the time, but after he left she said, "He didn't understand that he ate my food and insulted me at the same time." I don't think he really understood the connotations, the negative connotations that it had for us. But it meant a dirty, lazy Indian. And we were far from that.

Gordon White:

My name is Gordon White. I'm the youngest by ten minutes of a family of six, the youngest son of Calvin White. I wear the term jackatar with pride. And it was a very long time before I realized it was a derogatory term, meaning like a savage of some kind. I was on the schoolyard going, "Yeah, I'm a jackatar. What about it?" When you take the power away from a word, it doesn't do any damage. Someone could say "Oh yeah, you're a jackatar," and it's like, well, what does that mean? I'm both Mi'kmaq and French and born on the West Coast. Yeah, I qualify as that; there's nothing wrong with that.

Calvin White:

Every time I drove through my community…[or] I picked up somebody on the road who was unemployed, or somebody who didn't have the schooling or [know the] people that I knew, and every time I heard other people pass remarks about how lazy they were or how unambitious they were, that always bothered me. I always believed that those of us who are fortunate enough to be able to get ahead in life should never look down on other people who've been less fortunate because we don't know all the circumstances. So why should we judge them? So this was always bothersome to me….I wanted to make some type of a contribution.

Believe me, it was a challenge. People who you thought were your friends don't take long turning their backs onto you when you stand up and do something that is unpopular. I was portraying myself as a [native] person publically, not privately. And that was unpopular with a lot of people. Because it's the fear. I've had native people who had no way to escape their identity tell me "Why don't you leave well enough alone? Why are you doing this?"

Gordon White:

    I was always hearing of my father and I knew he was going away an awful lot when I was young. So I was always looking at him as something even bigger than he was. He was a god. Oh Dad is coming back! Oh Dad is gone off to Saskatchewan today. At those points I got ideas that this is what he was trying to do, this is what he working for—to make a difference for some people on the island.

Judy White:

    I got in lots of fights because of defending my father's position. There were lots of people not fully understanding what he was trying to do, people who supported what he did, and people who just didn't care. So going to school, especially in high school, I always had to defend what I thought he was doing.

Calvin White:

    A status card doesn't make you any more Indian than what you are without the status card. But it removes the doubt from the minds of the people because the system we live in is based on the acceptance of the law and the acceptance of the government. So we're schooled to believe in the acceptance of these structures in society. If these structures don't recognize you, then neither does anybody else…

Calvin White:

    …we wanted opportunity to be able to pursue a social and economic development among our people while maintaining our identity.

    I started meeting people who, in most cases, were elderly people who were very much aware of who they were themselves, but were somewhat reluctant to stand up and be counted because of the kind of experiences that they've had earlier in life. You know, of dirty jackatars and all this kind of stuff. I've had people in the very early seventies, when I got involved in the native movement…[who would] call me one o'clock in the morning and stay on the phone for about two hours sharing all their depressions with me and congratulating me for what I was doing. But yet those people would never show up to a meeting. Like they wanted to stay away from it because they didn't think that they could deal with the pressures, but still, they wanted it to happen.

    I can recall this one instance of this elderly lady who was probably close to eighty years of age, and who I probably saw just once in my life. I mean, just knew who she was. And I recall one time in particular that I went into the hospital and she was sitting there with her daughter in the clinic, and when I went in she reached for my hand. And she squeezed my hand hello. She didn't say anything, but she said a lot. Because she knew who I was and she knew what I was doing and what she was doing was motivating me. Because she wasn't trying to hide from me; she's wasn't ignoring me. I mean, the fact that she reached out to me was an indication that hey, here's a person who wants you to do what you're doing.

Calvin White (on a bear taking moose and vegetables from his property):

What I've always tried to school myself is that you have to take responsibility. That's where our society is broken down some: you pass responsibility. You pass on the blame to other people and in this particular case, it's another animal. It's not a person, it's not a human being; it's an animal. But I can't fault that bear for taking something that I left within his grasp. I have to take responsibility for that. If I had loaded that meat aboard the boat and taken it out to my truck and brought it out to the butcher, that bear could have never gotten that meat.... It only reinforced in my mind that when a human makes an error, he should be held responsible for it. And I made an error, and I'm responsible, not the bear. And the bear needs to eat.

Calvin White:

One of the very first things that I bought, and I recall having two children, my oldest, Judy, and Cal junior. They were probably about five years old. And I bought a set of encyclopaedias that I couldn't afford because I knew that these were the tools that my children needed. And we paid off those encyclopaedias with just as much pressure as I would have had to pay off a mortgage. Because [although] it was a very small amount, it was more than we could afford. But we did it because education was a priority. I wanted my kids to be competitive in the academic field. I had no difficulty with their aggressiveness. I knew that they were going to be aggressive, but in order to be able to fulfill that kind of a challenge, then an academic degree would also be one of the tools that they needed.

Judy White:

I am my father's daughter and I'm very proud of it. I guess that my biggest accomplishment was going off to law school and actually trying to use the tools of white man's society to actually carry on a dream of my father's and thus ours—ours meaning our family and our community.

Calvin White:

The ignorance of the critics is that people think that because I'm not taking the skins from the animals that I kill and making the clothing for myself and my children, and because I don't own a birchbark canoe, and because I don't live in a wigwam, that I can't be Indian. I don't see every Scotsmen going around with a kilt on and only playing the bagpipe.... Why can we not accept each other's differences? And accept the fact that we've moved into the nineties and it's no longer practical for me to burn my house and build a wigwam in my field just because I want to prove that I'm an Indian. I'm an Indian because that's who I am, because that's what I believe, because those are the things that I understand, because that's the knowledge I have, because that's my history.

When I look in the mirror in the morning I see the Calvin White who committed himself to an honest life and one that was never afraid of work, and one that would never expect from others what he didn't expect from himself. That's the Calvin White I see.

Humour: Forms and Functions
Herbert Lench Pottle

In so far as humour anywhere reflects the life style of the people involved, we have reason to hope that the various classes of Newfoundland humour, which we shall identify here, will serve something as tiles in helping to fill out the full Newfoundland mosaic. This part of the study will discuss also the purposes which Newfoundland humour has seemed to serve. The two considerations, taken together, and overlapping, as they are bound to be, will add up to basic homework if they reveal promising leads toward a possible theory of Newfoundland humour.

Humour as life enhancer

Traditionally, in the light of the adverse weather conditions of Newfoundland history, humour has been both an individual and a collective means of enabling life to be tolerable. At heart, as we have seen, the crucial issue for the first Newfoundland settlers was sheer survival. For in coping with the inexorable laws of nature the Newfoundlander was always cast as an unequal. The best he could do was to try and "bend the rules" so as to emerge, if only for a moment of time, as a seeming winner. When his best effort of raw ingenuity and dogged persistence failed, his last resource of humour came to the rescue.

This resort to humour, then, has to be seen not only as a kind of face-saving: it is in practically a biological sense lifesaving. It is applied not only to life occasions when there is some remnant of a chance in trying, but also when no such chance exists, since God's will must be done. The fatalist in the Newfoundlander persuades him to accept life as it is—it must go on. Thus, the sailor Lukey, in "Lukey's Boat," has just lost his wife, but there is no use, he figures, grieving and pining for the past. And so he keeps both eyes open, port and starboard, for a new mate:

> I'll have another in the spring of the year.
> Aha me riddle I day.

Humour as a changing of the old guard

It belongs to what we have just said to elaborate and to see Newfoundland humour at work, not only as a mellower of the harsh elements that constantly assail him, but as a direct challenge to them. To appreciate the significance of this more aggressive role for humour, it is necessary to recall a rather radical change in the lifestyle of Newfoundlanders over the generations. Having crossed the ocean to escape the repression of bureaucracy and the depressing experience of being rendered anonymous in a rapidly industrialized society, they had at last come into their own in a new human order. Not all of a sudden, to be sure, but out of the raw materials of cod and fog and bog they had, in the course of seemingly endless, tedious time, fashioned an identity for themselves, reassuring as a lighthouse in a blizzard, "as fresh as dulse." They had their own plot of land, without title but without question. The orders they had to follow were of their own making. They belonged to a society so immediate and so

manageable that they themselves counted. And that society was community in that it stoutly endorsed what they already as individuals held "to be grandly true." The typical community was a first-hand experience where, as I have rehearsed several times in addresses and in publications, the same church bell summoned everyone to the same altar, and where a single shout for help brought all hands to the beach.

Today the situation seems to be settling for another spinal change. The present temper is one of general euphoria aroused by greatly improved economic conditions. These are intensifying the individual rivalry for position and so altering at the roots the character of community structures. Nowadays the reliance of communities is not so much on local resources as on outside subsidy. The old-time stand-by, the local merchant, has been outdated by the big-time patronage of government. This rather sudden somersault of condition—the turn-over of traditional initiative to political handout—has not been lost on Newfoundland humour, compounded mostly of satire, which has been enjoying a roaring trade, the politicians being both suppliers and customers.

As a preserver of personal dignity

Of all that we know about the main purposes served by humour on Newfoundland soil, the fact that it enables the Newfoundlander to maintain his individuality is one of the most persistent and most pervasive. This is no little consideration within an encircling condition of threatening change and mechanized ways of living which defy even his picturesque language to describe. One has only to recall again his ancestral state of constant uncertainty to realize how utterly essential it has always been for him to be reassured of his identity, that he was at least as good as a 'skin-and-grief' model of Speedy Muffler's Somebody. And now even that insubstantial substitute for being was further threatened by invasions of his ancient markers which were once so sure as his trawl bearings on the "Offer Ledge." This sudden and baffling upset of his world order was a circumstance for which his tried and trusted compass was no longer of any use. My childhood experience of going astray at night in a fish-loaded boat, in dense fog, is only one momentary reminder of how shattering a helpless condition of lostness can be.

Neither here nor anywhere else in this study do I presume even to imply that a resort to humour is by itself a sufficient cure for all the ills which the Newfoundland flesh is humanly heir to. Humour, however á propos and potent, can make no such claims to an all-weather panacea as the Newfoundlander's hoary bed-mates, Sloan's Liniment and Dodd's Kidney Pills. But humour did and does have the invigorating effect of preserving upright his quality of person. It does so in many ways, such—for instance—as turning what otherwise could destroy his identity to supporting his life purposes.

Just recently a teacher in a Notre Dame Bay settlement recounted to a visitor the story of two men, Mose and Zebedee, going into the woods to cut firewood for the winter. Mose wore only one 'cuff' (mitten). When Zebedee noticed this, he said to his buddy, "Mose, what's the idea? You've got one of your cuffs on and the other off." And Mose replied, "Well, the feller on the news…he says last night…he give out 'bout the weather. He didn't seem to be sure 'bout what he was sayin'. He said, 'To-morrow, on the one hand, we might get ten degrees colder. But then, on the other hand, we might have it ten degrees warmer.' So I wants to be ready for both." Thus the forces of

science are bent along the line of everyday needs, and the reputation of the local sage for practical prudence remains intact.

A. R. Scammell, to whom I am indebted in several ways, describes another experience which points up the Newfoundlander's determination to maintain his private dignity, even if he must buck the recognized authorities to do so. He recalls one such instance from his grandfather's day. In his home town—Change Islands—road boards, as in other communities, were given small government grants to do local road extension and repairing. In this case, Justinian Dowell, the local teacher whose role in Change Islands I shall later recognize, was the board chairman. A crew of men were working at a crossroads and had sat down for a spell (a short rest) and a smoke, with their backs to the auxiliary road. They were watching the main road in case Dowell appeared to check on their progress. However, Dowell came upon them unexpectedly from the back road over the crest of a hill. One of the men jumped up, grabbed his shovel and said, "Hard at it, Mr. Dowell." "It's a dishonest way you're at it, Manuel," scolded the official. Retorted Manuel, "And a dishonest way you come, sir." He was nettled at not having the presence of mind to watch both roads. So in this way, by a quick repartee, the tables were turned and the guilt transferred to the bureaucracy.

By the same token, what was possible of private dignity to be salvaged in an emergency was thus availed of with one's personal natural resources.

Sometimes of course, as we might expect, this local striving to maintain one's reputation turns out to have unexpected rebounds, especially on foreign soil. Within the local setting the 'splitting table' is a strategic centre for preparing codfish to be salted away. One fisherman's daughter, who had served her apprenticeship at such a table, was later looking for a change of occupation in Toronto. She was asked by her would-be employer, "And what have you been doing up to now?" "Cuttin' t'roats, ma'am," was the proud reply.

Talking local

I have just drawn a few examples, selected from various living contexts, to illustrate how the force of humour is called in to garrison the defences of the person and his society against the shock and upset of a thoroughly altered set of conditions. What is necessary to underline here is not the shocking and upsetting impact of the new way of life—walloping as it is—but rather the deep-rooted and persevering quality of the old. In this section we shall continue to develop the role of humour in shoring up the vitality of the individual and his fraternity, disrupted by the ferment of intestinal and convulsive change….

When, now, the cherished language of his very household is being challenged by the big words and the high-sounding phrases of the new age, he tends to look upon the situation as a clear case of breaking and entering. And the fact that the new style is being adopted by natives of his own class and generation makes the offence no less pardonable. I recall, in a comparable situation, that my older brothers saved their choicest adjectives of caricature for those locals who never had a second suit of underwear, but, after no more than six months on the mainland, would return home high-heeled and feathered in the finest array.

What can the poor local 'angashore do at all to cope with this threat of having his mother tongue strangled? He can do what he normally does under such circumstances: he will use the weapon of the strangler, namely, the new lingo, and hurl it straight back in the dentures of the assailant. He will do this by the easygoing, seemingly effortless technique (humorous, if you will), of bending the impressive word to serve the more menial exercises of his daily routine.

Thus, when the late Ted Russell came to reckon with the new-fangled ways of describing the weather (one can hardly be optimistic enough to say "forecasting" it), he had to contend with such adversaries as "general synopsis" and "major disturbance." He knows very well that the Newfoundlander can do much better deciding on the state of the weather than the pretenders just by peeping through a crack in the storm door before bedtime. And so he sets these prophets in their proper stations—weather or no. What he does is to take their airy characters and transform them into real personages. In their ridiculous translation they now become General Synopsis and Major Disturbance. Nor is this just a clever semantic accident. For in this mutation the parachuted nobodies, sponsored by the well-paid weather man, now become impressive personages whom the Newfoundlander is bound to acknowledge out of his veteran respect for Queen (King) and Country.

If the eloquent habit of turning an alien language to one's own familiar account is not instinctive in the Newfoundlander, he certainly adopts it at an early age. This the Bishop of Newfoundland discovered when on one occasion he was visiting a day school. There he meant to put to the test the children's religious knowledge in a school situation where Religion is one of the Four Rs.

"What is confirmation?" he asked a hopeful looking youngster.

"Shirt and dra'ers together, me Lard," was the home-made reply.

There seems in fact to be no limit to which the language may not be stretched or re-cast to answer need in local terms, the Newfoundlander in the process becoming anything apparently for the purpose—amphibian, for instance.

There was the very senior citizen who was asked whether she had ever been bed-ridden.

"Dat I have," she spoke up briskly, "hunderds o' times. Twice in a dory."

Arthur Scammell has shared with me two stories which further confirm the tendency of Newfoundland children to convert the unknown to the known—a process producing humour for more sophisticated adults, but serious enough for the children themselves.

For instance, he once showed Willie John a picture card representing the miracle of the loaves and fishes, under which were the words "Feed my lambs." "Now," he asked Willie John, "can you tell me what this is about?" "Oh yes, sir," was the prompt answer. "It's a few pork buns and a couple of tom cods." In this way he had pinned down the miracle in terms of the vernacular: the ordinary food of the ordinary Newfoundland people.

The same tendency to reduce mysteries to the elemental language of everyday life was instanced by a little girl in church. Her parents had taken communion at the 8 o'clock service, and, having gone again to the 11 o'clock service, they were on the hand of leaving church before the communion, when she called out so that everyone around could hear: "Idn't you fellows gain' to stop for lunch?" In this way she was interpreting the mystery of the communion in terms meaningful to her, namely, as one of the daily meals.

This tendency to convert the foreign to the familiar as a means of preserving one's integrity for oneself and his fellows knows no break in the Newfoundland age progression. Thus, a Newfoundland adolescent at a private school attends a party to which her school has invited the male students of a neighbouring institution. She has met her partner and heard his name for the first time. When her turn came to introduce him to the Principal and his wife, the following formalities ensued:

"Dr. and Mrs. Organ, I'd like you to meet Mr. Hiccough."

"Burpee is the name," corrected her escort. And this ended the formalities.

At the adult level one is struck by the range and richness of those human situations which the ordinary Newfoundlander can cooper to his own making and his own purposes. These situations may not be causes of merriment for him; indeed they may be occasions for his anguish of spirit. But by the way he gets into them and the language he uses to work himself out again, he becomes a resourceful spring of humour to his neighbours. I recall one recent occasion when my taxi-man in St. John's was quite upset about the new 'artillery' road which, he claimed, was going to bottleneck east-bound city traffic into one hopeless snarl. It was only after I got back to my hotel, and enquired around, that I found that my driver, who was an army veteran, had been more than mechanically exercised about an arterial road.

The late Bob MacLeod, to whom I am glad to make acknowledgment, recited at mutually enjoyable length those fun-producing episodes which he had come upon either in his daily goings to and fro or in his earlier news reporting. These are even further illustrations of the ways Newfoundlanders— either consciously or otherwise— make the language (odd or otherwise) serve their daily purposes. And so the familiar drunk is described as "half-abbreviated." The local labour union gets an increase in pay, which is "radio-active." And a news item was once presented for Bob's bulletin, which advised: "For sale: a schooner, with wench attached, ready for use."

No experience along the Newfoundland shoreline seems exempt from this tendency to domicile whatever happens, especially of the unusual. And even the crises of wartime have to be counted in. Thus, a local commentary on German bombing during the Second World War:

"Did ya hear the bad news over the air last night?"

"No, boy. How's that?"

"Well, it said the Germans was droppin' bombs at Random. Dat's getting pretty close."

(The name "Random" covers a large area of Trinity Bay, including Random Island).

As banishing the baleful

The function of humour as a salve for the Newfoundlander's wounds from his constant conflict with nature is not confined to his biblically ordained "three score years and ten." Indeed, humour not only operates to make life bearable, but it serves also as a balm wherewith to soothe what St. Paul calls "the last enemy" which is death. In summoning up his lightness of heart within sound of the last trump, the Newfoundlander resorts to nothing like bitterness or sacrilege. For him, inasmuch as he has reflected on the question at all, life and death are very much of a piece; and he would find it difficult to visualize any after-life as denying the many blessings of this

present one. Something further needs to be said here which bears no less directly upon our theory of humour which we shall be elaborating later. It seems quite evident that the volume and variety of levity about death are increasing. While the event of death—as we shall shortly instance—has always tended to bring out a protective kind of banal behaviour which sets the Newfoundlander upon the surer ground of everyday life, today we hear expressions of good humour applied to death across a wide gamut of everyday experiences.

Lazarus Dwyer, of Gull Island, had been working in Halifax for a while, where he suddenly died. His body was brought home for burial, and when the lid of the coffin was lifted in his parlour, his relatives and friends found it hard to believe their eyes, for, with the face-lifting effects of modern embalming, Lazarus had never looked nearly so healthy when he was alive. One of his long-time buddies stared a while at the 'carpse' (corpse) and marvelled: "Boy, oh boy! Halifax sure done Laz' some good!"

"Jes' look, Mose, look, see dat t'ing up dere?"

"No, boy, can't see anyt'ing."

"Das coz he's gone under the cloud. Dere, he's comin' agin, I t'ink."

"I siz en now; yes, I siz en plain enough."

"An' can ya hear en? Like a 'arsestinger, boy. Jest like a 'arsestinger.'"

The thin line between life and death is drawn in the case of another funeral which was attended by a frail old fellow on his last legs. Said one of the younger generation to his buddies alongside: "'Tis hardly worth his while to go home."

Sometimes the truth in such items as obituaries comes out more strikingly than intended: as in the news report of the death of…, "which has caused great relief in the community."

As a general principle, the sense of continuity between life and death in the Newfoundland tradition is much more real than apparent, so much so that we may in truth reverse the ancient saying to read, "In the midst of death we are in life." In another funeral procession, for instance, during a winter month, one of the pallbearers slipped and broke his leg. Whereupon it was duly reported that the accident "seemed to cast a gloom over the whole proceedings."

A middle-sized settlement was peopled by the name of England. When a husky sample of the clan died, his body had to be taken over a steep hill on the way up to the burial grounds. At the foot of the hill one of the pallbearers, bracing himself, exhorted his companions: "Fellows, this is the time England expects every man to do his duty."

The light that never was on land or sea does not apply in this matter of levity on the most serious grounds, for it lightens up both land and sea. In these pages we shall have several occasions to honour the precious memories of those who "go down to the sea in ships." Many are the graveyards of Newfoundland which are marked with the words, "Lost at Sea." But the epitaph of one Doyle was markedly different: "Here lies the body of William Doyle: / His body lies here, but he died on the *Kyle*" (an old coastal boat, now rusting to her grave in Harbour Grace waters).

Humour as the great leveller

In Newfoundland where the estate difference between the rich and the poor is so pronounced, we might hardly expect this fact to pass unnoticed in everyday commerce and conversation. It doesn't. And humour gets a fair share of the proceeds. Mind you, humour does not originate in any compounding volume from the side of the rich. In fact, in the dispensing of humour, with some rare and notable exceptions, they are as miserly as Scrooge. The deposits in the humour account are made almost exclusively by "the toiling masses." These are not, as a rule, grudge items or, as we shall soon see, an investment in envy of the rich. They are as likely as not to be the poor man's way of cutting the rich man down to size.

There was the famous O'Brien firm whose senior partner, Terence, was very fond of fine clothes. One year he went away for a holiday and came back wearing a beautiful pair of tan boots—very likely the first time tan boots made their appearance in Newfoundland. He was very disappointed when none of his customers, coming to his shop, made mention of his fine boots. Having waited a long while for comment, he walked down to the wharf where one of his men was pouring pickle into a herring barrel. Still there was no mention of the boots. Whereupon he put his left foot upon the barrel, and there it rested for a while. Finally he had to give in. "What do you think, Mickey, of that boot? I paid twelve pounds for it in England."

"Well, Mr. O'Brien," replied Mickey, "all I can say is that if you paid anyt'ing at all for tudder boot, then you got a fine pair of boots."

The well-shod merchant probably saw no humour in the reply. And Mickey—well, for him it was one of those probably infrequent but not unwelcome occasions when he could put the local nabob in his place in his own way, with no rancour but with some relish.

It is at least fair to say that while popular criticism and even ribaldry may be directed at the propertied class, yet in Newfoundland there is, as we have just anticipated, the saving grace of very little envy. Many years ago in a moderate-sized community Walter Butler built a $20,000 house for himself which, by today's values, would fetch more like $200,000. In the local general store the subject came up for the Saturday night discussion, and Simeon Reader remarked, "There's only one difference between Walter's house and mine." At this point a free-for-all laugh erupted, because Simeon lived in an old weather-pocked shack behind the store. "How can you say that, Simeon?" someone asked. "Well," said he, "in his the water comes up from the floor; in mine it comes down through the roof." There was no envy here—he was citing a matter of fact which did not require a plumber to verify. Newfoundland is a mosaic of contrasts: the rich and the poor may be next-door neighbours in a spirit much more peaceable than détente. The poor, relatively speaking, for their part traditionally tended to be realistic about their condition; like Simeon, no doubt—placing a bucket under the drops.

Humour as social power

One of the most common purposes widely ascribed to humour is to help render the distressing conditions of life more tolerable—a factor we have already recognized at some length for its application to Newfoundland. Indeed, as Mercier states, the

humorist even exaggerates these conditions, so that "our laughter at [his] humour is in part motivated by a feeling of relief that things aren't, thank goodness, quite *that* bad."

The role of humour as a social agent, as the yeast of social awareness and cohesion, is central to the concept of humour itself as viewed by many observers. "Humour," says one, "is the nursery of social subjectivity."

The power of Newfoundland humour is a social fact to be reckoned with principally because it is so appropriately a power to enliven community, if indeed it is not already the birth-mark of community. It is quite safe to say that when Newfoundlanders get into a huddle, a humorous story is much more likely than not what brings them together and keeps them so. It is the sure sign of what they hold most surely in common—what Mindess sees as their community-minded conviction about those things that matter most to them.

Their common ground is so firm and so redoubtable that anyone who cannot share the same premises feels like an outsider. You have to know that ground, from which their humour springs, in order to "belong." There is the well-known instance of the stranger in a church congregation who, when all the others around him were laughing at something humorous, could not share in the merriment because, as he said, "I don't belong to this parish."

This sampling of the kinds of humour and the purposes they serve is little more than an intimation of all the possibilities here. In citing these I have been impressed by a fact already recognized, namely, the enormous variety of circumstances which humour can entertain, even within the relatively cramped quarters of Newfoundland. Later I shall be coupling humour with five broad institutional areas of Newfoundland life. Here I am gratified to note that, in the natural course of events, the forms and functions of humour just described relate in some fair degree to all five.

We have now identified a many-sided, responsible role for humour, and in doing so we have seen something of how Newfoundland humour comes to life out of the body of the Newfoundlander's habits—his odd ways and words. In this present study we shall be regarding this odd style of liveliness as a reliable sign of the total state of health, so to speak, of the Newfoundland society—in terms of its vigorous power to arouse humour from such vital organs as its politics, its religion, the sea, technological change, and the creative arts. In ranging so widely I shall be always conscious that my main homework is to discern and declare how Newfoundland humour says its piece within the prime settings of Newfoundland life—that is, its basic institutions, keeping the individual in open sight throughout the whole exercise.

It is only, of course, according to the sensitivity one brings to an enterprise of this kind that one can hope to discharge it with fidelity and conviction. That is to say, if the Newfoundland reality is aptly grasped, then the door is more than half-open to getting inside that reality and reflecting it freely and fully. Or, in something like the words of the Newfoundland compact, "If you tells me where you're at, I'll come where you're to."

Excerpts from
The Life and Times of Ted Russell
Elizabeth Russell Miller

Author's Preface

In one of the stories in Ted Russell's *The Chronicles of Uncle Mose*, Grampa Walcott has this advice for the prospective biographer:

> Grampa says that the only right and proper way to tell the story of a man's life is to begin at where he dies and to work back. I told him that most books about people's lives started at where he was born and went on from there. But Grampa said that anyone contrary enough to want to read about a man's life that way should be made to start at the end of the book and read it backwards. Besides, he said, this way of doin' it would stop people from the foolish habit of writin' books about a man till after he was dead, 'cause until then they'd have no place to commence.

Chronology

1904 (June 27)	Ted Russell born at Coley's Point
1919	Left for St. John's to attend Bishop Field College
1920-21	Teaching at Pass Island
1921-22, 23-24, 25-26	Teaching at Harbour Breton
1923 (Jan-Jun)	Attended Normal School at St. John's
1924-25	Teaching at Millertown
1926-28	Teaching at Channel
1928-29	Attended Memorial University College
1929-32	Teaching at Fogo
1932-33	Attended Memorial University College
1933-35	Teaching at Bishop Field College
1935 (Jan 6)	Married Dora Oake, formerly of Change Islands
1935-39	Magistrate at Springdale
1939-40	Magistrate at Harbour Breton

1940-43	Magistrate at Bonne Bay
1943-49	Director of Co-operatives with the Commission of Government
1949-51	Minister of Natural Resources in Smallwood government
1951 (Mar 24)	Resigned from Cabinet
1952-57	Insurance salesman for Crown Life
1953-61	*The Chronicles of Uncle Mose* broadcast on CBC Radio
1954-58	Wrote all eight radio plays for CBC Radio
1956 (Feb 8)	*The Holdin' Ground* stage production by Northcliffe Drama Club won Provincial Drama Festival
1957-63	Teaching at Prince of Wales College, St. John's
1963-65	Student at Memorial University
1965-73	Teaching at Memorial University
1966	Political memoirs published in *The Evening Telegram*
1972	*The Holdin' Ground* published
1973 (May 1)	Honorary degree conferred by Memorial University
1975	*The Chronicles of Uncle Mose* published
1977 (Oct 16)	Died in St. John's at the age of 73
1977	*Tales from Pigeon Inlet* published
1979	Recording of six *Chronicles of Uncle Mose* released
1981	First Ted Russell Scholarships awarded

Ted Russell turned his attention to imaginative writing late in 1953, spurred on by a combination of financial necessity and a realization that selling life insurance left certain of his talents unused. At the age of forty-nine, he made an appearance on the literary scene, bringing to pen and paper his wealth of experience as a teacher, magistrate, a co-operative worker, and a politician (p. 147).

Central to all of Ted Russell's writings is the setting, the fictitious Newfoundland outport of Pigeon Inlet. Ted was frequently asked whether his Pigeon Inlet had been modelled on a single Newfoundland community, and his answer was consistently "No." He did indicate, however, on several occasions that the community he knew which was most like Pigeon Inlet was Pass Island, the place where he first went teaching in 1920. Possibly it is more than coincidence that Pigeon Inlet and Pass Island share the same initials. But Ted was always quick to add that he had no one outport in mind when he created Pigeon Inlet; rather, it was meant to represent all of those Newfoundland outports that he knew and loved during his lifetime, "especially Coley's Point, Pass Island, Harbour Breton, and Fogo." Furthermore, there is no doubt that throughout his writing, Pigeon Inlet becomes a symbol not only of a Newfoundland outport but of a way of life, and of the qualities of living that the traditional Newfoundland lifestyle had to offer.

Pigeon Inlet is typical of hundreds of outports in pre-Confederation and early post-Confederation Newfoundland. These small settlements, scattered along the rugged shoreline of the island and of coastal Labrador, depended almost entirely for their existence on the inshore cod fishery. This fishery, with its economic uncertainties, its dependence on the unpredictable ocean, and its demand for hard work, helped to mould the characters of the men and women who inhabited the outports. "Combined with this," wrote Ted recently, "was the isolation of the settlements from the outside world, a factor which resulted in closer ties and a meaningful interdependence."

This is how Uncle Mose describes Pigeon Inlet in his introductory chronicle:

> We've got as good a harbour as you'd care to see, deep water, good holdin' ground. And if anybody ever wants to build a fish plant, we've got the perfect place for it, right at the mouth of Bartle's Brook.
>
> We're right in the middle of a stretch of Coast about forty or fifty miles long, with five or six smaller places spread out along the shore on each side of us (pp. 158-59).

The most prominent Noddy in the Chronicles is Uncle Solomon's son, Jethro, of whom Grampa says, "the only good thing you can say...is that he's a better man than his father was." Ted Russell himself once said that Jethro was his favourite character: "He was the character through which I could say unkind things about Newfoundlanders and get away with it." He is first introduced to listeners and readers by Uncle Mose, as the "odd one—who's not quite so hard workin' and industrious and independent as the others." It is not that he cannot work; rather his problem is that he is not a consistent worker. Uncle Mose tells a few stories about Jethro that illustrate this characteristic. For example, on one occasion the local merchant asked Jethro if he would like to earn a dollar; to which Jethro replied, "No thank you, sir, I've got one." Another time while Jethro was helping Joe Irwin build a wheelhouse on his boat, Joe noticed that Jethro was using a hammer to drive in a screw. Jethro's reply to Joe's retort about why there was a slot in the head of the

screw was that the slot was there for taking it out. Uncle Mose makes it quite clear that Jethro Noddy is harmless. The closest he ever came to outright dishonesty was the time that he tried to get family allowance for his billy-goat, King David. When the welfare officer came to investigate, "Jethro squirmed out of it by sayin' that he'd had King David so long that he seemed like one of the family." One thing about Jethro for which Uncle Mose makes no allowances for his appearance:

> Jethro is not exactly the tidiest fellow in the world. Ordinary times, I should say that Jethro remembers to shave once every week—Saturdays—but often times it slips his memory…. It's better to explain what Jethro's face looks like with two or three weeks' whisker on it….

> The only thing I can compare it to is the North West corner of the Gull Mash, just after you've crossed the barren part and you're gettin' near to the foothills where we go for firewood. Well, that section of the mash is all spotted—mostly bare spots with here and there a clump of ground juniper or a small patch of alders or a few blueberry bushes—or an old gnarled stump—stuff like that. I don't know if I'm makin' it clear but I hope that'll give you some idea of what Jethro's jowls look like with a two weeks' whisker on 'em.

The greatest problem with Jethro Noddy, however, is not Jethro himself, but rather one of his possessions—his goat. Christened King David by a school teacher who had admired the goat's ability to jump fences, the goat is now old and quite useless. "He's a bit like Jethro himself," comments Uncle Mose. "He just lies around the lanes and under the fences gettin' a bite wherever he can." But even though King David can no longer jump fences, he can still do plenty of mischief, especially around cabbage gardens. Uncle Mose tells of one such instance:

> I watched him from my kitchen window one Sunday morning. He hooked his horns in between two pickets. Then he turned his head sideways. Then he pushed in with the bridge of his nose on one picket and hove out with his horns on the other picket. He drew out the nail and pushed the butt end of this second picket to one side. He stepped back then and manoeuvred till he got one end of his yoke into the gap, then he slewed around and followed it….I admired him so much that before I collected my wits he had the heart chewed out of the biggest cabbage in the garden. When I drove him out, blest if I didn't believe for a minute that he was goin' to stop and nail on the picket.

Needless to say, the majority of Pigeon Inlet residents are upset by the goat's antics. Attempts to force Jethro to keep King David tied up have come to no avail; once when Uncle Mose insisted that the goat be tied, Jethro's reply was that "Since Confederation, King David is a Canadian goat and he got his rights." Once the residents were successful in forcing the issue, but only after they agreed to supply King David with scraps of food, his "family allowance." But before long the goat was on the loose once more and matters were as bad as ever. It took a Pigeon Inlet posse, organized by Uncle Mose, Skipper Joe Irwin, Fred Prior and Levi Bartle, to settle the matter once and for all.

After careful planning, they were able to arrange for Jethro to be positioned back on to an angry King David. Next day, Jethro Noddy came to Uncle Mose for a length of chain (See "The Posse" in *Chronicles of Uncle Mose*). Ted Russell lived a full and productive life, a life that demonstrated certain qualities that were the essence of the man himself. In spite of the fact that he pursued several different occupations, a characteristic common to all was his dedication. His philosophy of work is best expressed in his own words:

> I grew up believing that the world consisted of a vast number of human beings who were hungry for service and if I served them well, they would somehow or other make it possible for me to continue doing so. The important thing was the work (pp. 166-68).

Ted's dedication to work, whatever that work might have been, is evident throughout his whole career. Whomever he had to serve, he served faithfully, be it his students, co-workers or constituents. His dedication to a particular job was prompted for the most part by his belief in what he was doing: "I am unable to do work unless I believe in it." The fact that his most short-lived occupations were those of politician and insurance salesman underlines the principle that governed his attitude towards work: he was not at all convinced that he was suited to either. By far the longest portion of his working life he spent at teaching (a total of thirty years), a profession that he always stated he dearly loved; his wife Dora substantiates that, asserting categorically that her husband was happiest as a teacher. For teaching provided him with the opportunity to utilize those characteristics that dominated his personality, and to utilize them in the service of others: his own creative instincts, his sense of humour, open-mind and optimistic view of life.

Many of his friends and acquaintances remember Ted best for his sense of humour, a trait that can be found at every stage of his life. But Ted was much more than a mere teller of funny stories. His most humorous anecdotes invariably had running through them a thread of sound Russell philosophy, the wisdom of a man who had lived life to the fullest. Of remarkable credit is the fact that Ted never did use his humour and wit to the detriment of any other individual. Although he may have had reason to be bitter as a result of his political experiences, Ted did not use his abilities as a writer to attack or condemn. It is as if he accepted his unfortunate foray into politics as his own fault: "I wasn't cut out for it; it's as simple as that." His pen was never a weapon of battle, but rather an instrument of love. At the core a romantic optimist, he believed in the human being's capacity for good, given the climate in which the good might flourish. "The world is taking pills for imaginary complaints," he once told a Grand Falls audience. "All barriers between men and nations would disappear if they were ignored."

Every individual who knew Ted Russell has his own particular impression of the man. While his dedication and sense of humour seem to be the dominant traits that have impressed some people, others admired him for his intellectual capacities and his humility, a combination that cannot help but draw admiration. But all who knew this man agree on one essential point, that Ted Russell has left an indelible mark on the history and culture of Newfoundland (pp. 220-21).

Jethro Noddy
Ted Russell

One thing I'm always afraid of is that I'll get you tangled up by telling you about too many people at the one time. There are two more characters I've got to tell you about before you can get a proper insight into the goin's on in Pigeon Inlet. In a way these other two characters are related, although one of 'em is a two-legged character and the other is a four-legged character. The two-legged one is Jethro Noddy and the four-legged one is Jethro's billy goat, King David.

I think I'll tell you about Jethro Noddy first, although in some ways King David is a more interestin' character.

When I told you a few weeks ago that the men in Pigeon Inlet were the finest and hardest workin' in the world, I've got to own up that I was forgettin' about Jethro Noddy. I suppose every place has got the odd one—who's not quite so hard workin' and industrious and independent as the others. I know they have one in Hartley's Harbour and they had one in the place where I lived on the Sou'West Coast. In bigger places they've probably got two and in a place the size of St. John's I wouldn't be surprised if they had three or four. Anyway, Pigeon Inlet got Jethro Noddy.

Now let's be fair to Jethro. 'Twould be a sin to call him lazy because off and on he can work as hard as any man in the Inlet. Only he don't stick to it, and when he gets a few quintals of fish caught or a few dollars earned he slacks up right away. I can't guarantee the truth of this, but Levi Bartle, the merchant, tells how he wanted his fish store swept out one day and he said to Jethro: "Jethro," he said. "How would you like to earn a dollar?" And Jethro said, "No thank you, sir, I've got one." That story mightn't be exact gospel, because Mr. Bartle stretches it sometimes, but 'twill give you an idea.

And it wouldn't be fair to call Jethro a good for nothin'. After all, he has a wife and eight children. But he's no good on his own. He's got to be workin' under someone else, and even then you've got to watch him. Joe Irwin tells a story about how Jethro was helpin' him build a wheel-house on his boat and Skipper Joe saw Jethro using a hammer to drive in a two-inch screw. Skipper Joe bawled at him and asked him didn't he see the slot in the head of the screw. "Oh, yes, Skipper Joe," said Jethro, as he gave the screw another belt with the hammer. "Isn't that slot there to be used puttin' the screw in?" asked Joe. "No, sir," said Jethro. "What's it there for, then?" bawled Joe. "For takin' it out, sir," said Jethro.

Like I said, he's not much good on his own. This spring he's salmon fishin' with Luke Bartle. Then he'll be a shareman in Skipper Joe Irwin's trap skiff. After that you'll see him and his biggest boy out in their punt on fine days hand lining in shoal water. Other times you'll see him goin' in over the hills with his trout pole. Then he'll pick up a few dollars if any sports come to fish for salmon in Bartle's Brook. They all want him for a guide because he seems to know all the salmon in the pools just as well as if he was one of 'em. Oh, he'll get by all right. It might be a tight pinch…but he'll do it.

The clergyman was preachin' a few Sundays ago about bein' happy. He said it wasn't always what you had in this world that made you happy. It was what you could learn to do without. That fits Jethro sure enough.

I'll never forget how Jethro put one over on me one day last spring…and my leg is not too easy to pull. I was busy trying to finish a herring net and I had a few turns of birch wood in my back yard that I wanted to have sawn and clove. So I thought I'd ask Jethro to do it. 'Twas near the middle of the month, so I figured the Family Allowance was runnin' short and he'd need a dollar or two. So I said: "Jethro," I said. "Yes, Uncle Mose," he said. "Jethro," I said. "How much will you charge me for sawing up that bit of birch wood?" Jethro looked at me, then at the pile of wood, then back at me. "How much?" he said. "Yes, how much?" said I. He looked at the wood again—walked around it—you wouldn't know but he was a qualified scaler. Then he looked back at me. "'Bout three parts of a cord, isn't it?" he asked. "'Bout that," said I. "Now, how much will you charge?" "Nuthin'," he said. "Nuthin'?" said I. "Not a cent," he said. "But," I said, "Jethro, you can't do that. It's kind and neighbourly alright, but you with a wife and family—you need a dollar or two like the rest of us. What'll you charge for sawing it?" "I won't charge nuthin' for sawing it," said he. "Why won't you charge for sawin' it?" I asked. "You must have a reason." "Yes," he said, "Mose, I've got a reason." "What is it?" I asked. "Uncle Mose," he said, "the reason why I'm not goin' to charge 'ee anything for sawing it—is—that I don't intend to saw it." And off he went.

Well, like I said, Jethro's a character. There's no harm in him and his only fault is that he's the owner of the other character I've got to tell you about—the four-legged one—King David—the billy goat. If you think Jethro Noddy is a character, wait till you hear about King David. I'll try and get a chance to tell you about King David next week.

King David
Ted Russell

Last week I gave you a sort of outline of Jethro Noddy and promised you I'd go on to tell you about King David. King David is just about the best known character in Pigeon Inlet. King David is Jethro Noddy's billy goat.

He was christened King David a good many years ago by a fellow we had here teachin' school. 'Twas before my time, but this teacher saw the billy goat jump over Aunt Sophy Watkinson's cabbage garden fence one morning and named him King David there and then. He said that there was a piece in the Bible about how the King David in the Bible was quite a one for leapin' over walls. Personally I've never been able to find the text, but Skipper Joe Irwin found it once although he nor I can find it since. Skipper Joe says, though, that he's almost sure it's somewhere there in the Psalms.

Be that as might be, our King David is finished with jumpin' over fences or leapin' over walls. His jumpin' days are over and he's long past his labour. No one, not even Jethro Noddy who owns him, seems to know how old he is. To give you an idea, the teacher who christened him went overseas in the year the second world war broke out and hasn't come back since. And the goat was an old goat before he was christened—so, as I said—that'll give you an idea.

Why in the world Jethro Noddy didn't make away with King David years ago is a puzzle. It might be just plain contrariness. That goat is no longer any good to man nor

beast—and since he can't get an old age pension, what's the sense of Jethro keepin' him? Every mornin' for years now the other goats go over the hills to graze, but King David pays no attention to them. He just lies around the lanes and under the fences gettin' a bite wherever he can. He's a bit like Jethro himself. Perhaps that's why Jethro keeps him.

About ten years ago, just before King David give up jumpin' fences, he destroyed Grampa Walcott's cabbage garden and they had court work over it. 'Twas up in the school one Saturday mornin'. The Ranger (that was before the Mounties) measured the height of Grampa Walcott's fence and even brought the goat into court and measured his yoke.

Then after they took the goat outside and opened all the windows to let the fresh air in, the Magistrate come to and give his judgement. He said 'twas a very unusual case. Grampa Walcott's fence was a lawful fence and King David's yoke was a lawful yoke. The only verdict he could give was that King David wasn't a lawful goat. But there was nothing he could do about it. He said he had looked through all the law books and he couldn't find in any statute "in such case made and provided." So that was that.

Perhaps you're wondering what harm King David can do now when he's too old to jump fences. He can do plenty. He can still get into the gardens. Last fall I watched him get into my garden where I still had a few cabbages left. (I'm awful fond of cabbage.) Here's how he got in. I watched him from my kitchen window one Sunday morning.

He hooked his horns in between two pickets. Then he turned his head sideways. Then he pushed in with the bridge of his nose on one picket and hove out with his horns on the other picket. He drew out the nail and pushed the butt end of this second picket to one side. He stepped back then and manoeuvred till he got one end of his yoke into the gap, then he slewed around and followed it. He went through that hole in the fence with his yoke out ahead of him just like 'twas a boat hook and he was fendin' off from his stage head. I admired him so much that before I collected my wits he has the heart chewed out of the biggest cabbage in the garden. When I drove him out, blest if I didn't believe for a minute that he was goin' to stop and nail on the picket.

Off I went to have it out with Jethro Noddy. I might just as well have stayed home. "What's he been up to now?" asked Jethro. "Eatin' my cabbage," I said. "You've got to tie him on." "What law says so?" said Jethro. He had me there. "We'll make a law," said I. "A harbour law." "Harbour law is no good," said he, "unless we got a Town Council." "Well, then, we'll get a Town Council," said I. "Town Council law'll be no good either," said Jethro, "unless it applies to all goats. They'd all have to be tied up." He had me again. "You should tie him up, anyway," I said. "'Twould be cruelty to poor dumb animals," said he. "Since Confederation, King David is a Canadian goat and he has his rights." He turned for a minute. King David was lyin' right behind him chewing on a cabbage leaf. "No, Uncle Mose," said Jethro. "I can't tie him up. 'Twould be too cruel." So that was that. Like I said. Better if I'd stayed home.

This year I'm trying another tack. I cut new pickets last winter and I've got new spruce rails all 'round the bottom of my cabbage garden fence. I've put new 1/2 inch nails into the bottom of every picket, and if King David can get into my garden this summer it must be because he's even fonder of cabbage than I am.

Somehow I've got my doubts. He was lyin' down watchin' me nail on pickets last week and I was tempted to throw the hammer at him. I made an offer but he didn't

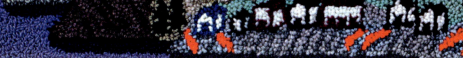

give it any heed. All he did was turn his head to one side and made a motion exactly as if he was drawing out the very nail I was drivin' in.

Well, time'll tell. I'm expectin' trouble and if I get it, you'll hear about it.

Edward Russell
24 May 1973

George Story

The eleventh epistle of Horace is addressed to a friend who, like Premier Moores during our recent Methodist Conference weather, has been cruising the wine-dark eastern Mediterranean. "What do you think of Chios, my friend?" asks the poet. "What of famous Lesbos and charming Samos?" Horace, with his tenacious sense of Roman identity, his small-holder's ambition satisfied by the Sabine farm, is skeptical of his friend's wanderlust. A man's happiness, he argues in the poem, depends not on his place of abode (even though it be Clearwater, Florida), but on his state of mind. And then, echoing Aeschylus, he says:

> *caelum, non animum, mutant qui trans mare currunt.*

Fairclough renders this, in prose, as: "they change their clime, not their mind, who rush across the sea"; and Conington, in verse, as:

> *when o'er the world we range*
> *'Tis but our climate, not our mind we change.*

But the perfect translation was neatly turned by the candidate who stands before you when, more than forty years ago, he construed the passage for John Lewis Paton as, "You can take the man out of the Bay, but you can't take the Bay out of the man."

That line, it will be recalled, is central to Ted Russell's most famous play, *The Holdin' Ground*. And something of its fierce sense of local Newfoundland experience and identity forms a persistent thread in everything he has set his hand to: as master teacher, outport magistrate, co-operative organizer, and politician. Uncommon in the written literature of Newfoundland, a precise and correct sense of place is also at the heart of everything Ted Russell has written, so that the world of Pigeon Inlet and Hartley's Harbour, of Uncle Ben Walcott, Skipper Joe Irwin, Aunt Sophy and Jethro Noddy, has become a rich example of what Robert Frost has called the "locative" in art: writing (which Frost admired above all else) rooted in the singularities of a place, and in the common language. Throughout these recent decades, which for Newfoundlanders has been so full of cultural and moral ambiguities, and in which politics, in the phrase of Ambrose Bierce, might be defined as a strife of interests masquerading as a contest of principles, Ted Russell's words, like his public actions, have rung true and untarnished.

I present at last, with special affection and pride, for the Degree of Doctor of Letters, *honoris causa*, Edward Russell of Coley's Point.

Special DADication
Kevin Tobin

When I was a young snotty-nosed kid in Stephenville, I never really felt I had a lot in common with my father. After all, it was from my mother that I inherited an interest in drawing. And it was my mother's calm view of the world that I've tried to copy and still live by.

Back then, it seemed my father watched the news a lot on our old black and white television. And if you dared disturb his concentration on the news about politicians or politics, you'd get a loud stern growl, "LISTEN NOW, LISTEN!!!" No three words spoken since have been able to shut me up as fast. And he also intensely read the local daily newspaper. And…Oh yeah, he loved to tell jokes about politicians, especially Joey Smallwood. Hmmm. Watching the news a lot. Telling jokes about politicians. I guess I do have more in common with my father than I ever imagined. His sense of humour and his way of telling political jokes is a lot like the way I approach my editorial cartoons—maybe a little "politically incorrect," at times.

And looking back, my interest in politics and politicians comes from the old days of my father listening keenly to the news on our old TV.

Yes, my ability to draw cartoons comes from my Mom but my ability to draw editorial cartoons comes from you, Dad. Thanks for everything.

The Outdoor Motor
Arthur Scammell

"Pride an' flusteration," said Skipper Neddie, stuffing the tobacco into his pipe bowl with a huge, spade-like thumb, "are two things that makes fools of people." When the old salt started making sweeping statements on human nature, I knew he was getting wound up for a good story.

"There wuz one man I knowed," resumed the Skipper, "who had both of them faults. Proud as a legharn rooster, an' nerviser'n a she-robin over 'er eggs. Luke Bolton his name wuz, an ornery little son-of-a-gun. Used to go fishin' in a punt be hisself. Had plenty of gall and wuz always tryin' to go one better than the rest of us. If he happened to be high-liner among the hook-and-line men any year, he'd go around proud as a peacock and brag that he used his brains and we didn't.

"One spring Luke got hold of one of those outdoor motors that hooks on the starn of a punt. The old buzzard wuz always talkin' 'bout the time he wasted, rowin' out to the grounds and back agin. One of the merchants here had this ingin come for his son, but the son died just afterwards, so his father told Luke about it. Got him all worked up over the nice, easy time he'd have, sittin' down, watchin' his punt zip along. Course Luke didn't know nothin' about runnin' the thing, but he got one of the fellers around here wot's studyin' to be an ingineer at college to larn him. Adder two weeks hard work, an' tearin' the starn off his punt and puttin' a new one on, he thought he wuz ready to leave the wharf-head.

"The second day the ingin come on the room, Luke's wife, Martha, packed up an' moved over to 'er sister's, until Luke had his course finished. She told how Luke 'ud get up in his sleep, go to the gramophone, thinkin' it wuz his outdoor motor, hitch a piece o'string on the post in the center an try to start 'ee. She used to send over a box o' Nerve Food every week. Luke never took 'em but he give 'em to the young ingineer, Joe Manning. Joe claimed that wuz the only thing that saved 'im fram goin' crazy while he wuz teachin' the old man.

"I remember the first day Luke come out fishin'. I wuz out on the ground, fishin' away, when all of a sudden I hears this queer hum. I couldn't make out first if it wuz an airplane or a 'hosstinger'. I looked all around, couldn't see nothin', but the hum got louder and louder. Then, up over a lop, I sees Luke's little crooked-nose punt, goin' like the divil terryfied, an' Luke back on the countersate, grinnin' all over his face. He cocked up his leg as he whipped along an' shouted out that he'd give me a tow if I wuz ready to go in when he wuz.

"Everything seemed to be comin' his way fer a while. He painted a name on the bow of his punt. Called 'er the *Hummin' Bird*, and hum she sartinly did. When Luke 'ud get in, just afore dark, all the young gaffers 'ud be down on the wharves, watchin' the *Hummin' Bird* dock, and all this attention made the old feller perk up still more. It got so bad that the rest of us wuz beginnin' to think about gettin' outdoors too, an' two or three of us had sent away for a catalog, when something happened which made us change our minds.

"One evenin' I got in afore Luke, an' a crowd of us was gettin' ready to go squiddin' when we heard the *Hummin' Bird* comin'. We didn't pay much attention till she got quite handy, and then somebody shouts, 'He can't stop 'er! Something's wrong with Luke's outdoor motor!' That made us look pretty fast. Sure enough, he couldn't get 'er shot off, so he had to turn 'er out to sea agin, or she'd uv stove 'er stem in agin the peer.

"Well, holy ole mackerel, then the fun sturted. Four times he hove around an' made fer the wharf, en' four times he had to sheer off. Luke wuz frantic. The outdoor wuz putterin' away as if he wuz two miles out to sea instid of 'longside his own stage-head. Everybody sturted shoutin' advice, but by this time Luke wuz too far gone to take it, even if it had been any good. 'Don't the *Hummin' Bird* know 'er nest when she gets to it?' bawled Bert Simmonds. 'What's the matter, Luke?' somebody else shouted. 'Did ya just remember the old woman promised ya a lickin' the minit ya stepped ashore?'

"By this time people had come from all around the cove and the fuss wuz tee-rific. An' then Luke got out his oars an' tried to stop 'er. But 'twas useless. He could only row about one horse power and the motor wuz four. We wuz all doin' our best to encourage 'im, goin' with our arms like we wuz rowin'. Aunt Sarah Coles, Luke's sister, rowed so hard, she fell over backwards, sprained 'er ankle, an' a couple o' men had to carry 'er 'ome on a handbar.

"All this time Luke's wife wuz tryin' ti find Joe Manning, so he could tell Luke wot to do. Well, sir, the last we saw of Luke fer a while, the oars had caught agin his chest, on account of the punt goin' so fast round an' round, an' knocked him down in the bottom of 'er outa sight. He wuz headin' straight out to sea then, an' the outdoor wuz goin' as strong as ever. He had filled 'er up with gas when he left the fishin' grounds. A full hour he had to keep cruisin' round the cove till she run outa oil, an' then he landed. The next day he sold 'er to Joe Manning fer half wot he paid."

"Hauled up and rotting..."

Uncle Mark White's Rat

Bruce Stagg

If you visit Roaring Cove and look down behind the post office in the town council compound, there barred in behind a chain-linked fence, you will see Uncle Mark White's rat—the pride of the whole town and the envy of all the other places up and down the coast. You see, Uncle Mark's rat is quite out of the ordinary; it is much larger than others of its kind and it has a different and unique shape. It came all the way from Texas, and the story of how it ended up in Roaring Cove is an unusual one indeed.

It all started one day in late June last summer when Uncle Mark and I went to Middleville to pick up a few supplies for a garden party that our newly-formed volunteer fire department was having to raise money to purchase a new fire truck. By lunchtime, the back seat of my car was full of paper plates, plastic forks and knives, admission tickets, stuffed animals, and other garden party odds and ends.

Our shopping was complete, so we went to the restaurant up on the highway to get a bite to eat before heading back to Roaring Cove. We ordered the special of the day and were waiting for it to be served when we heard this thunderous roar coming from outside. Through the front window, I saw fifteen or twenty motorcycles pulling into the parking lot. They ceremoniously circled several times, as if announcing their arrival, and parked in a neat row in front of the restaurant. The drivers dismounted, removed their helmets and sunglasses, and inspected their bikes. They congregated in the middle of the parking lot, held a brief discussion, and headed in single file towards the restaurant. Four or five people sitting near the back of the restaurant made a hurried exit through the side door.

"Maybe we should get out of here," I said to Uncle Mark. "I've read about motorcycle gangs like this. There could be trouble." I noticed a gleam in Uncle Mark's eye, and I realized that my comment had only fanned his lust for adventure.

"I fought the Battle of the Dardanelles, my son," he said. "I'm not afraid of a crowd the like a dat." He sat straight in his chair, ignored the meal that had been placed before him, and sized up the bikers as they entered the restaurant.

Around Middleville, they were a strange-looking crowd indeed. Most of the men wore long hair and beards of all shapes and styles. A couple had no hair at all, their heads having been completely shaved. There were only a few women. Their hair was held in place with handkerchiefs that were twisted across their foreheads and tied at the back. All faces were deeply tanned, and they looked as if a good bath would not have been wasted.

Both men and women were dressed identically, in black leather pants and jackets with high-heeled cowboy boots. Their outfits were decorated with silver studs that bordered the waistband and pockets of the pants and short pieces of chain that looped from the shoulder straps of the jackets. On the back of each jacket was a large yellow star. The words "Freedom Riders" were panted in red letters around the outside of the star, and in its centre was a symbol that resembled something between a set of bull's horns and a pitchfork.

These were not young people. Most of the beards were streaked with grey and the long hair was thin and wispy. I figured most of the people to be middle-aged at best.

They were noisy as they entered the restaurant, and they spoke loudly in slow, drawn accents.

"Queer lookin' crowd," Uncle Mark commented as he inserted his fingers into his soup bowl and extracted a salt meat bone which he immediately proceeded to strip of meat. He continued his assault on his dinner and his attention was fully taken up with his favourite pastime: eating. But, as he was waiting for his apple pie to be served, he noticed a bit of a show from one of the tables at which the bikers were sitting.

"Look there!" Uncle Mark said in a voice clearly audible to the three bikers at the table closest to us. "Buddy got a rat with en." He pointed his finger directly at the big, bearded man sitting at the head of the table.

My heart jumped into my throat, and I looked towards the man for some sort of a reaction. Much to my relief, the man's attention was focused on his huge hand that was outstretched over the table. A tiny hamster was running around his palm and in and out between his fingers. The man had removed his leather jacket; underneath he wore a denim shirt with the sleeves cut out. The little hamster ran over the bulging muscles of the man's tattooed arm and disappeared into his thick, bushy beard. It surfaced on the man's sideburns, climbed onto his head, and ran around and around.

The very amused Uncle Mark clapped his hands and laughed loudly.

Finally, the hamster ran down the man's neck and inside his shirt collar. Uncle Mark leaned forward in his chair and stretched his neck, searching for the little rodent.

"Dere he is! Dere he is!" Uncle Mark shouted excitedly, pointing to the hamster surfacing from the front of the man's shirt. It jumped onto the table and ran wildly, sliding and slipping on the smooth tabletop. Uncle Mark again clapped his hands and laughed, making a snorting noise as he drew in his breath. When the animal began sniffing at the sugar dispenser, the big biker scooped his hamster friend into his hand.

Before I knew what was happening, Uncle Mark was off his chair and was hopping over to the man holding the hamster. "Show Uncle Mark yer rat," he half stated and half demanded. The big man stared ahead expressionless and silently. "Come on, show Uncle Mark. Uncle Mark's not gonna hurt yer bloody old rat."

The biker raised his foot and kicked out the empty chair from the table. "Sit down," he said. As Uncle Mark squatted in the chair, the biker handed him the hamster. Uncle Mark cupped his hands and received the creature. He stroked and petted it as he engaged in conversation with the three men.

I could not hear what was being said, but it was evident that Uncle Mark was doing most of the talking. It was also evident that these strangers were not offended by Uncle Mark's intrusion because they were smiling and, on a couple of occasions, laughed loudly. Then I noticed Uncle Mark lift his shirt and show the men his bare back. I knew they were getting the full details of his active war duty, so I figured it was time for us to leave.

"Excuse me, Uncle Mark," I said as I approached the table, "are you ready to leave?"

"Come here," he said, "and meet these fellers." He introduced me to Joe, Sid, and the big man, Hank. "And this little rat here is called a 'amster," he announced, holding the pet out in his hand. "Cute little feller, en he?"

I shook hands with the three men and made small talk with them as Uncle Mark gathered his cap and coat. He placed his cap on his head and gave it that distinguished little tip forward before returning to the bikers' table. We said our good-byes and were prepared to leave. I was holding the door for Uncle Mark when he suddenly turned back to the men. "You know what?" he said. "We're havin' a garden party in Roarin'

Cove on Friday. All you fellers should come down to it; I guarantee a good time." I made my exit into the parking lot.

Uncle Mark's face was beaming with a broad smile when he got into my car. "They're comin' down to the garden party on Friday," he announced proudly.

"I wouldn't count on it," I said.

Around noon on Thursday, children lined the sides of the roads, old men leaned over the fences, and faces appeared in kitchen windows as a convoy of motorcycles invaded our little town. Like ants scurrying in their trails, the bikes wound their way along the narrow dirt road as the children chased behind. Revving the motors to echo the noise off the cliffs, the bikers drove to the end of the community, where the road meets a solid rock face. They stopped their bikes and got off. Some climbed up the cliff and looked out over the harbour; others threw stones from the road in an unsuccessful attempt to reach the water; a couple of men urinated over the edge of the cliff. Every move was carefully watched by all who lived below Sam Whiffen's shop.

Uncle Mark was on the road, waiting for them when they came back. It was Hank who pulled up alongside him. The first thing he did was to reach inside his jacket, pull out the hamster, and hand it to Uncle Mark. Uncle Mark held the hamster as he directed the bikers to what he calls "my big garden."

Uncle Mark's garden was a long, narrow, grassy field that was across the road from his house, down over the cliff near the water. He used it years ago to grow hay and graze his animals. Today, it is only used by youngsters to play a scattered game of cricket and rounders.

The bikes slowly snaked their way down the steep foot path, and the big garden was soon transformed into a camp ground as bright orange pup tents blazed in the green grass, and smoke from the camp-stoves climbed lazily up the face of the cliff.

By four o'clock, Sam Whiffen's shop was completely sold out of beer, and concern ran through the community. Uncle Mark's telephone rang continuously. "They're on your property, so you'll be held responsible," Thumb-On-Wrench Swyers, Roaring Cove's mayor, said before Uncle Mark could hang up on him.

The first night was noisy. The bikers hooted and hollered and burned fires on the beach for most of the night. The next morning, Toby Avery's lobster vat was empty—twenty-two lobsters stolen. Toby pointed the finger of blame at the bikers. A public meeting was called, and all the toilets on the beach—the ones the bikers were using ended up with padlocks on the doors.

The big concern at the meeting was the possibility of trouble at the garden party that night. Thumb-On-Wrench suggested that the party be postponed until after the bikers left. Uncle Mark stood up, buried his hands deep in his pockets, and said his piece, "I think you fellers are a bit quick to hang the cat. I thought the idea of havin' a garden party was to raise money for a fire truck, so I figured the more who attended the better—that's why I invited them fellers along. And besides, they seem like an all right bunch to me. We got no proof that it was they who stole Toby's lobsters—we've had lobsters stolen in Roarin' Cove before. And, as for puttin' padlocks on the toilets on the beach, I've had a toilet down there fer fifty year, and I haven't had anything stole out of it yet. And I don't suspect the bikers will steal anything from it now."

Well, most saw Uncle Mark's point, and the garden party went off as planned—and without trouble. As a matter of fact, it was the most successful and enjoyable garden party ever held in Roaring Cove, and it was the bikers who helped make it so. They arrived early in the evening and remained until a hint of orange sunshine glowed in the sky. They virtually bought out the concessions, and the beer tent turned in remarkable profits. They proved to be polite and friendly, and they socialized easily with the Roaring Covers. By the time the dance started, friendships were blooming, and plaid and leather blended well together. And once things got going, it was realized that the bikers and the Roaring Covers had something in common—they knew how to have a good time.

The floor of the old Fisherman's Hall was put to the ultimate test as it creaked and groaned under the assault of hundreds of dancing feet. The strangers were taught to dance the Roaring Cove jigs, but they proved that they could cut a square set as well as anyone. When Paddy Whalen's fingers got sore from playing the button accordion, one of the bikers produced a concertina and picked up where Paddy had left off. A little later in the evening, one of the biker women played her guitar and sang in a voice that would have sweetened a pickle. Paddy and the concertina player joined in with her, and tired feet were rested as the dancing gave way to a sing-along.

Sometime during the evening, Art Pearce went up to Toby Avery and asked if forty-five dollars was enough to cover the lobsters. Toby had no idea what Art was talking about, but he played along and got the entire story out of Art. Apparently, on Thursday night, Art, Joe Stead and the devilskin, Alfie Lambert were on a bit of a party up in Kellop Harbour. Sometime during the night, they figured that a good feed of lobsters was needed to add to the festivities. So, they came down to Roaring Cove and cleaned out Toby's vat.

The next day, Alfie, realizing that he was out of money and that the garden party was that night, lied to Art and Joe that Toby had found out that they had stolen his lobsters. Alfie then suggested that the proper thing to do was to pitch in fifteen dollars each and pay Toby. Of course, Alfie ended up with thirty dollars for the garden party.

When the sing-along was over, Thumb-On-Wrench Swyers went to the platform and called for attention. "Ladies and gentlemen," he said, "I have a couple of announcements to make. Before I do, however, as mayor of Roarin' Cove, I'd like to extend a warm welcome to our friends camping out in Uncle Mark's big garden, and I'd like to thank them for attending our garden party here this evening. Now, first, I'd like to announce that Toby Avery has found his lobsters. Secondly, I'm happy to announce that this evening we've raised a grand total of $2,234.22. I know we'll need many more fund-raisers before we can get our fire truck, but it is a good start."

While Thumb-On-Wrench was being applauded, the bikers congregated on the dance floor, and I noticed a motorcycle helmet being handed around and bills being dropped into it. It was Hank who dumped the contents of the helmet in front of Thumb-On-Wrench. He and Walt Churchill began counting. "Another $235.00!" Walt shouted. The applause was long and sustained. A perfect ending to a perfect night.

The next morning, the padlocks were removed from the outhouses on the beach, and Toby Avery gave his entire morning catch of lobsters to the bikers as an apology for wrongly accusing them. Aunt Mae White baked bread, while Uncle Mark carefully packed the entire batch into the wheelbarrow and delivered it to the campsite, in time to go along with the lobsters. Hank fitted Uncle Mark with a leather jacket and a helmet and gave him a thrilling motorcycle ride halfway to Middleville and back. Other bikers gave the children rides through the community.

On Sunday morning, the last three pews of the church were full of leather. That afternoon, old men leaned on their fences and waved good-bye; smiling faces disappeared from kitchen windows, to reappear in doorways, with more waving, and the children chased the bikes all the way to Bakeapple Marsh Road intersection. No one in Roaring Cove ever expected to see or hear from the bikers again—but Roaring Cove was in for bit of a surprise.

Summer had faded into fall and the Christmas season was quickly upon us. It was a still Saturday morning and everyone was busy stringing outdoor lights around almost anything that would support them. Suddenly, the screeching sound of a siren echoed through the community. Everyone thought it was the Middleville Santa Claus parade being led by a police car, and they lined the sides of the road to see it.

I was in Uncle Mark's shed watching him shape out a model dory. The two of us went outside, leaned over his fence, and waited for the parade to come along. We looked at each other with surprise when a large lime-green fire truck rounded the corner and rolled down the road towards us. It pulled up in front of Uncle Mark's gate. His jaw fell open and he turned a pasty white when I read aloud the words printed on the side of the truck, "PRESENTED TO THE TOWN OF ROARING COVE, FROM THE TEXAS FRONTIER OIL COMPANY—AND THE FREEDOM RIDERS."

Two unfamiliar men stepped out of the truck and, in a deep southern drawl, requested "to speak with Mr. Mark White." Uncle Mark proudly presented himself and shook hands with the two men. "This is for you," one of them said, handing Uncle Mark a rectangular shaped object covered in a leather case. Surprised and unsure of how to behave or respond, he took the object and removed the cover. It was a wire cage. Inside, a small hamster ran wildly on a treadmill, and fastened to the outside of the cage was a silver name plate with the word "RAT" engraved on it.

The two men were promptly invited inside, and Aunt Mae prepared a lunch. The men told their story. They were employees of the Texas Frontier Oil Company of which Hank, the biker, was owner and president. With several oil fields and as many refineries, fire trucks were standard safety equipment for Hank's company. The truck the two had driven from Texas to Roaring Cove was one that was being replaced with a newer, more modern one. Hank, also the president of the Freedom Riders Motorcycle Club, decided that the replaced truck would make an appropriate gift for Roaring Cove.

A public meeting was quickly called and a very astonished Mayor Thumb-On-Wrench Swyers was presented with the keys to Roaring Cove's first fire truck.

The story of the fire truck went through the community like a west wind, and by the time it reached Jonas Pickett on Manuel's Point, it was somewhat distorted and blown out of proportion. Old Jonas hurried in the harbour to see the big rat that had been given to Uncle Mark. He had heard it was so large that it had to be barred in the town council compound.

Well, that was it—the truck had acquired its name, and a few days later Thumb-On-Wrench put the truck in his garage and painted the words "Uncle Mark's Rat" in red letters along the front.

So, if you visit Roaring Cove and look down behind the post office in the town council compound behind the chain-linked fence, you will see Uncle Mark White's rat.

The Poor We Have With Us Always
Ray Guy

I went up into a dory

It is funny how the infant mind functions.

I can mind, when I was small, being lodged off down on the coats in the back of the school at dances.

This is where they put you at about two o'clock in the night when you commenced to get groggy and wanted a nap. There was a row of desks shoved in tight to the wall for all hands to put their coats on.

Sometimes there would be three or four of us at once laid out down there heads and tails, some on a half-doze, more with their thumbs stuck in their gob looking around, and others a cold junk sleeping it off.

Solid comfort.

I can recall hearing this very restful "RUMP-A-RUMP-A-RUMP" noise in the background. It was half a shuffle and half a stamp which caused the floor to heave rythmically up and down and rattled a few loose panes in the windows.

And I remember watching the light from the kerosene oil lamps dancing on the ceiling from the draft as they all swung around in the Reel and I can remember this strange noise threading through everything, rising and falling in tune with the flickering light.

The big puzzle occupying my infant noggin was: is that noise making the light or is that light making the noise?

That is the first thing I can ever remember about dances.

She came down into a flat

Of course, before many more years had passed I had put two and two together and figured out that this noise was coming from the fiddler who was playing an accordion. He was always called the fiddler regardless of what he played upon. Even a rack comb and tissue paper.

First they had the Sale of Work. Second, they had the First Table followed by the Second and Third Tables depending on how many was there. Then they might have a Guess Cake or Grab Bags and third they had the Dance.

Sale of Work was cloths and aprons and pillow slips hung across on lines and all worked out into cock sparrows and roses and double mitts, fancy for Sundays, and cushion tops all made mostly out of dyed wool and flour bags bleached out.

You never saw many figgy buns flung about at the First Table. There was always a steadier lot sitting in at it. They even had grace at First which had to do for the Second and Third tables too where you had more driving works and carrying on.

A mug-up in paradise

They used to sing grace.

Every word was stretched out to the extent of an elastic garter. This was because the Salvationers had the name of singing too fast while the Church of Englanders were known to drain through their noses.

When both got together the Salvationers started out dead slow in deference to the C of Es and the C of Es slowed her down even a notch more to prove that the Salvationers WERE racy.

It was the most dismal thing you ever heard. "Beeeeeprezzzzzent aayt oour taaay-ble Lord" and so on through, "Be here and everywhere adored; Thy creatures bless and grant that we; May feast in Paradise with Thee."

"AAAAAWWWWW MMMMEMMMMMM."

Then the Catholics from Southern Harbour blessed theirselves and all hands sat down and dug in.

Behaving the same as you ought

Generally, they had Meat Teas or Soup Suppers.

This was bully beef and potato salad of different sorts. Then jelly and blanc mange and partridge berry tarts and cakes and figgy buns and tea.

If someone who had a few drinks in, or some of the youngsters hove a bun at someone at the other end of the table or flicked blanc mange on their spoons across, then one of the women serving on the table would give them a click across the ear and tell them to behave the same as they ought.

When they had Soup Suppers you got a chance to be sent down to the house for the boiler.

Halfways up with it yourself and the other chap put down the boiler, took off the cover and drove your arm down to rummage a biggish bit of meat off the bottom.

This was a tricky business.

You had to be quick because they were timing you back at the school. If you took too much they would notice it because meat wasn't always that plentiful. And the stuff was burning hot.

So it was in and out of the boiler as quick as you could and then jam your arm down in the snow to take the sting out. Once, Gordon lost his mitt in the boiler and forgot to hook it out and got a lacing for it.

Doggedy, doggedy, bark at the cat

When the Last Table was nearly eat down to a shambles they started the dance.

Mostly they had sets which included such things as "Form a Line and Advance," "Dance to your Partner" and "Round the House." Sometimes they had "the Reel" or the "furginia Reel" and in later years, a "Wallace."

Everyone got out except for the small youngsters and women not feeling well. The oldish men were always the ring leaders of it. It seemed that the fiddler played a lot faster than Harry Hibbs.

There were two sides to a set and when one side stopped the other side commenced. To my knowledge, there is no harder or faster or longer dancing in the world unless among uncivilized races.

The windows were up with the snow blowing in, the door was open, the stove was let die down but whenever the fiddler stopped the men in their shirtsleeves with sweat running down their back would lurch for the door and fall across the bridge rail outside with the steam flying out of them in the frost.

And the women panting for breath with their hands to their bosoms would stagger off toward the kitchen to dip a cup in the water barrel. They would shake their heads at the other women in the kitchen and puff their cheeks and say, "Ohmygod! I'm just about dead."

The Reel was even worse. When someone would mention having the Reel there would be groans all around and people saying, "Oh, no, not the Reel. For God's sake not the Reel." Reels took an hour or more apiece.

Mussels in the corner

As a lad I was somewhat on the slight side. It is only these late years that I have fallen into flesh. So one of my worries then was that a woman might take me off my feet in the dances.

Some of them were upwards of 17 stone. There were very few there that any husky man could swing off their feet so generally it worked out to a tie. But imagine getting taken off your feet yourself!

Once I had like to but that was on account of the water they had sprinkled on the floor to keep down the dust making into ice down by where the door was open.

When you got swinging about 102 miles an hour they commenced to tighten their grip until you could feel your ribs lap over and your draft cut off and little spots dancing in front of your eyes.

If two people swinging happened to rouse into two more some bad injuries were likely to result. If you let go at top speed you would clear the floor like an oblong bowling ball and probably have to be dug out of the wall.

Only the poorest kind of dances ever finished up before it was daylight all abroad.

The poor we have with us always

By means of these affairs they built schools, churches and halls, assisted distressed persons, sent parcels overseas and helped put a stitch of clothes on the poor naked backs of heathens in other countries who, although odd looking, are created in our blessed Saviour's image just the very same as you and me.

Once when I was telling a person from upalong about Soup Suppers and so forth he shook his head and became down in the mouth and said: "You must have been very poor."

Strange talk. If we had been poor it would have been the other way around. People in other countries would have been running off Soup Suppers to send parcels over to us.

It is funny how the mainland mind functions.

This Dear and Fine Country—*Spina Sanctus*
Ray Guy

Well, we made it once again, boys! Winter is over.

Oh, but there is still snow on the ground.

So what? It hasn't got a chance. It is living in jeopardy from day to day. We should pity it because it will soon be ready for the funeral parlour.

It is only a matter of another few paltry weeks and we shall see it disappear into brown and foaming brooks: we shall see the meadows burning green and spangled with little piss-a-beds like tiny yellow suns.

Winter is over.

Oh, but there is still ice in the water.

So what? The globe is turning and nothing can stop it.

We are revolving into light.

The fisherman tars his boat on the beach and is heated by two suns, one in the sky and another reflected from the water, and the ice on the cliff behind him drips away to a poor skeleton.

It is only a matter of a few more paltry weeks and we shall see the steam rising from the ponds and from the damp ground behind the plow; we shall see the grandmothers sitting out by the doorstep for a few minutes watching the cat: we shall see the small boats a'bustle, piled high with lobster pots in the bow, and the days melting further and further into the night.

Winter is over now.

Praise God and all honour to our forefathers through generations who did never forsake this dear and fine Country.

Chimney Cove

A Fairy Tale
Ed Smith

Once upon a time there was a family. A typical Canadian family that lived in a typical Canadian town in typically Canadian Ontario. There was a father and a mother, a boy and a girl, and a dog named Mr. Muff.

One fine spring day, Father called the family together for a big announcement. For vacation that summer, he said, they would be going some place special. Perhaps 'special' was the wrong word, he said. Perhaps 'different' was more accurate.

The children clapped their hands for joy and Mr. Muff wagged his tail.

"Where are we going, Father?" they chorused. "Bermuda? British Columbia? The outer Hebrides? Somaliland?"

Father stopped the eager chatter with a laugh and a wave of his hand.

"Oh no," he said. "Nothing as common as that. We're going to—are you ready—Nufunlund."

The children stopped clapping. Mr. Muff cocked his head to one side quizzically.

"Nufunlund?" asked Peter.

"Where's that?" chimed in Susan.

"You can't be serious!" Mother said severely.

"Ah, but I am!" cried Father. "It's perfect! We may be the first people in our whole town to see it in its natural state. Just think of the adventure of it all!"

His enthusiasm was contagious. The frown left Mother's face.

"We once had a mailman whose mother had a brother-in-law originally from Nufunlund," she said. "It isn't as though it's totally strange." Father was getting more and more excited.

"We'll sell the car and buy a four-wheel drive," he enthused. "And we'll need four extra tires and extra cans of gasoline."

"Don't they have roads in Nufunlund, Daddy?"

"Of course they have roads, Susan. The logging companies put them in years ago. But the government hasn't got the money to keep them up so we have to be prepared for some rough going. That's all part of the fun, eh?"

"Nufunlund can't be very rich," observed Peter, "if they can't look after their roads."

"Poor Nufunlund is very, very poor," replied Mother. "The natives all fish for a living and they don't get paid very much, I'm afraid."

"Then how do they live?" Peter was obviously disturbed.

"I think Nufunlund is in some way a part of Canada," said Father, "although I'm not sure exactly how it works. But I do know Canada gives them all the money they need to keep going."

"And here's a lesson for you children," Mother went on. "Although they have so little, Nufunlunders are very, very happy. They're always laughing and singing and telling jokes, and they're very, very friendly, too."

"I bet they're friendly 'cause they 'preciate all the money we're giving them," cried Susan. "Oh, I'm so glad we're able to help them, Mommy. Do the children in Nufunlund go to school?"

"I'm sure some of them do," Mother said, "although not many ever learn to speak English well, and that reminds me, Mr. Crosbie, the cabinet minister, is from Nufunlund, isn't he, and he seems to have at least a basic education."

"That's true," Father said authoritatively. "But a little bad news here, kids, once we're on the Island, there's no more indoor potty. But they keep their outhouses in reasonable shape, and we'll take our own toilet tissue, just to be on the safe side."

"Can we take Mr. Muff, Dad?"

"Sorry, Son. Mr. Muff wouldn't last a minute in Nufunlund. The huskydogs would tear him limb from limb in seconds."

"Oh dear," said Mother. "What are huskydogs?"

"Huskydogs are the savage animals that Nufunlunders use for travel in winter when the roads are blocked with snow for six months at a stretch," replied Father.

"It's too bad we won't see an igloo, children," Mother said. "But by July most of them will have melted away and the natives will be in their summer homes."

"It sounds like grand fun, anyway," cried Peter. "Can we stay very long, Father?"

"Ah yes," replied Father. "Just as long as we pack enough provisions and gasoline, we can stay until the Gulf of St. Lawrence freezes up in late August."

"There, children," said Mother. "Now you see the advantage of having a high school principal for a father and a geography teacher for a mother!"

"Hurrah!" cried the kids.

Hurrah.

Mosey

Donald Gale

For many years an odd-looking man pushed a wheelbarrow around the streets of Stephenville, collecting usable items from the garbage, which he sold or just kept. His real name was Moses Murrin, but he was usually called Mosey, or sometimes, mistakenly, Mosey Burns.

Mosey had very curly grey hair, and a curly beard. He had a bounce to his step, even when he was old, and he had the brightest, roundest eyes you ever saw. He wore a lot of clothes. Sometimes he would have three or four coats on, along with an old hat and a big pair of overshoes, with winter boots inside, even on a fairly warm day.

Mosey often went to people's houses to ask for a cup of tea. Most people would give him one, and he would tell strange stories to whomever was there. My mother kept a special cup for Mosey, and we often heard his stories. He used to tell about a giant spider that did all sorts of damage, and then would get caught but always escaped again. This spider was sixteen feet long and would be trapped in a herring net by a bunch of men, but they could never keep it. It always got away to be seen in some other place.

Small children were often afraid of Mosey because of his unusual appearance, but they had no need to be frightened. He was never known to hurt anyone. However, people sometimes were unkind to him. He used to say that he did not like teenage boys because they often chased him or threw stones or snowballs at him.

Mosey lived alone in different shacks in the woods at different times. The last place he lived is near where Townview Road is now, between Hillview Avenue and the Hansen Highway. He also had shacks in what is now commonly called Area 13, and in Moonshine Valley, which we know as Brook Street.

Bernard O'Quinn, a retired fireman, tells about being called to a fire in Mosey's shack. He said that the shack had no plumbing or electricity, and was heated by a wood stove, the cause of the fire. In his own eccentric way, Mosey had placed his stove on top of a table. It was difficult to get into the house because of all the clutter in and around the small building. An RCMP officer entered the house with the firemen, and found Mosey asleep under a huge pile of old clothes. The firemen put the fire out and saved Mosey from sure death, but, instead of being thankful, Mosey was angry at being awakened and said that the neighbours had no business calling the fire department.

That does not mean that Mosey was ungrateful for kind deeds done for him. He just did not believe that anything bad would have happened to him. He was completely carefree, even about such dangers as fire.

Mosey lived in Stephenville, but was seen in many places on the West Coast. He sometimes went to Corner Brook and other communities. He came originally from Lark Harbour, in the Bay of Islands, and one of the names with which some people cruelly taunted Mosey was The Ghost of Lark Harbour.

Many stories are told about Mosey, attesting to his quick wit and shrewdness. One story is that Mosey was in Port aux Basques when the ferry arrived from Nova Scotia.

Some American tourists got off the boat, expecting to find very primitive conditions, and asked Mosey where all the "savages" were. Mosey replied that they were not all off the boat yet.

Mosey was said to be travelling on a ferry one time and had no money, so he dropped an empty wallet overboard and made a big fuss about losing all his money in the water. The people on deck all saw the wallet and felt so bad for Mosey that they took up a collection for him. He ended up with a wad of money and all it cost him was an old wallet which he probably found in the garbage anyway.

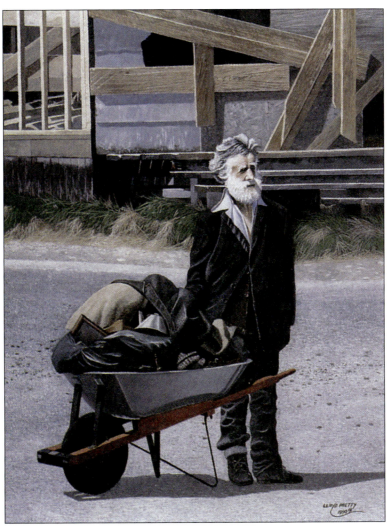

Mosey by Lloyd Pretty.

While sitting in the dentist's chair Mosey asked how much an extraction cost. The dentist replied that the first tooth was ten dollars and the rest were five dollars each. Mosey said that he wanted the second one taken out; the first one did not hurt.

When asked by a lady, who was giving Mosey a free breakfast, how he wanted his egg, Mosey said, "With another one."

I do not know whether or not these stories are true. They have been attributed to Mosey in the same way as other witty stories are attached to other similar people. People like Mosey provide us with a convenient character around which to build our folklore.

Mosey talked to anyone who would listen to him. He was sometimes hard to understand and sometimes he seemed to be talking nonsense. I once met him in the old Shoprite Groceteria where he told me that it was King George's birthday. "That's old King George," he said, "the Queen's father." I did not check out the date to see if he was correct or not. I guess all that really mattered was that Mosey was remembering the past and honouring the dead King. He was living in the past as so many people do as they get older. When there was no one around to listen, he often talked to himself as he bounced along giving frequent shrugs of his shoulders.

When I think of Mosey I am reminded of the Gospel of St. Matthew in which he quotes Jesus as saying that we should not worry too much about worldly things because we will be looked after. Mosey cared not at all about money or possessions. What someone else threw away was fine for him. That's probably why he did not worry about fire in his shack. If it was his time to die, then he would die; if not, then he would not be hurt.

The fact that so many people are interested in Mosey should tell us one thing: it is characters like him who give a community its unique character.

Mosey was definitely a colourful character. Some teased him while others were afraid of him. In both cases people were wrong. Mosey was dirty but harmless. I suspect that Mosey was a lonely man. There are persons in every community who, while not as extreme as Mosey, are nonetheless different from most people. These people are often lonely, too. The important thing is to be nice to them. They are people who deserve our respect. None of us knows what the future holds in store for us. Like Mosey, we may be in need of some patient understanding as we grow older.

Recipe
Gordon Rodgers

For your family, find a sheltered, deep-water cove with a place to haul up boats, land to sink a well. Clear the land of rocks and forest; keep the trees for fences or to split for firewood. Become a carpenter: build your house, your wharf, your boat, a shed for gear. During the summer season, start and keep a simple garden, dig a deep cellar to store the harvest. Preserve wild berries. Gather farm animals; dogs for hunting and sledding. Learn to use rifles for birds and moose; learn to set rabbit snares. Read weather signs in all seasons; study tides and navigation—sew nets, mend nets, cure the fish—and know your own coast. Keep your eyes open and put your hand to anything to survive the regular, random disasters. Most of all, hold your health: keep a barrel for cod livers. Let them stand and froth all through the brewing summer. Dip out a fingerful. Taste the pungent oil, the true tonic of this shore.

The Badger Drive
John V. Devine

Chorus: With their pike-poles and peavies and bateaus and all,
And they're sure to drive out in the spring that's the time;
With their caulks in their boots as they get on the logs,
And its hard to get over their time.

Billy Dorothey he is the manager, and he's a good man at the trade,
And when he's around seeking drivers he's like a train going down grade;
But still he's a man that's kindhearted, on his word you can always depend,
And there's never a man that works with him but likes to go with him again.

I tell you today home in London the *Times* it is read by each man,
But little they think of the fellows that drove the wood on Mary Ann.
For paper is made out of pulpwood and many things more you may know,
And long may our men live to drive it upon Paymeoch and Tomjoe.

The drive it is just below Badger and everything is working grand,
With a jolly good crew of picked drivers and Ronald Kelly in command.
For Ronald is boss on the river, and I tell you he's a man that's alive.
He drove the wood off Victoria now he's out on the main river drive.

So now to conclude and to finish, I hope that you all will agree
In wishing success to all Badger and the A. N. D. Company.
And long may they live for to flourish, and continue to chop, drive and roll,
And long may the business be managed by Mr. Dorothey and Mr. Cole.

Sharpening a traditional bucksaw.

Newfoundland Outport Furniture
Walter Peddle

Newfoundland outport furniture belongs to that broad category of painted furniture often referred to as "Country Furniture". It was made in the outports, or small coastal communities, from the days of early settlement in the early seventeenth century until at least 1949.

Until the late nineteenth century, furniture making specialists were rare in outport Newfoundland. This island was sparsely populated and the economy was focused almost entirely on the fishery. Outport fishers had to be self reliant and posses a number of skills, including furniture making, to survive. Consequently, even during the twentieth century, a large number of pieces of Newfoundland outport furniture continued to be homemade by a handy person, or by a local person who worked on a part time basis to produce items for others. For the most part balsam fir (a soft wood similar to pine) and white birch were used for construction. Beginning around 1900 they often recycled boards from shipping boxes or demolished buildings. These were used for backboards and interior parts which, under normal circumstances, would not be seen.

The origins of Newfoundland outport furniture, like other Canadian regional furniture, can be traced to designs introduced by early European settlers. In fact, many late eighteenth-century examples of Newfoundland painted furniture are virtually indistinguishable from counterparts made overseas. These pieces were usually built by British tradesmen brought to Newfoundland at the time of the migratory fishery. Local merchants recruited shipwrights, joiners and highly-skilled carpenters to construct and repair Newfoundland fishing premises and schooners. They came mainly from the West Country of England and southeast Ireland. Some settled permanently in Newfoundland.

Early Newfoundland outport furniture, based on specific regional British designs, often served as models for items fashioned by Newfoundland born furniture makers. Design elements from different examples from various regions were often combined to form a new design unique to Newfoundland material culture.

Newfoundland painted furniture, especially that which was made during the late nineteenth and early twentieth centuries, is notably distinguished by a high incidence of unusual combinations of design elements. Furthermore, models other than household furniture were occasionally used. For instance, a kitchen settee was made circa 1930 by Mr. Billy Wheeler, a fisherman who lived in Keels, Bonavista Bay. It had an open apron patterned after church windows of the day, and a back made of V-jointed matched lumber similar to that used in early twentieth-century church pews.

Because furniture making was relatively unorganized and a variety of models were used, many one-of-a-kind pieces of furniture were made in outport Newfoundland. Together, such furniture comprises one of the most colorful and distinctive groups of Canadian regional furniture.

Labrador travelling box

Keels dish dresser

Artist's Statement
Paterson Woodworking
Mike Paterson

I run a small woodworking business, Paterson Woodworking, in Upper Amherst Cove on Bonavista Bay, producing wooden furniture, crafts and architectural millwork. Much of our work is original in design, and is created in the spirit of local culture and tradition, borrowing on design and construction elements from older Newfoundland pieces.

I place a strong emphasis on a process which utilizes local materials, labour and tradition. Birch, tamarack, aspen, cherry, pine, balsam fir and spruce are harvested locally and cured, worked and finished on site by local craftsmen. My philosophy is to engage a high level of human involvement, keeping people working and machinery to a minimum.

The process of producing a piece of handmade furniture is as essential to good craftsmanship as is the finished product, and the subtleties of that process should be reflected in the final work.

From the forest to the finished piece, every step is an opportunity for us to test our skills and imagination and create something functional and beautiful.

Paterson Woodworking showroom

Rocking chair

Carved washstand

Bucket, Grub box / Lunch bucket, piggin.

A River Runs Through Her
Al Pittman

Coming on dark
the loons lament the slow closing
of the sky. And she's out there
having one more flick.

The rod, the reel, the line
are extensions of her self

Here (hidden in twilight)
I watch from the river bank
and wonder what some stranger
might think if she were his mother
out there in that current
going for the legal limit
at age eighty-three.

Would he stand here
in the shelter of these trees
where I stand safe on shore
shielding myself from the realities
that surround me, and think
"That's my mother. She's the flow
my father swam in?"

The last cast.
The feathered fly afloat.
The sudden splash.
The leap of the heart.
The frantic landing.

She rows ashore
in the dawn of dark.

I leave the trees, the loons, the river
and slip away
in the sudden comfort
of darkness.

I am the stranger.

Though she is my mother
I know nothing of this woman.
I know only that a river runs through her.

And I splash in her blood like a fish.

The Phantom Iceberg
Adrian Fowler

A couple of days ago
it looked like the Parthenon
in mist
on the horizon

the next day
a giant water spout
moving in

hours later
a gothic cathedral

melting spires pointing
to the sun.

Then
it dissolves
into the fog.

When the fog clears
the iceberg is gone.

Next morning
with powerful binoculars
I can see it

monolithic

an island

white sides rising
sheer
above the freezing green

a hundred lost sealers
pitted on its surface.

Iceberg
Nellie Strowbridge

If no man is an island,
can a woman be an iceberg?

That's what the high school boys
called me:
an outsider; an outporter
come to this inland place
on a school bursary.

I should have been flattered.

Iceberg: Queen of the sea,
nameless, for years untold, her look ageless,
her curves and regal body
sculpting her own throne.
Clad in her own mysterious self
of naked blue-pure-white body
she stirs in sun-glinted waters
under the caresses of a thousand winds
texturing her skin,
her shape changing against the sky
as she somersaults,
cavorting with the ocean tides.

Oblivious to predators that stalk her bed,
she gives birth with groans
that carry no pains
dropping tiny bergs,
never having to raise them.

She sails on,
herself
her own mast and rudder.

Not even Titanic could sink her.

Appeal to Parnassus
Irving Fogwill

    Sing us a song! Poets, of dirty streets
        In little towns, without a flower;
            With pavements gleaming
    Muddily, clammily, in filthy pleats:
        Where foetid things have their foul hour;
            And rain is streaming.

    Shadowy streets,
        With dark forms prowling:
    Where shy youth meets
        Prostitutes—scowling.

    Come down! my Poets, from the mountain-top:
        Sun is setting, yes—I know: its tune
    Has rung a million times: 'tis time to stop
            Its sickly dinning.
        Nor need you wait for the laggard moon:
    You've strummed its music until, drop by drop,
        Like water dripping on a rock—too soon
            My heart is thinning.

    Whom do you seek in your rapt-eyed searching,
        In the heart of the moon and the star?
    Are you afraid of your soul's besmirching,
        That you run from the world's grim scar?

    The sweet-voiced Shelley sat athwart a cloud,
        And sang his song to the wild west wind.
    The sad-eyed Keats in lonely splendour bowed
        His dying head to the bright star, and blind
    Milton found his God. Do you think that you
        Will tune a sweeter lyre than these three?
    Will breast a wilder wind than Shelley knew?
        Or find a brighter star than Keats'; or see
    A greater tumult in the Heavens?

                Come down!
    Come down from the heights to the dirty town:
        To the muddy streets; to the unwashed men;
    To the laughter and tears where sins are sown.
        Tune your lyre and sing your songs again.

Required Reading
David Benson

Dare I read Canadian Poetry?
Raise the covers of surreal uniformity
on the latest anthologies
or the latest granted collection
of the latest Great Canadian Poet
I had not heard tell of, hitherto;
Assimilation awaits and I am not game.
Russian poetry in bad translation
has more to say and is no threat
to my voice or my insomnia.
I do not wish to sound
like the latest year-class,
the latest recruits
in the Literary Army
of colonial Canadianism,
in whose serried ranks
all men sound like Irving Layton
and all women, like Margaret Atwood.
(Bless their socks though, for all that.)
I was given my own voice
by people unable to write,
though my tongue is rough
and my language is being lost.
Vocabulary is like employment here,
limited, short, ill-fitting and ill-paying,
and anger is seldom articulate.
Dare I say nothing?
When new Canadian writers
are rolled off
University assembly lines
like so many doughnuts;
cooked up, half-baked,
with their cores punched out
and a texture that runs
from soft to soggy to stale.
Creative fiction indeed!
"The Deficit"
"The Unemployment Rate"
"Foreign Overfishing"
are Creative Fiction titles.

And what, pray,
is Non-Creative Fiction
besides bad literature?
I will read Canadian poetry,
as I must,
as I would,
were it American or British.
I will write my own poetry,
as I must,
as I would,
were I Jamaican or Irish.

Exploits by Lois Saunders.

Mining
Christopher Pratt

Comes a thought
an observation
phrase—
just start writing
words,
following
as if it were a road—
a trail
into the mind's interior,
the soul's periphery.

Comes
a thought—
and it is like an outcrop,
rock,
maybe, bearing gold
always with potential
to locate
the mother lode.

But I am well outside my own,
well into
some ordinary similes—
none-the-less
that is the way of it:
poetry,
mining the mind,
dealing with,
scraping away an overburden
previously smothering
the soul.

The Money Crowd
JoAnne Soper-Cook

When I was a child, my mother pointed them out to me, as a means of signifying the gap between our respective worlds. We'd ride the bus downtown, usually on a Tuesday morning in the summer, when there was no school. We'd pass that neighbourhood on our way, and she would always say the same thing: "See those houses? That's where the money crowd live." And we'd stare at them with a certain mingled awe and resentment, the begrudging homage of the poor. The "money crowd." It was a ridiculous appellation, as if they were sitting around with bags of it, lying loose, littered about the carpet like so much rubbish. As if they got up to change the t.v. channel and crunched it underfoot, great crackling piles of it, like dead autumn leaves.

I wanted to be part of the money crowd. I wanted to cast off the shackles of my poverty like a shed skin, and be independently affluent. I had developed explanations as to why my current state was such an ill-mended rip in the bright fabric of my dreams: I was adopted. My parents were well-meaning peasants upon whose doorstep I had been left, a high-born orphan. I reasoned that my mother only dressed me the way she did so that I might better experience the local colour, and achieve that patina of elegance that derives its existence from an intuited superiority. Knowing the truth of my origins, I desired that ease of sophistication that was bestowed like birthright upon those titled others, those denizens of mysterious privilege.

I never saw them, passing by their houses on the bus. I wondered if they ever went outdoors, to put the trash out or get the morning paper. I imagined them passing into the outside world via a network of complicated underground tunnels: cocooned in their catacombs, safe.

We never had any money. My father tried his best, but was cursed with the kind of big dreams that tugged him ever onward, towards the next quick scheme. By the time I was twelve, he'd had fifteen different jobs, all of them lasting for various duration. His last had been as a representative for a Japanese coffin company, marketing a new brand of foldaway caskets. He'd earned a total of fifteen dollars, hardly enough to pay the phone bill. He and my mother argued for the rest of the evening, but civilly: hissed accusations and eviscerating whispers, couched in *sotto voce*. After that, he retired into a kind of shamefaced solitude and spent his days taking tea before the wood stove, his eyes blank and resolute.

My mother ran the household off a small inheritance from my grandparents, took in laundry to make ends meet. Her hands were always red about the knuckles, cracked and sore, a pair of livid gloves. On winter days, the house smelled of chlorine bleach, the sweet lemon tang of laundry soap.

She admonished me to stay in school, get a good education, perhaps a government job as a stenographer so that I could work my way up the typing pool. She recited the natural histories of various aunts, all of whom had achieved manifold financial success through shorthand. She reminded me of great-aunt Betty, who had come over from Scotland in the forties with nothing but a sharp number two pencil and a knowledge of

Forkner. She reminded me of departed classmates: Doris Tulk and Lisa Dodge, who had earned their fortunes with their typing fingers, at the tail-end of the Eighties' last big hurrah. These were women who (unbeknownst to my mother) had vanished into the curious darkness of economic disaster, the aftermath of Black Monday and the Crash.

I didn't tell her that I'd begun carrying a notebook with me, to record the various stray lines and bits of prose that drifted across the surface of my brain. I didn't tell her that I kept a shoebox underneath my bed, stuffed to the brim with a veritable catalogue of rejection slips. I didn't tell her that a lifetime in a government typing pool was as close to the torment of purgatory as I hoped to get. "Get a government job, Marianne," she'd say, as we rode past the money crowd on our ubiquitous Tuesday errands. "That's where the money is." And she'd rub her sore hands, hide her cracked red fingers in her pockets.

I took a job as a domestic in the largest house I'd ever seen. I took the job because it offered free room and board, free rent; free reign to pursue my literary fantasies. I'd begun cataloguing my rejection slips, had bought myself a bulletin board from a garage sale, upon which was pinned the winding trail of paper carnage. I'd made a collage of them, pinning them all up side-by-side, and I spent ages studying them, searching their smooth pale faces as one might search a bank of windows, for some hint of their hidden treason.

I served at dinner, swept the kitchen, and tidied the dining-room after parties. They gave me a black uniform with a tidy white collar and a little hat, and I felt like I was in a movie, a witty French movie where all the servants are clever, and know the discreet nuances of the household, where the money goes. I felt like I should learn to dance, be ready at a moment's notice to slide into a Ginger Rogers number, tap-dance on the smooth marble floors. I felt like I was always being filmed.

I learned to carry the trays like an expert; I tiptoed among them, offering tasty tidbits, blinded by their glare. I'd never seen so much money in my life: money draped across pale shoulders, money glimmering on slender fingers, money glistening in great chunks, nestled in the hollow of the throat. They always hired an orchestra for these things, a full dinner-coated symphony with drums and horns, and the leader swinging his baton like Paganini.

The money crowd.

I hated them. As much as I was drawn to it, as much as I wanted it for myself, I was repelled by it. They were like some kind of alien race, inscrutable and bizarre. There was something inherently fake about them, something that jarred the mind, set the teeth on edge. They were followed always by the stink of decadence, a subtle fetor of corruption.

It was the way they talked, the way they laughed, it was every small and elusive thing about them. Head thrown back, one hand pressed against the bosom, *Oh my dear, you can't possibly be serious*, that sort of thing. An affected gaiety in the face of swirling music and tinkling crystal and unimaginable affluence. The soul thus bent by wealth and privilege into a tortured rictus, forced into the dance.

It was a secret society, their milieu. It required rituals. It required the use of Long Island Lockjaw: a private-school accent, sounded mainly through the nose. They took afternoon drives (or were driven) in the country, in order to absorb it, suck the essence into themselves as if that was their right. "Oh look, Dahling, it's a fahmuh." They went about ingesting experiences. They preyed on situations. They used a special language.

They did this as insurance against the creeping dessication of their ways. This was the thing I had wanted, in my previous incarnation, when I was young and impressionable. This was the distant Eden after which I lusted. This was the luxury of sight to which my youthful eyes had now become adjusted. I felt very righteous, thinking this.

People with money weren't like us, my mother always said, they had different standards. This was my mother's word for it: standards. What was important to other people wasn't important to them. What was tragedy for normal people wasn't tragedy for them; everything was easily repairable by the application of large quantities of money. When the unthinkable occurred, you could pay somebody something and it would be alright. You could throw a party and your friends would come, and Buddy Dexter's Midnight Lovers would blow their horns, and Buddy himself would swing the baton, and it would be alright. You could swirl into the dance, and forget about it, and someone would come by in the morning to sweep the scattered bits of things from the gleaming marble.

The woman who hired me was named Carol. She was tiny and blonde, with eyes of a surrealistic sapphire. The husband, his name was Robert. I'd hear her calling him, from somewhere in the upper reaches, her voice sliding down to us, over the winding staircase, the monumental scree of ornaments, expensive art and artifice. "Bryan Robert—" Bryan Robert Something Something the Third.

"Marianne, could you kindly take these things up to my wife." He would load them obediently into my hands. He was nice to me. He often tipped me extra for carrying the trays at parties. He expected things of me. He talked late into the night, on the telephone to Overseas; he ran off faxes in the early hours of the morning. He would still be sleeping when I went in to dust his study, when I lingered jealously among the rows of gorgeous bindings, elegant leather spines. I made a ritual of it, I walked along the shelves and touched each one with my fingertips, listened to the staccato tick-tick-tick as I went by. The study reeked of him, saturated with his presence and his cologne. The leather armchair smelled like money.

Once I stumbled into their bedroom, late in the morning, to dust the bureaus and make the bed. He was still sleeping in it, curled like a giant fetus in the cocoon of blankets. His wristwatch was lying on the nightstand, and I hefted its weight in the palm of my hand, testing its heaviness. I considered putting it into my pocket, and I wondered if he would miss it. I leaned over him, peering at the fringed juncture of his closed lids, wondering if he were truly asleep. His body reminded me of some giant insect, some horrific mutant pupa, curled into a chrysalis and waiting to be born.

When he finally approached me, it was at a party, and he was curiously hesitant, as close to solictitious as he ever was. I'd been tippling unseen from half-empty glasses in the kitchen, and drifted now, light-headed, my feet some small distance from the ground. I'd discovered that I liked being like this, that it was much more bearable if I were drunk. I'd discovered, too, my own inebriate threshold, that I could more easily imagine myself of their milieu if my sensibilities were bathed in a thin film of alcohol.

I'd spent ages testing it, conducting my experiments with a certain seriousness: I smuggled a bottle from the kitchen, something they kept for emergencies, Wild Turkey. I learned to drink until I could no longer feel the muscles of my face, until the noises in my head were reduced by my intoxication to a slow, luxurious clang. I was thus assured of a fixed smile, and a certain slow float of motion, hovering just above the ground.

I expected he would give me some kind of polite directive: "Marianne, I wonder if you could circulate among the Henderson party." I expected he would be ready with remonstrations, stark evidence of my servile lack: "Mrs. Henderson says you haven't been by with any of the shrimp yet. Do try to cover all the room." I expected he would have orders for me. He cornered me by the refrigerator.

"Sir?"

"Marianne, I need a favour." He cast about him wildly, glancing into all the corners, listening. "It's rather complicated, and I don't have time to explain right now." He cast a discursive look at me, eyes travelling quickly over my figure, with a certain contained distaste. "Go into Carol's closet and pick something. Take Simone—" the chambermaid "—to help you dress."

And I stared at him, still unsure of just what he was asking. I felt muzzy with booze, unsteady. I wondered if I could do it. I wondered if I'd studied long enough to pass this unsavoury muster. His thick fingers reached towards me, caught my hand and pressed a crumpled wad of bills into my palm.

I drifted up the stairs as if pulled by the music of some distant harp, and secreted myself inside Carol's vast closet. It was a grand cathedral in itself, a monument to style: racks and racks of Dior and Armani (I knew them by their tags), vast carrels of shoes, ranked about in staid rows like a battalion of dead soldiers; the evidence of wealth in leather and fine fabric.

She had gone away and left nothing behind her. I fancied that some aura remained of her, some drift of fragrance as ethereal as a curl of dying smoke. I wondered if she dropped her underpants behind the bathroom door: a passing scrap of silk, lying desolate and damp beside the bidet.

I chose a Dior: fire-engine red, bias-cut; it draped about me like an embrace. Simone, goggling near the racks of shoes, helped to zip me up. I pulled a boa of blue-dyed ostrich from a standing tree of belts and scarves, tossed it around my neck, allowed it space to flutter between my shoulder-blades, so much cool ebullience. I felt like Veronica Lake.

I padded barefoot into their bedroom, opened the great mahogany chest of jewels and chose a double string of pearls, opera-length; to this I added a weighty collar of rubies, heavily encrusted with diamonds, a pair of earrings in the shape of African elephants, each cut from a single blood-red ruby. The air about me was bright with noise and shapes, sharp with the animal tang of a noonday savannah. I was on safari.

I pushed Simone outside, shut and locked the door behind her. It was necessary that I savour this alone. It was necessary that I prance and ogle before the glass, audience to myself. It was necessary that I feel the weight of money at wrists and neck; money, twinkling in the hollow of my throat.

And so I stood there. And as I stood there, something rose up from deep within my belly, something rich and dark and throbbing, something hot as blood. I smoothed the fiery Dior about my stomach and my bosom, pressed the double strand of pearls deep into my throat. I desired that they should leave their imprint, and that I should leave my scent. I desired that they would know me, and remember.

I pointed my toes and raised my arms above my head, and twirled to see the skirt fly out around me. I executed a shaky step in a sort of bastardized *en pointe*; I preened and smiled at myself. I found a feathered hat with a veil and pinned it into place. I riffled through the top drawer and found a pair of red silk opera gloves, smoothed them over my hands and arms with something approaching ecstasy.

From Carol's cosmetics bag, I grabbed a lipstick and painted in my mouth, plumed bright peacock colour across my eyes. I practised walking, swiveling my hips like Gloria Gaynor. I smoked from an imaginary holder. Mother of pearl.

This was it, then. This was the advent of my movement into this coveted milieu, and what matter if Carol had gone, what matter even if Carol came back?

I was certain he would see me in a strange new light, Bryan Robert Something Something. I was certain he would see fit to redeem me. I was certain he preferred me in Dior.

When I descended the stairs, I waited for the wash of their applause. I was certain they rumoured (even now) that we were linked inextricably together: the kitchen maid and Bryan Robert Something Something The Third. I put ecstatic foot to stair, secure in the promise of my advancement into society. I had arrived. I was one of the Money Crowd.

They parted for me as I descended—like Moses presiding over the Red Sea. I wondered if perhaps they perceived some sort of discrete power, clutched between my fingers like an invisible staff. Even now, it hummed along my veins, throbbed like liquor in my breast.

The orchestra stopped playing, and every one of the Midnight Lovers (including the ubiquitous Buddy Dexter) turned to stare, open-mouthed. I was every gorgeous woman that had ever lived. I was Helen of Troy, I was Cleopatra, I was the legendary Hero, breathlessly awaiting Leander's treacherous negotiation of the Hellespont.

And at the apex of it all, standing at the bottom of the stairs like Rhett Butler in a dinner jacket, was Bryan Robert Something Something.

The Third.

He did send me off with a nice reference, I will say that much for him. And a generous bonus. And Carol let me keep the Dior, naturally, although she did request the return of the ostrich boa, when I'm done with it.

I ride the bus with Mother every Tuesday morning, past the houses of the Money Crowd. I tipple from a bottle in my bedroom. I have three hundred rejection slips on my peg-board.

And a double strand of opera length pearls.

The Time That Passes
Agnes Walsh

The time that passes between my mother and me
is more measured in what's not said,
and plain words are felt like samplings of fabrics.

Body, she said, we never said body then,
it was too bold, we said system:
tell the doctor what part of your system hurts.

I linger,
hold onto the feel,
the rub in the mind.

If they left it alone, Mike said,
and someone got hurt, then they'd be blempt for it.

I hold onto before, before our
tongues were twisted around corrected speech.

He was so grand he couldn't say Okay,
like the rest of us,
he said *Oh Kah*.

I ranted that we're educated into ignorance,
but can get jobs on the mainland
or at radio stations,
our voices do sound so homogeneous now.

> But you watch it, my mother said,
> it's your tongue too that was dipped
> in the blue ink, and do go leaking iambics
> all the day long.

Marriage
Hilda Chaulk-Murray

When couples who were "going together" decided to get married, they might inform their families and start preparing for the wedding, but there was no formal engagement. No ring was given until the wedding band was placed on the bride's finger. Sarah Chaulk, however, said she had a "sort of engagement ring." She wore "a heart and a half" ring which her "fellow" gave her before their marriage. Another woman, married in the 1940s, said: "No engagement ring. I didn't get mine 'til long after I was married."

It seems the majority of girls in Elliston in the early 1900s were married before they reached their mid-twenties. Many of my informants were married between the ages of seventeen and twenty. There was no "proper age" for marriage; it depended on the individuals involved. Aunt Hilda, when asked if people got married younger in the old days than at present, replied:

> Well, it was the same then as it is now. Not many reached the age of twenty-three or twenty-four. Some were married at eighteen. On the whole perhaps it was in their early twenties they were married. It depended on the circumstances. I think it was just the same then as now. I see changes. There's quite a change, for each generation says, "I don't know what this new generation is coming to!" I don't find one generation any worse than another.

Weddings were more informal than they are nowadays. There was no attempt to have the wedding party dressed in any uniform fashion; all wore their best, the men their Sunday suits, and the girls their best dresses. Usually the bride tried to have an especially nice new dress, plus other accessories, and the groom invested in a new blue serge suit. The bride didn't worry about a "going away" outfit for there was no honeymoon.

Some of the brides in the early 1900s wore veils, but frequently they wore white hats instead. And in very early days, it seems the brides wore special "wedding bonnets." One which was worn by my great-grandmother Tilley, a bride in the 1850s, was straw with fancy embroidery around the crown. It was very small and must have just "perched" on the crown of her head. Brides in the early 1900s usually wore white gloves, white stockings and white shoes even for a winter wedding, so they must have had some sort of feeling that it was right to have white at a wedding, even though the wedding dress was usually not white.

Dresses were street length and until the forties, of course, this meant mid-calf, or even ankle-length. The material chosen for the dress depended on the bride's circumstances. Sometimes it would be made at home, but more often than not such an important dress would be "storebought." It would be bought off the rack, perhaps in one of the Bonavista stores which had a wider selection of clothing than did the Elliston ones. If the bride-to-be were better-off than average, she might send to one of the St. John's department stores for a suitable dress and accessories. A soft crepe material seems to have been the choice of most women for this important dress. However, one woman, Emily (Pearce) Tilley, wore white lace over robin's egg blue satin for her wedding in 1914. Her veil was shoulder-length with a wreath of flowers on the forehead. This veil was a gift from the groom's brother who bought it in St. John's.

My mother, a bride of the late 1920s, wore a mid-calf length, apricot-coloured crepe dress with long sleeves. Her veil was shoulder length and was attached to a circlet of wax orange blossoms. She wore a string of beads which exactly matched her dress.

The so-called "traditional" long white bridal gown was not traditional in Elliston in the early years, nor in the 1940s. Most brides favoured blue. "Married in blue, always be true" was the saying. Although most girls knew the rhyme:

> Married in white, you have chosen all right.
> Married in grey, you will live far away.
> Married in black, you will wish yourself back.
> Married in red, you will wish yourself dead.
> Married in green, ashamed to be seen.
> Married in blue, he will always be true.
> Married in pearl, you will live in a whirl.
> Married in yellow, ashamed of your fellow.
> Married in brown, you will live out of town.
> Married in pink, your spirits will sink.

One informant mentioned someone she knew who had been married in yellow. She remarked: "She was ashamed of him all right. She only lived with him for six months or so and then she left him." Generally a girl chose a dress that would serve her "best" for a few years after the wedding.

The bridal bouquet of natural flowers has become fashionable in Elliston only in recent years, for there were few flower gardens and no "nurseries" nearby. Besides, weddings were rarely held in the summertime as this was the season for work. They might take place at any other season of the year and then natural flowers were unavailable. So if a bride carried a bouquet, it was of artificial crepe-paper flowers made by some woman in the community. The men in the wedding party wore paper roses in their lapels. Often instead of a bouquet, the bride carried a prayer book decorated with ribbons.

The wedding ceremony was never rehearsed beforehand. The titles "maid of honour" and "best man" were not in use. The chief attendants were the "father-giver" and the "mother-giver," and the other attendants if there were any others, were dubbed "bridesgirls" and "bridesboys." The father-giver was a cross between the "father" and the best man; he performed both duties. On the one hand, when the minister asked "who giveth this woman" he responded, but he still stayed in this position and "supported" the groom. However he did not carry the ring; the groom himself had this. The mother-giver had the same responsibilities as today's maid of honour.

Although people were poor, the wedding ring was never handmade as seems to have been the custom in some parts of the United States; the husband always managed to have a gold ring for his bride's finger. This plain wide band, costing ten dollars or so, was in later years probably bought in Elliston or Bonavista, but in earlier days had to be bought in St. John's. It was often the incorrect size, but if it were a bit big, the wife might wear some cheaper ring as a guard to keep it from slipping off. Since no woman would think of taking her ring off at any time, it was not uncommon to see a woman wearing her wedding ring on the middle finger of her left hand when she was washing clothes or washing fish. I remember my mother wearing hers on her middle finger.

When both bride and groom came from the same section of the community, they walked to the wedding—bride, groom, attendants and the congregation. For instance, if one or both of them were Anglican in Maberly (Muddy Brook), the marriage ceremony would probably take place in the Anglican school-chapel on the "Schoolhouse Hill." One couple, Jane and Aubrey Pearce, married some fifty years or more, recalled that for their wedding in December it snowed a bit, "just nice for walking." Usually if either the bride or groom were Anglican and one came from Elliston Centre while the other came from Maberly, the wedding ceremony would be performed in the little Anglican church located at Elliston Centre. If the wedding reception were being held in "The Cove," the bridal party usually walked. If the reception were being held in Maberly the couple and their attendants would ride in horse and carriage (buggy) in spring, summer, and fall, but on horse and riding sleigh in the winter time.

A couple married in the Anglican church could not have a surprise wedding for their banns had to be published for three Sundays previous to their marriage. Neither could they be married in Lent. If for some reason they wanted to marry during that time they had to ask a United Church minister or a Salvation Army officer to perform the ceremony.

Couples who were married by the United Church or Salvation Army did not necessarily have a "church" wedding. Sometimes the marriage took place in the church parsonage or in a private home. The number of people who attended the religious ceremony had little bearing on the number who attended the reception later. Most marriage ceremonies were performed in the late afternoon or early evening: three and four p.m. were hours mentioned for afternoon weddings, while seven p.m. seems to have been a popular time for evening weddings. People knew the rhyme:

> Monday for health
> Tuesday for wealth
> Wednesday's the best of all
> Thursday for losses
> Friday for crosses
> And Saturday no day at all!

Few considered any day unlucky for a wedding, though one woman had her reservations about Friday.

It was customary for men to "fire off" guns along the route taken by the wedding party after the ceremony.

No informants could recall any runaway marriages, but there were cases of quick or surprise marriages. These people slipped off to Bonavista or Catalina and were married there with no fanfare at all. But such cases were few and were a favourite topic of gossip for months afterward. There was also considerable gossip if there was a great disparity in age between husband and wife. Usually such marriages were between older widowers and young girls, rather than between an old bachelor and a young girl and although people gossiped they recognized the necessity of the man's marrying. In a fishing community a fisherman had to have a woman to take part in the operation, if he were partners with someone and not just an ordinary shareman. If his mother or a sister could not perform the necessary work in the stage or on the flake, he had to look around for a suitable helpmate—one who could pull her weight. A man who was skipper certainly was expected to have female help as he very probably got the lion's share of the "voyage" (proceeds from the sale of cod).

Up until the 1940s, a wedding was thought of as a community social occasion. Invitations were given orally by family members, and people would sometimes come to the reception even if they had somehow been overlooked when people were being asked to the wedding.

Everyone liked to contribute in some way, especially if the couple were well-liked in the community. Cakes, pies, and pastries, all manner of sweet delicacies, would be brought or sent to the reception by the women of the community. Often the dish on which a cake was brought to the wedding was the wedding gift. Wedding gifts were ordinarily brought to the reception instead of being sent to the bride in advance as is the custom nowadays. An area was set aside for the display of the wedding gifts, and guests might see what the young couple had received.

There was no set rule as to where the reception would be held. Sometimes it was held at the home of the bride's parents, sometimes at the groom's parents, and not infrequently in the new home of the bridal pair. Until the 1940s all receptions were held in private homes. Guests crowded into every room in the house and took up all available space. There was not much room for many kinds of games, but there was a lot of talking, joking, and "carrying-on." If the bride and groom were to sleep in the house where the reception was being held, some guests would be sure to play a few tricks on them. The favourite was fixing the bed so that it would collapse when the pair got into it.

The reception would carry on late into the night, and often a wedding reception was a two-night affair. Those who could not make it the first night tried to get there on the second. The second night guests were usually the older, more sedate members of the community and things would not be so boisterous as on the previous night. Perhaps because of the temperance movement, which was strong in the community during the first decades of the century, no liquor was served at weddings.

There was always a special "wedding cake." This was usually a rich fruit cake, very like the traditional Christmas cake. Everyone at the wedding had to have a piece of it. A young unmarried girl never ate her piece of wedding cake at the wedding. She wrapped it carefully and placed it under her pillow "to dream on" when she went to bed that night. Many believed that if a girl slept with a piece of wedding cake under her pillow she would dream of her future husband. This bit of folklore is widespread and was a common practice in Dorsetshire and other English counties, as is noted by Udal in his Dorsetshire Folk-Lore. This is not surprising since the ancestors of many people in Elliston were from Dorset and other West Country counties.

Here is how Aunt Hilda described a wedding reception around 1910:

> They didn't send out invitations then. It was all after the bride and groom had their cup of tea. They went around to all the houses in the immediate vicinity and asked them to come. After the bridesmaids and boys had their tea, they would leave them and go around. Just the bride and groom would go. Several weddings around that time were conducted in this fashion. They have more means now for doing things but even in those days everyone had a large reception. Everyone in the community was invited. No matter how poor you were. For they all brought a contribution to set the table.

The length of time the newlyweds had been "going together," and their ages, would determine what material effects they had to start married life with. Some brides who were older, or who had been courting for a long period, had chests full of the following items: bed clothes, sheets, quilts, pillow slips, pillows, etc.; tablecloths, often decorated with fancy stitching; dresser sets in knitted or crocheted lace; colourful hooked mats; cushions already stuffed with feathers, and so on. Others, barely eighteen years of age, perhaps just getting by on a servant girl's wages, would have less to contribute. A youthful husband would rarely have a home of his own to take his bride to, so the couple would live with relatives for a while at least. Here they would not need the items required for maintaining a separate household. They used what was already in the home and both fitted into the work team of the household as best they could.

Most young men, however, did not do serious courting until they felt they could afford to keep a wife as well as she had been accustomed to, for "sensible" girls looked for a "good provider" and he had to be able to make a living for a family. There was nothing in the way of government assistance to fall back on, and many in the earlier years, unlike today, were too proud to rely on such assistance. A man felt at a disadvantage, for example, if he was a fisherman and the girl he was courting was a teacher, for not only was she supporting herself on her salary, but also she was often helping out at home as well. He would have to be very sure that they could live comfortably on his earnings before he asked her to marry him. A man courting a "servant girl" in Elliston certainly did not have this obstacle in his way, for her wages were very low and she might have been in service since she was twelve years old. If she married young, she would be working just as hard or perhaps harder, but at least she could feel she was working for herself.

Wedding photo, 1940

Harbour Le Cou

Traditional

Oh boldly I asked her to walk on the sand,
She smiled like an angel and held out her hand;
So I buttoned me guernsey and hove 'way me chew,
In the dark rolling waters of Harbour Le Cou.

My ship she lay anchored far out on the tide,
As I strolled along with this maid at my side;
I told her I loved her she said, "I'll be true,"
As I winked at the moon over Harbour Le Cou.

As we walked on the sands at the close of the day,
I thought of my wife who was home in Torbay;
I knew that she'd kill me if she only knew,
I was courting a lassie in Harbour Le Cou.

As we passed a log cabin that stood on the shore,
I met an old comrade I'd sailed with before,
He treated me kindly, saying, "Jack, how are you?
It's seldom I see you in Harbour Le Cou."

And as I was parting, this maiden in tow,
He broke up my party with one single blow,
Saying, "Regards to your missus and wee kiddies too,
I remember her well, she's from Harbour Le Cou."

I looked at this damsel a-standing 'long side,
Her jaw it dropped down and her mouth opened wide;
And then like a she-cat upon me she flew,
And I fled from the furies of Harbour Le Cou.

Come all you young sailors who walk on the shore,
Beware of old comrades you've sailed with before.
Beware of the maidens with bonnet of blue,
And the pretty young maidens of Harbour Le Cou.

Two Dresses from St. Pierre

Ruth Lawrence

The baby blue one has a lace bodice
that must have fit your delicate form
like an August rain could if you
ever thought to allow it.
The sheer nylon bands
crossed your waist and married
with the pleats that laid flat
against your barely rounded hips.

When I look at the size you were
after squeezing four lives out of you
I look at myself naked in the mirror.

Your yellow dress is wrapped
around the babies around your legs
by wind coming in from the harbour
past the doctor's garden through the path
to Nanny's house on the hill.
I see you wearing this one perhaps
because, like you, its plainness is its beauty
but more than likely the colour suits you best.

I imagine St. Jacquesers watching you pass
saying there goes Burnsie in a yellow dress
that Tom brought from St. Pierre.

What would she say now if she could see them
hanging inside clear glass
pinned onto cardboard cream in a plain wood frame
out in my sewing room
and inspiring creation inside these swiss white walls?

I know.

She would say I'm foolish.

A Harmless Deception
Anastasia English

The Christmas snow is slowly falling, not drifting and whirling in fierce gusts, but slowly and gracefully floating down in its unsullied purity, covering road and byway, tree and housetop, with its soft, feathery mantle, till nothing is visible outside but a white world. From the window of a wealthy suburban residence in St. John's city, a young girl of twenty gazes out upon the peaceful scene. She is slight and graceful, with a bright, beautiful face, on which is portrayed too much pride and sensitiveness for her own happiness.

Her thoughts are with the past, and she pictures a different Christmas Eve from this one, when a loving mother, a kind father were there to share with her the joy of the holy festive season. Both are dead, and she is now an inmate of her uncle's household, Richard Huntley, who, with his wife and two daughters are her only relatives. An unwelcome addition she is to the family circle, and well she knows it. Often has her heart rebelled against the taunts and unkindness she so often receives from her cousins and aunt.

Her heart is rebelling now, for, though it is nine o'clock at night, and they live in a lonely part of the city, she has been told that she must go to Water Street to purchase a particular kind of silk blouse which is needed for the morrow. That she has been there three times already the same day, does not trouble them.

As the door opens she quickly dashes away the tears from her eyes and turns round. A tall, well-dressed woman of about fifty enters.

"Here Lena," she says, "is the money. Ella says to get as delicate a shade of pink as you possibly can, and hurry because it is getting late. Your uncle may have a visitor with him when he returns, and there are still some little things to be seen to before midnight."

Without a word the girl takes the money and, turning up the collar of her coat, departs on her errand.

Meanwhile Mrs. Huntley retires to the drawing-room and throws herself into a cushioned armchair, drawn up to the fire. Her two daughters, who have just put the finishing touches to the Christmas decorations, are sitting a little distance away, fearing that the heat of the fire might spoil their complexions. Both are tall and good-looking, but of very uncertain age.

The Huntleys moved in the best St. John's society. Both girls might have married long ago, but they were not of the type who marry for love, and the eligibles were scarce. A few months before Mr. Huntley had paid a visit to an old friend of his who was living in New York, and whilst there won a promise from the son that he would spend the coming Christmas with him in Newfoundland, and he was expected to arrive tonight. Lena had been spending three months with a school friend in one of the outports, and only arrived in town a week before Christmas, so knew nothing of the expected visitor.

"What a sullen disposition Lena has," remarked Mrs. Huntley. "She did not deign to answer me one word just now when I gave the message about your blouse, Ella."

"That girl should be made to feel her dependence more than she does," answered Ella, who was the elder of the two girls.

"She shows no gratitude for what has been done for her," remarked her sister, Maude.

"It is not every girl whose father died and left her penniless, would be offered a nice home like this," said Mrs. Huntley.

"It is a great mistake, Mamma, and a drawback to our prospects, to have Lena living in the same house with us. Of course she is younger, and, people seem to think, prettier, and then she has such a natural talent for claiming the attention of the male sex, that, humiliating as it is to acknowledge it, we are neglected when she is by. I do wish she had remained away till Charlie Fane's visit was over. She has heard nothing of his coming, mamma, has she?"

"I just mentioned to her now that a visitor may arrive with her uncle. I did not say from where."

"We must try and keep her in the background as much as possible," said Maude. "Papa says that Mr. Fane is worth ever so much money. Do you know at what hour the *Silvia* is due, Ella?"

"The papers say about twelve," she answered. "Of course Papa will wait and bring him in."

Meanwhile Lena walked on towards town. The snow falling so softly and peacefully down had a soothing effect upon her, and, by degrees, the swelling indignation melted from her heart. It was Christmas, the time of peace and goodwill, and she resolved to lay aside all unkind and bitter thoughts, and do her best to be happy and make others so.

Water Street was dazzling. The shops were ablaze with lights. Gold and silver flashed in brilliant array from jewellers' windows: everything bright and rich looking gleamed forth from those of the other stores, and all that could please the palate and sharpen the appetite was temptingly arranged in the grocery and fruit stores. Throngs of people rushed hither and thither.

Lena was young and buoyant, and soon all weariness and unpleasantness were forgotten, and her spirits rose as she mingled with the merry, moving mass of humanity. She had much difficulty in getting the blouse the exact shade which was required. She tried every shop from the West to the East End, and she began to fear she would have to return without it, when, to her relief, she found the very shade for which she was seeking.

She had also purchased a pretty Christmas card for a friend of hers, and thought that, as she was not very far from the place, she would go and leave it at the door. True, it was a lonely spot; but she decided to take Water Street until she got right opposite the house before she turned up. When she came to the unfrequented part of the street she glanced timidly around, feeling a little nervous, for it was now near ten o'clock.

She held by a chain in her hand a small purse which contained her money, and, as she quickly turned a corner leading to the next street, a man who was leaning against a door, and seemed to have imbibed too freely, rushed quickly out, and, snatching the purse from her hand, dashed past her.

Lena gave a cry of terror, and looked helplessly around.

In a moment she saw a tall, manly form stride past her in pursuit of the drunken ruffian, and in a few seconds he had him by the collar. Wrenching the purse from his hand, he then flung him to the sidewalk, saying: "Only that I cannot see a policeman about, I would give you in charge."

He then walked back to Lena, and raising his hat said: "Permit me to restore your property. I fear that scamp has given you a severe fright. It is quite fortunate that I happened to be on the spot, and saw him snatch the purse from your hand."

As he gazed upon the girl's face, he thought—even in the uncertain light—that he had never seen one to compare with her. Some dark curls had escaped from under her hat, and on them a few feathery snowflakes had found a resting place; her cheeks were deeply flushed from her walk, and a pair of large, dark eyes, eloquent with gratitude, looked up at him.

Lena knew that he was a stranger for he had the unmistakable American accent. She liked his face, not that it was handsome, but it was one that she could trust. He had a pair of honest blue eyes, was light complexioned with a golden brown moustache.

"It was indeed most fortunate for me," she answered; "not that my purse contains very much. I should not have come down here so late. Thank you a thousand times!"

"It is a great mistake to be out alone at this hour," he said, with a very grave face; "it would not do if you were living in New York."

"Oh, you are from New York, then!" she remarked.

"Yes," he replied; "I just landed from the *Silvia*, and I rejoice at the impulse which prompted me to do so, since I am so lucky as to be of service to you. The gentleman to whom I have come was to have met me, but we have arrived somewhat earlier than was expected, and I suppose he is not aware of it; so, being Christmas Eve, I thought I would take a stroll up Water Street and have a look at the stores."

"Thank you again, so much," said Lena, "but," as he seemed inclined to linger, "don't you think you ought to hurry back to the steamer, your friend may now be looking for you there?"

"I could not dream of leaving you alone and unprotected at this hour," he said. "You must allow me the privilege of accompanying you to your door."

"Oh, I could not think of troubling you so much," said Lena, "I shall be quite safe now, thank you."

"I am not so sure of that," he replied; "who knows but that scamp may be on the look out and follow you."

This was what she herself feared, but still she remonstrated: "You may miss your friend."

"That makes no difference," he answered; "I have his address, and can go there. I trust you will pardon me, young lady, if I say that I must insist on seeing you safely home, for I feel it my duty to do so."

The ring of genuineness in his voice, and the deep, respectful reverence of his demeanor, gave Lena the feeling that she was quite safe, and, with a sense of newly awakened pleasure stirring in each heart, they walked on side by side. They conversed quite pleasantly and at perfect ease during the walk. Once Lena shook out the very thin paper bag which held her cousin's silk blouse, saying, "I fear the snow will melt through this paper and spoil the silk."

"Give it to me," he said, "I have a long, loose pocket in this overcoat, and can put it in without crushing it," and he took it gently from her hand. "There," he said, laughing, "you did not think when buying this that a stranger from New York would bring it home for you. Perhaps you may give me a thought sometimes when you wear it, if it is anything wearable."

Lena laughed softly as she said: "I'll never wear it; it isn't mine at all."

"And you took the trouble to go all this distance so late to buy it for someone else. You must be very obliging."

"No, I'm not one bit obliging. I stormed and raged inwardly at having to come, though outwardly I was quite calm."

"Will you think me very unkind if I say I'm glad you came?" he asked.

"I will," she answered, archly, "and I will also think you very unwise to say such a thing."

"Why?"

"Because I'm sure it's not true. I know that you are also storming and raging inwardly at being forced to perform such an onerous duty."

He looked at her a moment and then said, "I will not argue the point now."

"No," she retorted, "you have not time, for here we are at the door. Thank you so much," she said holding out her hand, "and a merry Christmas to you."

He took it, and said: "Well, I won't say I'm sorry the journey is ended, for you may tell me I'm fibbing again, but—" and he looked up at the house—"I shall see you again, unless you forbid me."

"I certainly shall not be so ungenerous," she answered, "when you have been so kind."

"My name," he said, "is Charlie Fane, at you service; would it be too presumptuous of me to ask yours?"

"I'll tell you half of it," she said, with a little touch of coquetry, "it is Eleanor," giving her full name instead of the abbreviation, Lena.

"That will do," he replied. "I'm thankful for half; it is a sweet name."

Lena laughed. "Why do you laugh?" he asked.

"Because," she answered, "if I had said it was Judy you would say the same."

He smiled in spite of himself. "Do not tell me the name of your street," he said, "or the number of your house. I'll find it out. It may prove to you, if I take a little trouble to see you, that I am possessed of more sincerity than you give me credit for."

"That's a bargain," she cried gaily, "but I'll bet you won't find me."

"We shall see," he answered.

"Shall you find your way back?" she asked, her mood changing to grave seriousness. "I almost forgot that you are in a strange city."

He laughed musically, as he said: "Oh, trust an old dog for a hard road. I'm quite used to strange cities. I daresay my friend will have found out about the arrival of the *Silvia* by the time I get there. Good-night, and a very happy Christmas to you," as he raised his hat and strode off.

As Lena entered, she was met in the hallway by Mrs. Huntley. "What a time you have been, Lena," she said, crossly; "go up to Ella's room, she is waiting to try on the blouse."

Lena had removed her hat, and was just divesting herself of her coat when, to her dismay, she remembered that the blouse was still in Charlie Fane's coat pocket; and, oh—what was she to say. Of course, when he discovered it, she felt sure that he would bring it to her immediately; but how, in the meantime, could she explain things? She would not go into all the details of what had happened. It was certainly a harmless deception, but could she have foreseen all the unpleasantness that would arise from it she would never have practiced it. She was certainly in an awkward plight, and, acting on the impulse of the moment, said: "I have not got the blouse, Aunt Emily, but I will have it tomorrow. I left it somewhere to keep it from getting wet and forgot it."

"You have not got it!" she replied. "Did you buy it at all!"

"Yes, I bought it."

"And where did you leave it? Did you lose it?"

"No, aunt, I have not lost it. All I can say is that Ella will have her blouse tomorrow. Here is the change," she said, taking some money from her purse and handing it to her.

"Well!" exclaimed Mrs. Huntley, "If this is not cool impertinence, never mind it."

Ella and Maude, hearing voices in the hall, came downstairs. "I've had a long wait for my blouse," pointed the former.

"It seems you are to have a longer one," said her mother. "She has bought your blouse, Ella, my dear, and lost it."

"Lost it," echoed the two girls.

"I did not say I lost it," said Lena, the indignant blood mounting to her forehead.

"No, because you are not truthful enough, I suppose," said Ella Huntley.

"How dare you!" exclaimed Lena. Then, turning to Mrs. Huntley, she said: "Aunt Emily, as I find I am only subjected to insult by remaining, I will go to my room. I have told you that the blouse is safe, and you shall have it tomorrow. I can say no more." And she ran quickly upstairs, before the passionate burst of tears escaped her in their presence.

About eleven o'clock Mr. Huntley and the visitor arrived. Lena, standing at her window, was the first to see them, and knew at a glance that Mr. Huntley's companion was her champion of the night. She descended the stairs and stood at the door. The light from the hall revealed her face, and, to his astonishment, Charlie Fane recognized her.

"Well, Lena, my dear," said Mr. Huntley, "have you come down to welcome the stranger? Here he is. Mr. Charlie Fane, this," he said, turning to the young man, "is my niece, Lena Huntley."

They shook hands and exchanged glances of amusement. "So I found you," he whispered.

"Ah, but only by chance," she answered.

"Lucky chance," he said.

"Quick," she murmured, "now," glancing at her uncle, who was removing his overcoat. He understood her, and hastily drawing the parcel from his pocket slipped it into her hands.

"What a blockhead I was," he said in a low voice. She smiled, and running quickly to her room threw it on the bed and was down again by the time Charlie Fane and her uncle were entering the drawing room. All the unpleasantness was now forgotten; her hero was there in the house. If she had only told him her name, all the disagreeableness would have been avoided. Her aunt and cousins frowned upon her behind the visitor's back, but she did not mind them. When it was near midnight, and supper over, they separated for the night, Mr. Huntley saying that their young guest must feel tired after his long voyage.

Lena is standing again at her window, thinking of what a happy Christmas it has turned out to be after all. It had stopped snowing and she wanted to hear the bells when they ushered in the Christmas morn. Suddenly she remembered the blouse, which still lay upon the bed. She took it quickly from the paper bag and shook it out fearing it might be wrinkled. As she did so a light knock came upon the door, which was immediately opened and Mrs. Huntley entered. Lena quickly dropped the blouse upon the bed and turned part of the counterpane over it, but not before the quick eye of her aunt had caught sight of it, and, hastily turning back the coverlet, she demanded, in angry tones, as she held it up: "Pray, explain what this means. Why are you hiding my daughter's property? Why did you pretend you had not got it?"

"I did not pretend anything," answered Lena. "I had not got it then. How, or where I got it makes no difference, since, as you see, it is quite safe."

"This explanation does not satisfy me, Lena Huntley," said her aunt. She left the room for a moment and summoned her two daughters, to whom she told all. Lena stood with her arm leaning on the bureau, a look of indifference upon her face.

"Did you intend appropriating it to your own use?" demanded Ella.

"Will you please explain!"

"I will explain nothing," answered Lena.

Stung to anger by the girl's seeming indifference, and heartily wishing that something would happen to take her away from the house during Charlie Fane's visit, Mrs. Huntley said: "Then nothing remains for us but to suspect you of having pretended to lose the blouse, and, when the fuss had blown over, taking it to the store again, and getting the worth of it for yourself." The girl grew pale to the lips at the insult, and her eyes blazed. "You must remember that by your silence you place yourself under suspicion," she continued, "and whilst you keep so you must find another home. We will make arrangements after tomorrow. Come girls!" and they left the room.

Lena stood like one dazed. Was it possible that she, Lena Huntley, was accused of dishonesty and called a common thief by her own relations? Her first impulse was to seek her uncle and tell him all, as he had always been kind to her; her second, was to fly from the place forever. How dared they do it? she passionately asked herself. She dressed quickly, and, unheard by anyone, descended the stairs and noiselessly opened the hall door. She stood for a moment irresolute. Where could she go at that hour? Over the snow-clad hills and through the frosty air came the musical peal of the bells, breathing their message of peace and gladness to all, speaking to each human heart of charity and forgiveness, of pity and love, of goodwill towards men—but no peace found a place in her stormy, passionate, rebellious heart now. She felt bitterest anger, bitterest indignation against her kinsfolk. This was her Christmas, which, a short time ago, she thought was going to be so happy—alone on a lonely road at midnight, not knowing where to go, accused of dishonesty, and by a great condescension permitted to remain under her uncle's roof till they found a suitable place for her. Ah! Did they think for a moment that she would tamely submit; that she would accept, for one hour, the shelter of this house after such an accusation. Suddenly she thought of an old woman living some distance further on, who had but one granddaughter living with her. She was called Granny Doran, and was always fond of Lena, whom she had known in happier times. So Lena decided to seek shelter there for a few days till she could make other arrangements. She found the good woman at her door listening to the "merry bells of Yule," for, as she said, "It may be the last time I will ever hear them."

"Mercy on us!" cried Granny Doran, as Lena came up to the door. "What is the matter, child?"

"I have come to spend Christmas with you, Granny, if you will have me," said the girl. "I have quarrelled with my aunt, and I'm never going back again."

"And right glad I am to have you, dearie," said warmhearted Granny Doran. "Come in, you must be half frozen. I'll get you a cup of hot tea, and then the best bed in the house is yours as long as you wish to stay. I always said the Huntleys were not half kind enough to you."

Many young men and maidens, living near Granny Doran, often went to her to have their fortunes told, and when Lena had finished her tea, the old woman proceeded to "toss the cup" in the endeavour to cheer her up a bit, and predicted for her a speedy marriage with a tall, handsome man, when she should be robed in white, with veil and orange blossoms.

About nine o'clock on Christmas morning at Huntley's, all sat down to breakfast. Charlie Fane looked longingly towards the door, expecting every moment to see there the face of which he had dreamed all night. When her absence was commented upon by Mr. Huntley, his wife remarked that "she must be taking an extra long nap this morning."

"That is unlike her," he said, "she is always an early riser."

Soon after breakfast Mrs. Huntley and her daughters discovered the girl's flight and feared the consequences if Mr. Huntley found out the truth; so when seated at dinner Mrs. Huntley told him that Lena had gone to spend a few days of Christmas with a friend. "Strange that she should wish to leave us on Christmas Day," remarked Mr. Huntley, "I do not like it."

Charlie Fane sang and laughed, and talked with the Misses Huntley till they thought him charming. When nine o'clock came he could stand it no longer, and he managed to slip out unseen by anyone. The night was bright and fine; he lit a cigar and began a brisk walk on the road. He felt pained beyond measure that Lena should treat him like this. He walked on till he came to Granny Doran's house; a light gleamed from the window, and he stood watching it for some time. As he gazed, he saw a hand raise a corner of the blind, and a face looked out. His heart gave a great bound as he recognized Lena. In a moment he was at the door, and she ran out to meet him. "Answer me one question, Miss Huntley," he said. "Did you leave your uncle's house to avoid me?"

Lena answered, "No." She did not tell him everything; only that she had quarrelled, and she was not going back. So, every night for the next week he managed to go out alone, and Granny Doran's was his destination.

Soon he and Lena discovered the same thing: that one could not live without the other. One night he bade her good-bye for two or three days, as he was obliged to keep a solemn promise made to his mother before leaving New York, which was that he would visit a particular friend of hers who was living in Harbour Grace, to which place his mother belonged.

Over a week had passed and he did not return. During all this time the Huntleys endeavoured, without avail, to discover Lena's whereabouts; Charlie having, at her request, kept silent about her. Mr. Huntley was much annoyed and puzzled at her behaviour.

One night a servant of Mrs. Huntley's dropped in to Granny Doran's to have her fortune told. Granny "cut the cards" and told the girl that she was soon going to a wedding. "Oh, that's true," she answered. "We are to have one at the house tomorrow night. Miss Ella is to be married to Mr. Fane. He is in Harbour Grace, but he will be home tomorrow." Lena, who was in the next room, heard all, and her faith in mankind died. "And so," she thought, "he was but amusing himself with me after all."

"You heard, dearie, I know," said Granny Doran, coming into the room when the girl had gone, "but wait a bit. I don't care if the wedding is arranged a thousand times, there's a hitch somewhere. I have not used my eyes for nothing, and that young man is honest. I'd stake my life on it."

Next morning, as Lena was sitting near the window looking over the want-column in the morning paper, a sleigh drove up, and Charlie Fane got out and walked slowly, and with a slight halt, up the pathway to the door. Granny was out, also her granddaughter, so Lena went to the door. She was determined not to betray herself in any way. "Good morning, Mr. Fane," she said, drawing back as Charlie opened his arms, "I hope you enjoyed your visit to Harbour Grace." He looked both hurt and puzzled.

"You are aware of how I enjoyed myself, Lena," he answered; "this does not look much like amusement," and he pointed to his foot, on which he was still limping, then showed his hand, which was bound with linen.

"Have you hurt yourself?" she asked; "I am sorry."

"Did not my letter explain all, Lena?" he said.

"I received no letter," she answered; "but of course I make all allowances. A man who is preparing for his wedding cannot have much time for letter writing, and I think it is with your intended bride you should now be instead of here."

"My intended bride!" he repeated. "What are you saying, Lena? You are my intended bride, if you will make me happy by being so. I wrote you begging that you would be prepared to marry me tonight, as a few days ago I received a cable message informing me that unforseen and important business connected with our firm required my immediate presence in New York. I cannot delay longer than tomorrow, and, Lena, darling, I wrote, explaining all this to you, for I cannot leave Newfoundland without you. I could not come sooner, for the day after I arrived in Harbour Grace I was thrown from a sleigh whilst driving. My foot caught in the runners, spraining my ankle severely. I also hurt my wrist, so that it was with much difficulty I managed to write a short letter to you. I wanted to give you a little time to be prepared for our marriage tonight."

As he spoke, all Lena's faith in him was restored, and she laughed at herself for doubting him. "Perhaps you do not know, Charlie," she said, drawing nearer to him, "that we are out of the city limits, and our letters are not brought to us."

"Oh," he said, "that explains it."

"I am sorry you have suffered so much," said Lena, with sweet, womanly pity and love shining from her eyes, and then she told him of what she had heard on the previous night.

Charlie only laughed, saying, "Ella Huntley may be getting married tonight, but it is not to me. I have not written one of them a line since I left."

"It is strange," murmured Lena. Then a suspicion flashed across her mind, and she said, "Tell me, how did you address my letter?"

"Miss Eleanor Huntley, No.—Road."

"Why, that is Ella's name also. We are both named 'Eleanor,' but our abbreviations are different."

"I did not know your cousin's name was Eleanor," he said, and they looked at each other for a moment.

"They do not know at Huntley's that I am here. They always send for their letters, and, oh, Charlie, do you know what has happened? Ella thought the number was only a mistake on your part and that the letter was for her, and she is prepared to marry you tonight."

"Good gracious, Lena, do not picture such a catastrophe. I would not wish such a mistake to happen for worlds. How could I ever face Mr. Huntley again."

"Well, you are free; go and marry her tonight, and everything will be straight: I shall not mind much," said Lena.

"I don't believe you would: but I do, and I would not marry her if you were never in the question."

"I was only trying you, Charlie," she replied, smiling fondly up at him. He smiled back and both were content.

"Our stupid mistake about the blouse on Christmas Eve, and my deception afterwards, has caused all this unpleasantness," said Lena, and she told him all about it.

"It is a terrible piece of business," he said, growing quite serious; "how am I ever to explain to them."

"You should go there right away, before things go any further," she said.

"Go there? Why I'd rather face a ravenous wolf."

"Do you know what, Charlie?" said Lena. "I am the cause of all this trouble; if I had explained all to them that night this would have been avoided, and now I will take it upon myself to smooth out things as well as can be."

"Heaven bless you, Lena, you are an angel," exclaimed the young man delightedly. "In some cases men are moral cowards, and this is one of them." So Lena wrote a note to her uncle, requesting him to come to her, which he did, and then she explained everything to him. He was pained beyond measure at the humiliation his daughter would have to endure, but, in his own mind, had to acknowledge that she deserved it.

"If there is anything which I can do to make this mistake less painful to Ella, I am willing to do it, uncle," said Lena.

The rage, mortification and indignation of Ella Huntley, when she heard her father's explanation, can be better imagined than described. "I'll sue him for breach of promise," she declared, when Mr. Huntley had left the room. "To think of that sly manoeuvring girl having the laugh on me like this. I can never live and stand it. I'll die with mortification," and she burst into a storm of tears.

A little timid knock came upon the door. It was opened gently, and Lena entered. In her great happiness, her generous heart was ready to forget and forgive everything.

She felt her cousin's great humiliation, and would not be in her place for untold gold. She went to her, and threw her arms around her saying: "Oh! Ella. I would give anything to undo all this. I am to blame for it all, but I was too proud and stubborn to explain to you that night. Of course, I know none of you meant the things you said, it was only because you were vexed with me."

"It is all very well for you, Lena Huntley, to come here now when it is too late to undo what you have done," cried the miserable girl, rising to her feet. "I shall be the talk of the town."

"No, no, Ella, I can fix everything if you will only listen to me. No one but ourselves need ever know of this mistake. There have been no invitations sent?"

"No," answered Ella."

"You have had no time to get any dresses made?"

"No, only a veil and orange blossoms were ordered."

"Well," went on Lena, "the veil and orange blossoms were ordered for Miss Huntley, and I am Miss Huntley. The servants could be told that you all knew I was to be married when Mr. Fane returned, and that it was only for a joke you pretended it was yourself, and I can wear the veil and orange blossoms if you will permit me."

"And how am I to explain to Mr. Fane?" asked Ella.

"Tell him you did not intend to accept him; laugh at the fun about the mistake of the letter, and prove your indifference by acting as my bridesmaid." Lena had not the heart to tell her that he knew all.

"Are you sure you will never inform on me?" asked Ella Huntley, doubtfully.

"I pledge you, upon my word of honour, Ella," she replied, earnestly, "that he shall never hear the slightest allusion to it from me." And they knew her well enough to believe her word.

And so the wedding took place at Mr. Huntley's house, and Lena, true to Granny Doran's prediction, was robed in white, with veil and orange blossoms. Ella Huntley was bridesmaid, and all went "merry as a marriage bell."

Interview with Grant Boland
Shannon M. Lewis

Boland:

The painting *September* was done in 1996 and it was the first significant painting with a human figure in it for me. It's not something I've really approached before. *September* was actually a key painting for the work to follow. I had the idea for this painting in high school and I didn't paint it until after art school. So I had that idea for about six or seven years before I painted it.

Lewis:

Do you find you think about your paintings for a long time before you paint them?

Boland:

I don't mull it over, I have the idea and it's big at the time. Then I kind of push it away for whatever reason and then it will pop up. I don't even have a choice in the matter. It just comes. Generally what will happen is that the idea will ride you for a few days and then you have no choice but to sit down and do it. It's kind of a cliché but a lot of painters have said it, the paintings generally happen on their own. They make the choices themselves. What this painting did for the rest of my paintings was it opened up the idea that it's not really necessary to spell everything out for your audience or viewer. This painting and the paintings which followed were more or less snippets of a play. In retrospect, it's obvious how influenced I am by the cinema. I even do that now. If I am watching a movie on video I will pause it anywhere and size [the frame] up as a painting.

Lewis:

One of the things we noticed about *September* when we were viewing it is that it almost seems like a frame in a movie. You don't know what happened before, and you don't know what's going to happen afterwards. Because of the look on the woman's face, you're not sure what's going to happen, you have to surmise it. Was that deliberate on your part?

Boland:

Completely. I like the idea of giving the viewer credit. Some people like to spell everything out and leave no holes, but it's no fun that way.

Lewis:

There looks like there is a pre-Raphaelite influence in your work.

Boland:

The pre-Raphaelite influence surfaced and it is there. Artists in general are like sponges, they retain things. They're not always aware when those things surface, it's

September, 1996, oil on canvas, 4' x 5' by Grant Boland.

the same with people in general, you just retain things and stuff will creep up. It's more evident in literature or visual arts. At a glance, my paintings seem really innocent until you really size them up. Then there are normally darker undercurrents. They could be innocent but on closer look, it's not like that at all. Some people say my art is lovely, but other people shudder when they look at it.

Lewis:

Do you find it difficult to be an artist in Newfoundland? Is there enough material here for you to paint?

Boland:

There's tons of subject matter. I wouldn't draw my subject matter from anywhere else. I am culturally close to this place. There's loads of subject matter and it doesn't have to be about wharves and dories and fish stages and stuff. Those things have their place.

Lewis:

Your paintings do not have those elements in them. You expand the idea of "this place."

Boland:

The thing about "that stuff" is that I'm probably too close to "that stuff" being from St. Mary's Bay. I like to explore things I'm not familiar with, and things that other people are not more familiar with as well. But it's all culturally linked. All paintings after *September* are linked. *September* was a cornerstone. It is the beginning of the work I'm doing now. It started me off in a whole new direction.

Lewis:

Do you find emotions play prominently in your art?

Boland:

It has to. Well, it doesn't have to but in mine it does. Well actually some paintings you can look at and you could claim that they are void of any emotion but actually the reverse is true. Because that's an emotion, that coldness.

Lewis:

What does it mean to be an artist?

Boland:

I have no idea. I'd like to say total freedom but then there's the slavery part attached to it. Like I said, you don't have a choice in the matter. You could never walk away from it. It's like anything. What you do is what you are. That affects how you think. Like if you're a carpenter, you're a carpenter, that spills into your social life, it spills into everything else. Nobody can really walk away from your job at the end of the day. They take it with them. I think as a visual artist you tend to look at things differently. I always wonder how somebody else looks at the world. It varies from painter to painter and artist to artist, too.

Lewis:

So what other sorts of influences do you think are in your background, what did you study?

Boland:

It's not what I studied in art school. One thing I know is that the light in all my paintings this wasn't known to me at first is heavily influenced by Italian painting, in the vein of chiaroscuro: lights and darks, heavy, strong light. When I look at things I generally look for light. Just the way the light will hit a chair or a table, that will totally excite me and I'm sure it would not get a lot of other people excited.

Lewis:

To my eye, your light is reminiscent of Mary Pratt's work.

Boland:

Actually, Mary Pratt took me under her wing when I was in high school for about a year or so. She cleared a lot of things up for me. Her influence would be there regardless, I think. It is very difficult to answer questions like why do you paint that way, or why do you choose realism, or why do you choose abstract? No one can answer that. Those questions I hate. They're always there. At school they challenge you a lot that way, to define your art. You can be psychoanalytical when you're looking at something but not when you're doing it because that can really fool you up....The key to *September* painting and most of the paintings that follow is the ambiguity, the questions that are left to the viewers' minds. You're given a basis to start but ideally the audience or viewer will make their own narrative, and finish the story.

The Price of Bread

Gregory Power

One bright October day they laid
The keel, and soon as school was done
We came to watch them ply a trade
Far older than the Flood, and one
That had no need of manuscript,
Or rigid formula, to store
Their expertise. They simply dipped
Into their pool of tribal lore,
And built themselves a ship—while we
Looked on, and marvelled at their worth;
And at the flawless symmetry
They wove into her length and girth.
Their wizards went far beyond
The compass, or the draughtsman's rule—
The axe was their magician's wand;
The eye was their precision tool.

When snow had come to stay, and frost
Had edged the winter wind, till it
Was keen as shattered glass, we lost
No opportunity to sit
Beside their fire of hazel chips,
And learn about the role of wood
In the anatomy of ships.
Before too long we understood
The ancient parlance of their craft,
And used, with some authority,
Such words as rake, and pitch, and draught,
In terms as salty as the sea
And in the cold December sun
We stoked the fire, and watched her grow
Into a full-ribbed skeleton
That cast weird shadows on the snow.
In our romantic minds she bore
A likeness of the names of things
That ruled the Earth aeons before
Our kind were its acknowledged kings.

They didn't waste much time on talk,
Except to pass the time of day,
But bent their backs and hewed the balk,
Until the last light drained away.

And in the frosty dawn we woke
To hear again their axes ring,
For fate did not allow these folk
The luxury of lingering;
Nor was there time to sit and dream,
To climb a hill and stand at gaze,
Or stroll beside a woodland stream
On aimless, unencumbered days.
Luck seldom smiled on them, and yet
They kept their faith, and reared their brood,
And bore the everlasting debt
That guaranteed their servitude.

They'd heard of worlds beyond the Cape,
Where pay was good and goods were cheap,
And no man had to pinch and scrape,
Or work his heart out for his keep.
But these were vague, and far away
From his sights and sounds the heart held dear,
And when a Bayman left the Bay
He shed his bondage with a tear.
They said: No matter where he roves,
Or thrives beyond his native bawn,
His soul will haunt these lonely coves
And misty headlands in the dawn.

When the robins filled the wood with song,
And trout were running in the brooks,
Our truant souls did not belong
In the prosaic world of books.
And when, it seemed, the classroom walls
Were closing in upon us there,
The rhythm of the caulking mauls
Was borne upon the soft spring air.
And we were spirited away
To islands of eternal Spring,
Where sirens sang their roundelay
When bold men came a-seafaring.

Around the end of Easterweek,
When all the Arctic ice was gone,
And springtides hovered near their peak,
The word was spread—the launch was on.
They came as custom said they should,
The young and strong, the old and wise,
To give whatever help they could,
To heave, or haul, or criticize.

And after due considering
'Twas tacitly agreed by all,
That those who built that handsome thing
Were justified in walking tall.

With all her scaffolding removed
She stood there, naked to the eye,
And when, perceptibly, she moved,
We raised a quick, exultant cry.
She stood bolt-upright in her glide,
With every line in high relief,
And floated on the rising tide
As lightly as a fallen leaf.

They rigged her in their mooring dock,
And when her masts were stepped and stayed,
They did deft things with rope, and block,
And marlin-spike, and even made
A small concession to the use
Of ornamental fiddle-fad—
Since every artist would seduce
His audience and when they had
Her ballast stowed, and canvas bent,
She rode majestically at ease,
A trim, efficient instrument
For harvesting these teeming seas.

At long last, they were outward bound,
With every inch of canvas spread,
And headed for the fishing ground,
In their relentless quest for bread.
And through the endless days of May
They came and went, like all the rest,
As in their philosophic way
They worked—and waited to be blest…
Till suddenly, one night that Spring
A sullen East wind went berserk
And howled past all imagining,
While it erased their handiwork.
It made a cauldron of the Bay,
A shambles of the leeward shore
And smashed things in its mad foray
That waves had never reached before.
And those with menfolk at the Keys,
Whose world was being torn apart,
Kept hoping against hope, that these
Had run for shelter at the start…

Until the dawn it ripped and reamed,
And at first light we rose to face
A ransacked world, where nothing seemed
To be in its accustomed place.

The schooners limped back, one by one,
And there were awe-inspiring tales
Of fury never yet outdone
In the mad repertoire of gales.
Soon, only one was overdue,
And as each sad day followed day
Without a word of ship or crew,
We knew that they'd been cast away…
And then, some shoremen in their skiff
Were following the caplin scull,
When, high and dry, against a cliff,
They spied her broached and battered hull.
Although they combed the shore for miles
In every cove, from head to head
And, in and out, among the isles
They found no vestige of the dead.

By custom these were days of rest,
While once again the village grieved,
And neighbours came, dressed in their best,
To touch, and comfort the bereaved.
But life went on, and thereabout
Work was an anodyne for pain
So, well before the week was out
The boats were at the Keys again.

One Sunday afternoon we went
Around the cliffs to see the wreck.
We climbed her stranded hull, and spent
The sunshine on her splintered deck…
We saw where she had come to grief,
That awful wind-wrenched night in Spring,
Upon the ugly half-tide reef,
That wallowed like some unclean thing,
A cable's length or so from shore…
We marked each detail of her rived
And ravished hull, that heretofore
We'd seen painstakingly contrived…
We watched the unrelenting sea
That claimed so many of our dead,
And wondered why the gods agree
On such a dreadful price for bread.

The *Caribou* Disaster
Cassie Brown

October 14, 1942

It was war time and the *S. S. Caribou* was steaming steadily across the Gulf of St. Lawrence in the early hours of a cold fall morning. At 3:35 a.m. a torpedo from an enemy submarine hit the proud ship a mortal blow, and within minutes the only trace left of the passenger ship was a few humans struggling in the icy seas. She went down in the deepest channel in the Gulf, twenty-five miles Southwest of Channel Head in the vicinity of St. Paul's Island.

The night was cloudless and too bright for Captain Ben Tavenor's peace of mind, he had a premonition that something terrible was about to happen, but his passengers were unaware of it. He voiced his fears to the purser, Thomas Fleming, just two hours before disaster struck.

A passenger, William J. Lundrigan of Corner Brook, returning home after treatment in the Royal Victoria Hospital in Montreal, also had the feeling of impending disaster. Like many other men he had given up his cabin to women passengers and was sleeping in the lounge, but the feeling of disaster was on him so strongly, he could not lie still and rest. He paced the floor continually. Another man, Charles Moores, ticket agent for the Newfoundland Railway, was also uneasy. He remained fully clothed, ready for disaster.

Tom Fleming was the purser on the *S. S. Caribou*. He was a young man about twenty-seven years of age, and had considerable experience as a radio operator in the Merchant Navy in the early part of the war. He'd already made several trips across the Atlantic, had been on ships that had been chased and attacked by subs, and he was quite happy with his present position on the *Caribou*.

Nor was this a safe cozy berth, for subs were lying in wait in the Gulf of St. Lawrence, and continually chasing and attacking ships passing through the gulf.

On this fateful morning, some time after midnight, he was in the chief steward's room before returning to his office. The chief steward was Harry Hann, and he had in his office businessman Bob Newman of Petites, who had hurried aboard the *Caribou* in North Sydney at the last minute; Corporal W. B. Howse of the RCAF, and a couple of other men.

Young Corporal Howse was returning to his native Newfoundland on furlough, to marry a certain Miss Doris Welylon, whom he had met at Deer Lake. Right now, as the *Caribou* was speeding towards her doom, Corporal Howse was receiving the ribbing of his life as the men teased him unmercifully about marriage.

Presently, Tom Fleming left and went to his own office in the radio room on the bridge deck. He had many things to do, many lists to type up, statistics for the customs and the immigration authorities, for their passengers consisted mainly of Canadian and American service personnel.

His young assistant, twenty-year-old William Hogan of Carbonear, was there ready to help. They worked away, getting everything ready for the early morning docking, when about 1 a.m., Captain Ben Tavenor walked in.

S. S. Caribou *and Captain Ben Tavenor*

The captain was a heavily built, distinguished looking six-footer, much loved and respected by his men. He and young Tom Fleming were good friends, and had spent many happy hours fishing together at the captain's cabin at Red Rocks.

The captain was restless and uneasy that they only had one escort ship this trip, nor did he like the course they were steering on orders from the navy, which made them steer an alternate course every trip.

He invited Tom to stroll around the deck with him, and as they walked in the cool fall night, voiced his uneasiness about the course they were steering, which was near St. Paul's Island, near the entrance to the Gulf of St. Lawrence. He was convinced that subs were lurking in that very area. "On a night like this our smoke can be seen for miles," he said.

He was a worried, uneasy man when Tom Fleming left him around 1:30 a.m. to finish his paper work. An hour later he had finished, and he and young Bill Hogan lay on the two berths in the radio room to catch forty winks….

Charles Moores checked his watch and saw that the time was 3:30 a.m. He thought that the danger was over and there was less likelihood of an attack, so for the first time that night, he removed his shoes and lay on the berth…his companion was Harold Chislett, a businessman of Rose Blanche, who was already asleep.

William J. Lundrigan could not sleep. To him the night seemed ominous and forbidding, he *knew* something terrible was about to happen. There was no explaining this feeling, but it was there.

Other passengers prowled the deck uneasily, and William Lundrigan deliberately made himself lie down five times to try and woo sleep, but it would not come, and five times a strong feeling of urgency compelled him to rise and pace the deck—back and forth….

Once more he lay down in the lounge, forcing himself to remain there until he eventually dozed off.

The torpedo struck the *Caribou* admidships, causing her to roll sharply. The sea rushed in claiming those below her decks, hit the dynamoes within seconds and plunged the ship into blackness.

There was terror and confusion as the ship continued to steam ahead and under, and within two to five minutes the only trace left of the *Caribou* was a bit of debris and a few humans struggling in the frigid waters of the gulf.

Something woke Tom Fleming. He recalls it was a severe thump which threw him and his assistant out of their bunks. He was wide awake and alert in a second, and he said quickly, "We've got the works, Bill."

In the moments before the lights went out, he could see the radio equipment was smashed, the wall panelling had fallen in and there was a tangle of wires all over, then the lights went and he made a grab for their safety gear hanging on the wall. It consisted of a waterproof flashlight and lifebelts.

Young Bill Hogan was in his shirtsleeves, and Tom passed him a spare coat he had hanging on the wall. They got into their lifebelts and left the office.

On deck, they saw Captain Ben Tavenor struggling into his coat, and Tom paused to help him. He saw the captain go up to the bridge with young Bill Hogan following.

The *Caribou* was still steaming ahead but settling at the bow. Tom could hear the hiss of escaping steam from her broken pipes, and he knew there was no time for anything. He immediately made for the life raft to release it. Men were gathering on the deck....But the raft wouldn't release, the mechanism stuck and they dashed to the boat deck below to try and release it and as they worked frantically, the *Caribou* was going steadily under and the deck was beneath the sea.

She was going under fast and Tom leapt to the rail to jump overboard, but even as he did so, the rail also slid under, giving him no time to jump clear. The *Caribou* slid underneath the waves, carrying Tom Fleming with her.

Charles Moores heard a crackling noise as he was thrown from his berth, but apparently it wasn't sufficient to waken his companion, Harold Chislett. He shook him awake and the two dressed quickly as possible, but before they had a chance to properly adjust their lifebelt, the ship was plunged into darkness.

They left their cabin and discovered that the main deck was already awash. In the blackness, children were screaming, but Charles recognized no one.

Already the stern of the ship was rising as she slid beneath the seas, and Charles made his way to the quarter deck. Here, men and women were shouting and screaming, trying to get rafts into the sea. One woman, with a lifebelt fitting her snugly, hung onto the railing like grim death, crying with fear. Charles forced her to release her grip and made her jump into the sea, then something hit him in the back and flung him overboard....

William J. Lundrigan was rudely awakened by falling debris and crashing glass. He dashed out of the lounge to the bedlam on deck, but he found a boat and managed to get it launched.

Other passengers piled in and in a few minutes the boat was clear of the sinking ship, which quickly slid beneath the sea.

Around them, people were clinging to pieces of wreckage, and depth charges were exploding. Women were hauled from the sea, into the boat, and in the darkness, a black shape glided noiselessly through the water.

Was it the enemy submarine?

Terrified, they all laid flat in the boat and remained quite still until the ship disappeared into the night, then some sort of order was restored when a seaman on the boat took charge.

Thomas Fleming was horribly conscious of the fact that he was being pulled down by the suction of the ship, but being a strong swimmer, fought against it. There were no despairing thoughts in his mind, only the determination to reach the surface. The struggle seemed endless but finally, when his lungs were near the bursting point, he broke surface and gulped in the sweet pure air.

He was dazed and confused and the shouts of people, the explosion of depth charges around him, confused him further.

Then close beside him he heard the cry of a baby, and right in front of him floating on the surface of the sea was a baby. He reached for it, automatically, and it registered on his brain that the baby was wearing rubber pants. This, he thought remotely, is undoubtedly what kept the infant afloat.

Around him many different rafts were floating, each loaded down with people. He passed the baby to one of the rafts but did not attempt to get on any of them.

The rafts drifted away and Tom, his mind clearing, looked around for something to hang on to, and he found a piece of wreckage and crawled upon it.

Charles Moores found his way to the surface of the sea minus his lifebelt, which he hadn't time to secure properly, and being a good swimmer moved away from the sinking *Caribou*. He grasped a piece of wreckage and held on while watching the ship list and disappear.

Suddenly, the water was illuminated by a light and he heard the distant rat tat tat of a machine gun, then the light disappeared and Charles Moores swam about until he reached a larger piece of wreckage. There were four people up on it, one of them he recognized as Tom Fleming the purser. He crawled up on it, but other people came swimming out of the darkness and soon there were too many bodies trying for safety on the piece of wreckage which kept turning over and over, spilling them back into the sea.

Tom Fleming and Charles Moores released their holds and swam about in the night looking for larger pieces of wreckage….

Swimming around in the icy seas, Tom Fleming was not conscious of the fact that the seas were icy. He was still mildly confused but knew he had to find something on which to rest. Then, above the distant shouts and confusion, he was aware of the great solid form of a man threshing his way through the water right at him.

He thought he recognized him as Bob Newman, the businessman of Petites, and in alarm called out. "Bob, the other way. The other way!"

The big man obeyed blindly, altering his course enough to avoid a collision, and at the same time a raft with half a dozen people on it drifted by. Tom Fleming grasped at it and pulled himself aboard, then turned to give Bob Newman a helping hand. Charles Moore also pulled himself on the raft.

Others swam out of the darkness to the raft and presently it was overcrowded, and was completely submerged and the sea was sloshing around their hips. There were twenty-two people in all, including three women and two children, and one of the tots was suffering from exposure. Charles Moores took the little child and tried to shelter it from the sea with his coat.

Tom Fleming was most uncomfortable for one young man who had been in an air crash in Battle Harbour only a few days before, was sitting right across his legs, nor could the man move because any movement on the overladen raft might mean disaster.

The young man pleaded, "Mister, rub my back."

Tom obliged.

The men were surprisingly cheerful and well behaved. Bob Newman had swallowed a considerable amount of salt water and was feeling sick. All around them in the black night, they could hear the survivors singing to keep up their spirits. From one direction they could hear women singing "Nearer my God to Thee."

The hours dragged horribly, and there wasn't a sign of the escort....

Tom Fleming, occasionally answering the young man's plea to rub his back, urged the men not to lose hope. He explained that the escort ship had to track down the sub if possible, to try and drive it away from the vicinity. "We'll be picked up eventually, don't give up hope," he urged.

Meanwhile the little tot suffering from exposure died.

Five hours after the sinking of the *Caribou*, the raft with Tom and Charles was sighted and the survivors taken aboard the escort ship.

One hundred and thirty-six persons died with the sinking of the *Caribou*, while naval craft rescued one hundred and one from the icy waters of the Gulf of the St. Lawrence hours after the ship went down.

Captain Ben Tavenor, his two sons, Stanley the first officer, and Harold the third officer, went down with the ship, and it was said that the Captain tried to steer his sinking ship at the submarine, but that she slid beneath the waters before reaching the enemy craft.

Among the missing persons was Corporal Howse who was returning on leave to be married.

Businessman Harold Chislett of Rose Blanche was never seen again.

The dreadful disaster so close to home left twenty-one widows and fifty-one orphans in Port aux Basques and Channel.

On Tuesday, October 14, exactly five years after the sinking of the *Caribou*, a memorial was unveiled and dedicated in Port aux Basques, and on your next visit to the CNR terminal here in Newfoundland, pause a while and pay tribute to those who died by the enemy hand.

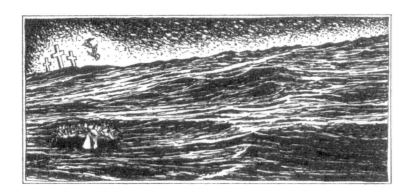

S. S. Eagle:
The Secret Mission, 1944-45
Harold Squires

In 1944 at the height of World War II the British Admiralty commissioned the sealing ship S. S. Eagle, owned by Bowring Brothers of St. John's, to go on a secret mission to Antarctica to establish a base camp. The Newfoundland ship was chosen because of her durability especially in ice-infested waters and the skills of her experienced captain and crew, all of whom were Newfoundlanders. The following incident is written by Harold Squires who today is the lone survivor of that epic voyage.

The storm was growing stronger by the moment and visibility in the driving snow was nil. I quickly made my way back to my cabin and set about contacting the shore base. (At first, I had no luck, for the "Walkie-Talkie" radio was off at the shore base.) As I was trying to contact the shore, without warning, all hell broke loose. The old ship lurched so violently that I was thrown against the cabin door and came face to face with old Skipper Tom Carroll who was just about to enter my cabin.

Skipper Tom was as near to tears as I had ever seen him come. He clutched my arm and roared over the howl of the wind, "We're going to lose her, Markie, we're going to lose her." The tears in Skipper Tom's eyes were not for himself—he had no fear of death—but for his beloved old ship, the *Eagle*.

I lifted my eyes at that moment and through a slight ease in the snow squalls saw a huge iceberg gliding past the *Eagle*. The iceberg had our bowsprit and part of our bow sticking out of it. Some of the rigging and a portion of the rail from the forecastle deck were also embedded in the ice. It was obvious we had collided with the berg and suffered serious structural damage.

At the sight of the iceberg Skipper Tom grabbed my arm and it was only by a stroke of luck I kept him from falling to the deck below. I was not so lucky, for in holding Skipper Tom back, I missed my own footing and fell to the deck below, landing with a great thump that shook every bone in my body.

To make matters worse, just as I landed, the *Eagle* rolled violently and I was in danger of being swept overboard. It was only by jamming my legs against the railing and holding on for dear life that I managed to keep my position.

Although badly shaken, I wasn't seriously hurt and with a bit of effort made it back to the wireless room. I was just inside the room when the *Eagle* scraped along the side of another iceberg. At this point, the shore base switched on their radio, and I made contact, telling them we had parted our anchors, and had to put to sea, and had suffered structural damage from the ice. I asked them to keep the radio on in case of other messages. Then I left the wireless room and went back to the bridge to report to Captain Sheppard. He told me we had collided with two icebergs. The first one tore away our bow, the second had scraped our side. With the prevailing weather conditions it was impossible to assess the total damage to the ship. In such a blizzard no one could venture on the forward head to see what had happened. He asked me to go back to the wireless room and contact the shore base.

"Tell them," he said, "we've lost both our anchors and eighty fathoms of chain. We've hit two icebergs but can't assess the full extent of the damage we have suffered. We think we are somewhere south of the base. Ask them to stand by until we contact them again."

We knew our damages were serious for each time the *Eagle* dipped the ocean flooded into the forecastle, forcing the crew to seek shelter in the stern of the ship. Then, there was more bad news when the engine room reported flooding, and the pumps were unable to keep ahead of the water which was steadily rising.

This news came as I was leaving the bridge to try and contact the shore base again. When Captain Sheppard heard that the water was rising in the engine room, he made an instant decision.

"Cancel that first message to shore, Sparks," he said, "the situation has changed. Tell them we have no hope of weathering the storm, and I'm going to try and get her into Eagle Cove. Ask them to go there as quickly as they can, and bring ropes, and anything else that may help the crew get safely ashore."

My hopes for survival fell. Eagle Cove was a rocky beach strewn with boulders and the huge seas sweeping over our ship would tear her bottom out long before she was beached. I knew it was a hard decision to make, and either way death stared us in the face.

I went back to the wireless room, and although the storm made reception difficult, I managed to relay the Captain's message. They received it on shore, and answered that they were on their way to the Cove. A few minutes later Captain Sheppard sent for me to come back to the bridge. He had just gotten a bit of good news. The pumps in the engine room now seemed to be dealing with the water which had just started to recede.

At this point Captain Sheppard called all hands to the bridge and explained our situation. There were only two alternatives, stay with the *Eagle*, and hope the pumps would continue to handle the leaks until we made it back to Port Stanley in the Falkland Islands or attempt to beach her in Eagle Cove. He was of the opinion we should try and make it back to Port Stanley, and asked the officers and crew if they would trust to his judgement.

There was total agreement to try and make it back to Port Stanley for we all knew the dangers of trying to land at Eagle Cove. When the crew had spoken, Captain Sheppard turned to me and said, "Contact the shore Sparks, and tell them we're going to try to make it to Port Stanley."

Just as I made contact with the shore base, there came a change in the weather, the wind eased a bit and the snow stopped. Even as I gave the operator on shore our decision, he told me they could now see us turning our battered bow seaward and wished us Godspeed.

So, with Captain Sheppard on the bridge, and Skipper Tom Carroll standing beside him, short of fresh water, and with bunker running low, we began the long, slow trek to Port Stanley. But, there was hope, for we trusted Captain Sheppard's judgement. As old Skipper Tom Carroll said, the *Eagle* had weathered many an Arctic gale in her forty years at the northern ice fields, and he was sure she'd do as she always had done, and bring her crew safely home.

Captain Kirk Surveys the Seal Hunt, or, To Boldly Go

Joan Strong

I see them all, up there, shining in the sun.
Captain Kirk, piloting his shuttlecraft—
a helicopter, spiraling, cameras gazing down
upon the swilers.
Superman's girlfriend travels with him,
Margot Kidder, recently returned
from therapy and LA
lets a new man of steel
carry her through the Labrador skies bluer, whiter than
any ice planet set she's ever seen.
And of course, the
inimitable Cynthia Dale,
vixen lawyer from the CBC's
Street Legal—though what
her kind of law has to do
with this place
I cannot imagine.
Still, I suppose their point of view
is largely corporate.
They don't, for instance,
tangle with McDonald's hamburgers
or interfere in salmon wars in the west.
The US and its transnationals
are our friends, and we
who work the ice, of course, are aliens.

Fascinating, Captain.

Shatner's prime directive now—
look good, and don't upset your sponsors.
But the swilers are okay.
Such little men they look, the swilers,
from up here. The Captain and
his lieutenants peer down. Shatner doesn't land
but circles at right angles.
The sealers use guns now as much as gaffs.
Travel out here to the pans as did
their fathers, and theirs before them.
Driven then by captains who condemned
them to lose themselves to

storms and hunger
fear and madness
freezing death and drowning
all for the sake
of the families at home
who survived by each other's toil
until
a government bought the place with welfare
cheques, no solution—another problem
so that Canadian goods could be consumed
in the east
to drive the central markets.
New masters on the ship, who prefer unemployment high
and the bank rate low, since it's good for them.
The only options open, consume or be consumed. Become one with
the centre. The federation. Was there ever a chance to become masterless men?
Not for the poor. Not for the hunted. Who got skinned, is skinned, for the price of
the market and its publicity?
And the little men, black smudges on the white ice ledger, whose sacrifice stands
as big as the stars in the night
to guide the ships, gave us in their work a culture
of enterprise, dignity and respect for nature—
for who knew and feared and loved nature more than we?—
those little men who bloodied ice
with honour
are disgraced by a few
who do not belong to the many of this craft.
Those late-comers selling penises to men who need them—
throw them out.
But, Captain Kirk, do not, from your lofty look
mistake those few fools for what is right and necessary here.
You, and Lois Lane and Cindy and Farley
Hardly-Knows-It Mowat in the back, writing his new
testament for the Inuit of our time.
We missed you when the cod died, but I guess the timing wasn't right on the
photo-op that day.

To Boldly Go—

that's what I'd like to see you do right now,
folks, if the lines of your script aren't so old that you've forgotten them.

Newfoundland Sealing Disaster: 1914
after Cassie Brown

Enos Watts

It is a story of
heaving blood-slicked decks
banshee shrieks in riggings
sun-hounds portentous
in the east
and nightmare's drift across
uncertain dawns;
a tale
of distances
between colonial men
who knew their stations
all too well
and ships with whistles silent
in March gales

Quiet men
who'd turned their backs
on tribal tyranny
raised faces against a storm
challenged the howl of death
till each last
voice and breath
became the wind

Their eulogies
were etched
on the scarred bows of ships
questing a pitiless harvest
somewhere
west of the Front

Excerpt from

But Who Cares Now?
The Tragedy of the Ocean Ranger

Douglas House

While the *Ocean Ranger* disaster has already begun to fade in the memories of most Newfoundlanders, for the families and friends of the victims it is a permanent, living reality. Peoples' lives have been saddened; they have had to become tougher and harder: they have become more skeptical of the pronouncements of those in positions of authority. While some have become embittered and cynical, most family members have begun painfully to adjust to their new lives, sadder but wiser in the ways of the world. Not only have their circumstances changed, but they have changed as people.

The parents of the victims, at a later stage in their life cycle, have changed less than the widows and younger family members, but they feel very strongly a permanent sense of loss. Mr. and Mrs. Gordon Hatfield, a couple in their seventies, wrote to us jointly about their son Tom.

> We lost our youngest son, the child of our old age, the dear baby of the family. He had three older brothers and one sister, and was a dear uncle to eleven nieces and nephews. He had innumerable friends all across Canada, and was loved by all our neighbours. We shall always be proud of the memory of our son Tom. He was a strong family-related person. He loved people and was particularly considerate of those whom he felt did not have his advantage in life.

Little anecdotes are a particularly poignant way to bring the image of a lost child to life. Mr. Scotty Morrison reminisces about his son, Perry.

> It wasn't until after Perry was gone and people from all walks of life would tell us stories about things that he had done that we never knew anything about that we realized how he had touched a good number of people. I guess one of the funniest stories, if you could picture this happening, he was going with a girl he went to high school with and they lived down the Kingsway. Her mother was having a pool party this day with all of the ladies dressed in their finery around the pool having lunch. Perry happened to be there painting. He used to wear these very short shorts, or cut off jeans. He was busy painting this day and he had come down off the ladder and walked around the pool, and just before he got to this one lady whom he knew very well, he knew her daughter very well, he dipped the paint brush in the paint can and as he walked by put a streak from the top of her shoulder to her arm, and then just kept on walking as if nothing had happened. All of the other ladies were horrified that this idiot would do something like this, but the lady that it happened to just laughed and said, "This is typical Perry!" She told us this story at Mass one day and we just shook our heads.

While the wives of the victims can expect to have more time in which to heal their emotional wounds, their life situations have been more profoundly changed by the disaster. Some have not been able to progress very far towards building new and satisfying lives.

> My mind is working strange: it has never been the same. I can never go back to what I was. I had a lot of stress and I've been in a lot of shock. I was bought off—I presume that is the word—bought off for what happened. I know I have an obligation to my children, but I have an awful lot to change. My mind has been totally screwed up. I can't think straight anymore, I can't trust anyone any more. I find that I've isolated myself: that I've had an awful lot of nervous problems lately. I fear everything I'm doing. I've got no confidence left in myself. I just feel totally blah type of thing now. I guess the hardest thing in my life right now is trying to play the role of a mother and a father. I'm feeling burned out: I'm tired. I'm exhausted. I carry too much anxiety in my head.

Not only is it difficult to adjust to this new double role vis-à-vis one's children, but the new status of widowhood changes one's relations with one's friends as well.

> I've learned from this whole experience that you should never give up your independence to depend on someone wholly, because it takes a long time to get back to being independent. We never had any kids, and everything we did we did together: went fishing and camping—everything was together. So it really was an adjustment for me. So I say, don't depend on anyone too much. I think I have become a stronger person, a bit more leery. I watch people more, suspicious I suppose you would call it. I've learned that some people can be very rude. I'm a widow now, and I've noticed first just talking to people—married friends—I've got the feeling that they didn't want me there any more because perhaps I'm a threat to their family, their husband. So I gave up a lot of friends because of that.

Most of the women who felt that they were adjusting reasonably well echoed this idea that they had had to become tougher and more independent.

> I guess I've learned how to come through with something like this. It's the first time I've ever experienced anything like it. I've learned how to be tough, I guess, tough in the sense that, well, I have to take it. I have to deal with it.

> I've learned how to cope with a lot. There have been a lot of problems dealing with lawyers and different companies. I guess you learn to cope with things that you never thought would happen to you. You learn how to make sure that the same things won't happen again. I've become a strong person, and more independent too.

Most of the women who had lost their husbands have since moved to a new house or even into a different community. This symbolizes their determination to pick up the pieces and start a new life. Some have taken new jobs, or begun courses at university or other educational institutions. Part of the personal philosophy of those that have

Ocean Ranger *monument and plaque (Stuart Montgomerie, sculptor)*

adjusted well was the decision to take one day at a time, and to adjust gradually to a different future. Marg Blackmore explains:

> I like to think I've learned a lot, especially about myself and other people and the companies concerned, and about society. I suppose people are basically good, you know, and when something like that happens you really realize how good they really are. They can be so helpful. But then, six months later when everything is straightened out to a point, people can be mean too. They can be envious and jealous, and all of that comes and you really don't know how to handle it sometimes.
>
> I do have some long-range plans, but I'm sort of living them one month at a time. I suppose that's one thing, for sure, that this disaster has taught us. I heard my mother say, 'What man appoints, God disappoints.' I have some long-range plans with regard to furthering my education, and possibly re-entering the workforce. But, as I say, I'm sort of living them one month at a time. My biggest concern now is that my baby is starting school in September and in getting my children through, getting them interested in something so that eventually they will end up with jobs. I hope it won't be offshore!

Even women who have adjusted as bravely as Marg Blackmore continue to have their difficult moments. As Marg explains in a conversation with Pat Hickey, an air of unreality still hangs over the whole tragic affair.

> You know, Pat, even now when I go to the cemetery, and even though I know Ken's there, the gravestone is there and the name is there, it's still not real. You know, I don't believe in thinking like that. It's not that I'm backing away from it or anything like that. I know logically that, yes, the accident happened: he's gone and he's not coming back. I know where he is and that I have to go on with my life and raise the boys, but sometimes it seems so abstract and unreal to me.

Eventually women and families that manage to make the painful adjustment can begin to think of the possibility of a new husband and father. The new mate will not replace the old, but will fill a new role in the family's life. For happy families, the beloved husband and father will never be forgotten. Jocelyn Maurice, who had a very difficult adjustment at first, has the final say in this book. She reflects upon the promise of her new life while paying homage to the happiness of the old.

> We lost our source of strength when Michael died. He took a lot of the bumps for us. He protected us a lot. But his greatest gift to us was the ability to make us laugh. In the past two-and-a-half years we have not had much laughter. At least not the kind he was able to provide for us. But I notice, as the pain subsides, that my son and daughter have the same gift. And I thank God for it. One day soon we will be a family again. We have someone special in our lives now, and we are in the process of building our lives over again. I know this remarriage has the blessing of God—and Michael.

When Orchards Green

Genevieve Lehr

And they never hear of boats
or storms, or gardens in summer—
no, they never heard of the tragedies
of widows on nights like these
when a wind blankets the world in
wailing
and children cry out in sleep;

they never hear, being up there
with other immigrants and misplaced
persons—
they never know we are waiting
submerged in Atlantic mists
wistful in the scent of Spring
like now, in dandelion May
when buds unfold their careful
homes;

O where when orchards green
and fields waver in their turf-black
odours
Where when a railway pierces
its jet-deep trail through hills and
lakeland spruce…

surely they will return
the sons and fathers
who hunt in dreams the moose and
hare
and spear the fish in shallow beds—
surely on days like these
we will hear the countless missing
voices
of families and friends who have
gone
searching for what they already had
on these shores that wake them with
their calling.

Your Last Goodbye

Bruce Moss

She's the finest in the land, designed and built by man,
To withstand all that nature has to offer.
And the *Ocean Ranger's* crew numbered eighty-four men true
To their homes and their sons, wives and daughters.

Chorus: Look away to the west, there's a storm upon the wind,
Bringing rain, snow and seas four stories high.
Look away to the west, will you see your homes again?
Or is this the time to say your last good-bye? Your last good-bye.

Then there's trouble from within, the rig is listing once again,
And the gallant crew are ordered to abandon.
But the hurricane's too strong, when the morning comes she's gone.
Not a soul survived to tell us what had happened. What had happened.

Husbands, fathers, sons and brothers leave behind so many others,
Who will not forget the price their loved ones paid.
Was it fate that dealt the hand, or the carelessness of man
That lead so many to an early grave? An early grave.

Chorus.

May God grant peace and serenity to our brothers lost at sea,
Give their families strength to bear the grief and pain.
And if our men must sweat and toil in pursuit of offshore oil,
Pray to God to bring them safely home again. Home again.

Repeat first verse.

Final remnant of the Ocean Ranger

Those Thirsty Critters
Gilbert Lynch

There's a story told
A long time ago
Of a wily fox
And a wise old crow;
Those thirsty critters
Hot and dry
Must find some liquid
Lest they die.

A long neck jar
Those critters found
With precious liquid
A long way down.
Said fox to crow
"Not a single leak
For my pointy nose
Or your handsome beak.

Since my pointy nose
Isn't long enough
And your saucy neck
Cannot reach the stuff."
With a foxy grin
He had to go
And leave the jar
With the wise old crow.

As the raven pecked
He began to think
Of another way
To get a drink,
By that long neck jar
The wise crow found
Some little pebbles
On the ground.

"I'll find a way,"
Said the wise old crow
"To reach that liquid
Down below
Then pebbles, one by one
I'll drop

Till the liquid grows
To the pitcher's top."

The wily fox
Of his thirst was killed
And the old crow drank
Till his craw was filled.
In an old *Royal Reader*
Of long ago
I read this yarn
Of that wise old crow.

Now Mr. Oilmen
Please take note
Of the wise old crow
In the poem I wrote.
Examine all that I have said,
Put a concrete jar
On the ocean's bed.
To get that liquid
In our reach
Take all those pebbles
On the beach
Drop 'em down
Like that wise old crow
Till the Grand Banks crude
Begins to flow.
Then the lion will roar
And the crow will peck
At the offshore oil
From a concrete deck.

Bogwood

Gregory Power

The year we plowed the river field, we found,
Deep in the silt, the warped and blackened bones
Of ancient trees; and most of them were sound,
Though every bit as heavy as the stones.
Among them there were ribs, backbones and knees,
Thin fingers that had held green leaves, or fed
White blossoms to the wind, lost springs, when these
Made magic here. For days we harvested
These bones of trees from soft, black furrows where
The land was wet; and when the field was done
We left them in loose tangles, here and there,
To season in the summer wind and sun.

Around the coast, old custom sets a time
For certain work, and in our neighbourhood,
When April comes we tidy up and lime;
December is the month for getting wood.
So, while the meadows slept, benumbed and white
And skies were little more than half-awake,
We cut them into junks, and they were light
As feathers now, but hard enough to break
An axeman's heart. One bitter night we burned
This wood that time had tempered in the mire.
It charmed those hours of rest, when we concerned
Ourselves with dreams, and made a ghostly fire.
Beyond its blue, transparent flame, we saw
The heat waves dancing in a parched July;
Its light, transformed by some enchanted law,
Was hoarded sunlight from an age gone by.

Address to Convocation
Edythe Ryan Goodridge

Mister Chancellor, Honourable Member, Mister President, Members of the Board of Regents, Members of the Senate and Faculty, Members of the Graduating Class, distinguished guests, ladies and gentlemen, family and friends. I wish to thank the Board of Regents and the Senate of Memorial University for this honour. I am deeply touched and will take a moment of this special occasion to acknowledge my personal debt to this institution.

But first I would like to extend my sincere congratulations to those of you graduating from Memorial today. While we share a common understanding of both the pain and passion that has shaped so much of our recent history, I fully recognize the role your generation must play in defining and determining our place as a society in the century ahead. I wish you well on your chosen journeys.

It was thirty years ago I entered the hallowed halls of Memorial as a member of its early Extension Service. Through a decade of intense learning and labour, I was accorded rare privileges: among them an opportunity to discover the boldness of spirit of our people and to share in the power of the creative imagination of our contemporary artists. For these privileges, I acknowledge a debt of gratitude to Memorial University.

It is the artists to whom I wish to pay tribute today. To do so I have chosen a simple passage from the extensive writings of the late George Story, who so generously enriched my years at Memorial and assisted me in the formation of the Newfoundland and Labrador Arts Council, as its first chairman.

"It is our creative ability that ensures our survival as a recognizable people and culture, and enables us to contribute to the enrichment of the nation of which we form a distinctive part."

I believe this simple and eloquent tribute defines the complex role artists play in our society, and marks a significant change in our shared perception as a people.

For most of our history, we have seen ourselves as others see us. With rare exception we have had but the narration and illustration of colonial masters and observers by which to measure our worth. Our collective memory is cluttered with their ragged tales of bitter poverty and the numerous efforts they made on our behalf, to change our ways.

It is this dominant portrayal of our history which has coloured so much of our sense of identity in the past, and lingers still in the minds of many. But in recent decades, there have been those who dared to search the recesses of that history for other interpretations, and to confront the brutal social and cultural engineering advanced by the ideologies and doctrines of their time.

One such doctrine was resettlement. As it gripped our communities and disrupted our traditional way of life, individuals and groups throughout the island and along the Labrador Coast engaged in active discourse and debate. Fearless of consequences, and undaunted by the ridicule of politicians, planners and civil servants advocating these changes, they began their challenge.

Among the opposing voices were a handful of academics and journalists, and a large contingent of artists. Through their energy, wit and passion they constructed a counter environment in which the stigma of poverty and colonial apologia were at last confronted. From these tensions and trauma, they expanded our understanding of the past and defined a daring vision for the future.

What united these voices was a deep conviction that there were choices for this society, other than those offered by the prevailing ideology. They believed that by strengthening our traditional values and reinforcing our collective voice, we could, like our North Atlantic neighbours, offer our young a vibrant future that was both post-colonial and post-industrial.

It was then that the work of the artists began. Some were committed to rescuing our rich resource of ballads and lore, epic tales and heroic deeds—all hidden under a cloak of shame. Others were determined to celebrate our traditional art and crafts and to defend our proud built heritage from demolition. All were intent on reforming our shabby institutions, demonstrating the dignity of our traditional skills and labour, and exposing some of the myths of progress.

Through their creative energy, the artists illuminated our values, achievements and invention. By addressing the complexities and contradictions of our human condition, they explored and defined the inner geography of our imagination: giving us a new narrative through their theatre, writing and painting. It is this narrative which I believe has resulted in a dramatic change in the mindscape of this society.

Today younger artists are expanding this mindscape, adding fiction, film and new music to our images and language. So too are younger scholars continuing to navigate the fog-bound channels of our history. Together they maintain the challenge set down by an earlier generation, confronting those among us who still insist on reducing our invention and art to entertainment and souvenir, producing cultural sentimentality and nostalgia for our amusement, and the delight of our visitors.

For artists do not amuse or entertain. Their works are not sentimental or nostalgic, but rather a probing reflection of our past and present experiences. Artists are engaged in a learned practice situated well beyond idelogy and doctrine. Like their counterparts in academe, their passage of meaning conveys imagery and language that conjure up hidden memories and remote truths that pose difficult questions for the future.

But in our time, few artists are honoured, and fewer still recognized or remunerated for their generous gifts or rich labour. If we are to be sincere in our efforts to value their contribution, we must accord the artists the dignity of status, by recognizing the critical and complex nature of their role in our collective deliberations. We must respect their voice in our political life, insist their commentary is reflected in our broadcasting, and ensure their work is located in our educational and custodial institutions.

As we complete the final chapter of yet another century of our long and arduous existence as a people, we are again experiencing a harsh and disruptive period in our history. Perhaps by ensuring our artists continue to play a critical and creative role in our affairs, we may discover within our shared memory and imagination the attributes essential to shaping what we all seek, a bold and proud future for this tenacious society.

Thank you.

An Interview with
Mike Massie of Labrador
Matthew Fox

Matthew Fox:

First of all, what is your general impression of Labrador Inuit art?

Mike Massie:

There is some nice work coming out—textile work, like moccasins and parkas—and there seem to be many more carvers than there used to be. Maybe that is a result of the Labrador carving workshop sponsored by the Inuit Art Foundation in 1991. Overall, work is looking very good.

Fox:

How do you think Inuit art in Labrador is different from Inuit art in other parts of Canada?

Massie:

Labrador artists are just starting to come into the mainstream. I have travelled in the North, to Gjoa Haven and Iqaluit, and I was able to see some of the styles there. Labrador artists certainly have their own style, particularly those who are serious and who have been carving for a number of years. The carvings that I have seen over recent years are much improved. Unfortunately, there isn't enough emphasis on art in Labrador. Just when something starts up, it gets shut down—the facilities aren't there, the qualified instructors aren't there to help, to show examples of other Canadian art. That is the problem, I find. Labrador artists base a lot of their work on what's going on in their environment. I find my work is representative of what is going on, too. In Gjoa Haven, the work is more spiritual, more mystical. In Labrador, the work is based more on everyday happenings.

Fox:

You are not what many people would consider a typical Inuit artist. How do you see yourself fitting into that description of Labrador art?

Massie:

Grade Six was the last year that I had anything to do with art. It was depressing because it was one of my fountains that I could go into and be relaxed. I had been drawing since I was about five or six, and I always enjoyed it. When I finished high school, I knew I wanted to get into the arts, but I didn't venture out to see what was there. I did a commercial-art course in St. John's for a year, and then I came home for a couple more years and I was confused about what I really wanted to do. In 1986 I went back to school in Newfoundland, where I did a visual-arts course. That was the big turning point for me. Finally I was able to sit down with a lot of other Newfoundland

Snowy Owl by Mike Massie.

artists. I might have been the only one from Labrador at the time. From there, I went to the Nova Scotia College of Art and Design and did four years of study, with three years in jewellery. It is just something I have always wanted to do. There were so many different types of art to work on sculpture, jewellery, painting, drawing, printmaking and photography.

Unfortunately, in Labrador, there wasn't any other place to do it. The facilities aren't there, which is depressing, because there are a lot of very talented people who seem to be quite interested in doing art. People don't like to venture out into larger centres; they find it too distracting and confusing which is understandable, especially if you come from a small community. But I just wanted to do whatever I could with art. With my teapots, earrings and brooches, I have a tendency to go back to a story years ago when I was down at my grandparents' old house, when I was camping with my father and we came across an old ulu. I have always kept it as a souvenir, and I have always been intrigued by its shape. I never really grew up in the Inuit culture. I didn't grow up living off the land or anything, I grew up in a white community. I hunted and fished, but it wasn't my living. I always found it interesting trying to understand my background, and to understand and try to relate to what Inuit do and how they live.

Fox:

Do you feel like you are part of two different worlds, being part Inuit and yet being brought up in a southern environment?

Massie:

I must say that it gets kind of confusing at times. I remember that in one of my first jewelry classes, I was making some earrings I think they were komatiks [sleds] and a lot of my ulu designs were just starting to emerge. The instructor came up to me one day and said she wasn't too impressed with students who were trying to copy other cultures. I asked, "What do you mean?" and she said, "Well, if you are African…." She didn't really say it but I got her point. She was saying that I shouldn't be copying what I didn't really understand. I told her that I was part Inuit and that I was trying to understand this. At the time, she didn't realize that I was Inuit. It gets confusing. While I was teaching up north, one of my students told me that I wasn't an Inuk, that I was more a Qablunaaq. And I said, "That's true, I did grow up in that environment, but I have always tried to understand how cultures are, especially being part Inuit." I have always wanted to understand the Inuit and their beliefs. Teaching in the North for two years helped me to understand people and their culture.

Fox:

And do you feel more a part of that culture now?

Massie:

More than I ever have. Even now, people ask me why I am making Inuit art and I just tell them that I am part Inuit, and right now, that is what I am comfortable with. I really

want to try and understand it more. I just want to be able to put it out visually. It's interesting because my painting doesn't take on any Inuit images whatsoever, but when I do some stone carving I really don't know why, but these are the images that are coming out. I didn't sit down and plan it; I didn't work out those designs it just came about. And with jewelry I've heard that Inuit should not be making jewelry because it's not traditional. I say that experimentation is what it's all about. It doesn't matter if it isn't traditional. I think experimentation is a way to understand, if you are interested in art.

Fox:

Do you feel that formal training helped promote that sort of experimentation?

Massie:

Yes, because when I went to school here in Stephenville, the first year we had to do everything. In the first three months, you might do photography, sculpture, painting and printmaking. And the next three months, you would do three or four different things. It gave me a chance to try these mediums, which was good because if you got tired, or if you really didn't want to try painting this time around, then the next semester you could try something else. When it came to my teapots, if I had a problem with a spout or a handle, I would sit down and talk about it and work out my problems with one of my best friends, who was into ceramics and who also made teapots. Because ceramics and silversmithing are a lot alike, in experimenting you discover that a problem in one area might help you with a problem in another area. It's those kinds of things that interest me, because we are only here for a short time and, in my opinion, it's more exciting to try as many different things as you can, in as many different mediums as you can. I think that art in general is nothing but an experience of life.

Fox:

How do you think other people perceive you as an artist?

Massie:

People have made comments about the strange objects that I make or the elegant objects that I have made. I was at the CNE [Canadian National Exhibition] in Toronto last August, and I received some great responses from the people who own galleries and from the general public. I wasn't there to worry about making money. I just wanted to go up and see what kind of response I was going to get. Unfortunately, I had only one finished teapot and other partially finished teapots to show, but what they saw they liked. The response I am getting is the one that I am looking for. I haven't really had a negative response yet, but if I do, that is fine too. Not everyone can agree.

Fox:

I am going to make an assumption here and I may be wrong in this, but I would think that a lot of galleries dealing with Canadian art would want to show your work and present you as a Canadian artist, rather than strictly as an Inuit artist. There are a lot of Inuit artists whose work would only be shown if it portrayed stereotypical Inuit images, because Inuit are always put into a pigeonhole. Now I don't know if that assumption is right or not.

Massie:

I kind of agree because one of my really good friends, who was also one of my first instructors, asked me one time why I was making Inuit art if I didn't really understand it. Well, a lot of times I do feel that I am caught between two worlds. So what I try to do is incorporate Inuit images, like the ulu. When my teapots are finished, hopefully they will convey what I am trying to get across here. I am part Inuit and part Qablunaaq; I might as well combine the two and come up with something different. I don't really want to be considered a stereotypical Inuit artist in that sense. All I really want to do is express what I see. If it comes out as being Inuit, then I think that is fine; if it comes out as being contemporary, that is also fine. I think a lot of times I have a tendency to put the two of them together to see what happens.

Fox:

Do you sometimes get angry at what seems to be a system in which Inuit artists if they are not working in a certain type of stone, or drawing certain types of images, are not going to be shown in galleries?

Massie:

Yes. That really gets me. I had that experience in Goose Bay this year. I was talking with a gallery owner who said she didn't like to get any wood carvings from Inuit artists. I don't understand that. I don't understand how people can think that just because you are an Inuit artist, you have to carve in stone. I don't agree with that; it is too limiting to an artist. Beauty—like I tried to explain to my students—is not in the material itself, but in the work that is produced. What I find quite interesting is that Inuit pick up techniques and the function of tools instantly; it seems natural to them. They pick up things so quickly and so easily. It is very restrictive to an artist to do things only one way. I saw one carving student while I was working up north—he wasn't my student—and his work in sculpture class was okay, but when he was given a video camera, it was amazing the way he produced images on the screen. He was more comfortable with the video camera than he was with the carving tool. I have a problem with these restrictions, because once you start offering different things to different people, you are going to start finding that they might prefer to do painting over stone carving, or they might prefer to do textiles, cinematography, anything at all. When people are given the opportunity to experiment, that is what I appreciate.

Fox:

How do you think other Inuit artists break out of that stereotype? You seem to have done it quite successfully. Is there any specific advice you can give or any comment you can make on that?

In My Dream, We Were Together As One by Mike Massie.

Wise To Who From Within by Mike Massie.

Massie:

Well, trying different mediums is one. If you find it hard with one, try another. There is nothing wrong with that. Also, be true to yourself. Don't ever take offence when someone says they don't like it. Not everyone will like what you do, that is only natural. As long as you are true to yourself and if that is what you are comfortable with, go for it. I never did agree with the idea that you have to please others before you please yourself. I have always found that you have to please yourself, and while you are trying to please yourself you please others, especially in your work. If you are out there just to please others all the time, a lot of times what you want to do or what you really want to say gets lost. Never be afraid to experiment.

Fox:

Do you have any concerns or problems? Are there certain challenges that you are facing that you would like to overcome?

Massie:

Well, financially I am not doing the greatest. The biggest thing I would really like to have for myself and that I am trying to get by next summer is my own studio, where I can work in stone or metal, both in the same building. Right now, those seem to be my two strongest areas. The only other concern I've talked about with other carvers is the problem of Labrador artists getting any funding whatsoever to do anything in the arts. I would like to see some sort of facility in Labrador that would be well looked after by responsible people who are trying to meet the needs of the artists.

Fox:

What do you have planned and where do you want to take your art?

Massie:

I would like to incorporate silversmithing with stone carving somehow. I have been thinking about that now for the last couple of years, but so far I have only come up with a few simple ideas. I really want to put the two of them together. But until something comes to mind, I'm just looking at other art, Inuit art and contemporary art. And if there's something that catches my eye, what I will do is make a quick sketch of it and put it in my sketchbook. For now, I just want to work on a carving here and there. If I get a bit tired working in stone, I would like to be able to start working in metal again and be able to go back and forth, or work on them at the same time.

Fox:

Was your first experience with carving when you were at the workshop in Nain?

Massie:

Yes. I did sculpture at school here in Stephenville and over at the Nova Scotia College of Art and Design. But it [the Nain workshop] was my first experience with stone, and it was quite enjoyable. I was quite timid at first to try it, because I had seen the work that other people do and I didn't expect to be as good as them starting off. But you can't expect to be good for the first while. So I think working with the two materials together is what I want to do once I finish my teapots. I would like to stop working in silver for a while and work in stone. When I was working in Labrador, I was able to make a few soapstone carvings on my own and I enjoyed it. It's a different medium, and it's exciting.

Fox:

Is there anything that I haven't asked about that you want to bring up?

Massie:

I'd like to thank the Inuit Art Foundation for having those workshops, because that's basically where I got a kickstart. I would also like to thank the colleges I've worked with for giving me the opportunity, and for all the people I've met and the information they gave me. The opportunity to do interviews like this; to have that chance. Other than that, for artists who aren't quite sure what's out there, just contact a college or get hold of somebody in your community and see what you can find out. There is lots of schooling available for whatever kind of art you want to do. I know it's difficult to go to the South, I understand that, but it might help if there were a couple of people who went down together. It makes a big difference if someone you know is there. I know it's kind of intimidating at times, but that intimidation always goes away.

Fox:

Do you think that formal training has a lot of other things to offer without taking away from what artists have learned by themselves?

Massie:

I know that some places will have a tendency to kind of restrict you from doing what you normally do. One thing I've found is that if you go into class and your instructor wants you to try something different, you should just try it, because you never know what might come out of it. But there is no reason why you can't continue to do the same thing you would do if you weren't in the school. I think that the South has a lot to offer, and there are colleges in the North that have a lot to offer, like Arctic College. The idea is, I think, to experiment as much as you can while you can. It doesn't mean you have to follow the rules; you make your own rules, really. You can learn as much technique as you want, but the idea is to be able to come up with your own ideas and use your own rules, as long as you don't break them or abuse them. I think that the more information you get, the better off you are. Goose Bay is not a very big place, but I was fortunate that my parents took me to Montreal and larger cities when I was younger. The more experience, the better.

Middle Son
Patrick O'Flaherty

Jimmy Byrne had chums, but he knew from early childhood that his real friend, the one he could always look to for a helping hand, was his brother Colin. Although Colin was a year older, they were in the same grade at school, two behind Alphonsus. The eldest was headed for great things. For years money had been set aside for his education. He was to go to St. Bon's College in St. John's, then on to university in Canada to train as a lawyer. Their Aunt Aggie, a spinster nurse who visited Long Beach from time to time to keep an eye on her aged mother living with the Byrnes, offered to support this aim, which had been first defined when Alphonsus was ten or eleven. From then on, legal ambition was to be the centre of the family's life. A Long Beach Byrne a lawyer! That was something worth scrimping for. Well known to have plenty of brains, Alphonsus stuck to his books and led his class throughout his school years. Destiny awaited him.

Coming up behind, Jimmy and Colin weren't exactly neglected, though what was to be done with them hadn't been worked out. No money had been put aside for them, that was clear. There was only so much to go around. Paddy Byrne was a fisherman and times were hard. "Long Beach's day is over," he'd say when he dragged back from hauling trawls on the offshore banks; and his wife Molly, who came from what she regarded as a more respectable place up the shore, Northern Bay, agreed.

She encouraged Paddy to leave fishing altogether to go to work in the mines in New Waterford up in Nova Scotia. One of her sisters lived there and was doing well. "Anywhere at all will do," she said, "but for God's sake get me out of this hole." And he did try the mines, the docks in Halifax, a labourer's job on the new airport in Gander, and carpenter work in St. John's. But he always left his wife and children behind, and then, after getting a bit of money together, came back to fishing. "Back to misery," she'd say bitterly. He was a very good fisherman, as he had to be to feed a growing family in Long Beach. After Jimmy there was a gap of some years, but then came three daughters in quick succession. When his youngest sister, Janey, started walking, Jimmy saw his father smash the cradle to pieces over the cabbage-garden fence, an action which the passing of time would reveal to be premature.

With Alphonsus growing into his teens and starting to chase the girls, their father away from home or consumed with fishing and other toil, and their mother looking after babies, once they did their chores Jimmy and Colin were mostly left to themselves. They played together and competed with one another in and out of school. Though young for his grade, Jimmy was a whiz at Arithmetic and English, and often ended up ahead of Colin in the class. Tom Johnson, a trucker's son from Northern Bay, would come first, Jimmy second, Colin third or fourth. Jimmy was skinny, sickly, and had poor teeth. The teachers made a pet out of him, and he would get to give recitations at the school concerts or make presentations to visitors. One summer he was picked to present a scroll to Governor Macdonald, who was making his farewell tour of the island. "I know he's sorry to be leaving," Molly said. "No mistake about it."

Colin's talents were less apparent. He was good at drawing, science, and history, but "slow to middling" in other subjects, as one teacher wrote on his report card. And this was the prevailing view. Normally subdued and retiring, he was somewhat more robust than Jimmy and would take his brother's part in the fist fights that broke out in the school yard. What made him formidable in these encounters was less his strength, for he too was thin and pale, than his savage temper when roused. "He's a deep one," Jimmy heard one of the teachers remark of Colin who, when asked one day in class what Newfoundland's main industry was, answered "American bases." Everyone else in the room knew it was the fishery or pulp and paper. It had to be one or the other.

Another day the class was asked to write on "The happiest day of my life." All the pupils knew the day in question was the one they had received their First Holy Communion. All except Colin, who wrote on "The Day a Black Bear chased me in the Woods." Jimmy didn't know what to make of that, because he and Colin picked berries together and went trouting in the brooks and ponds all the time, and no bear had ever chased them. If Colin had seen one when he was wandering on his own, he would have mentioned it when he came home. But he hadn't. There were no bears, black or brown, in the Byrne family history. When Colin started reading out his composition, Jimmy turned around and stared at him. But he was smiling and chucking softly as he read it. Nobody said a word until the story of the bear was over. Then the teacher had a lot to say about the importance of telling the truth. Colin said nothing. "It was a hard topic to write on," he told Jimmy later. It was queer to hear his voice in class because he sat in the back and most of the time didn't answer questions. The few answers he gave were humdingers.

There was a chirping one day in class, and the teacher found a bird in Colin's pocket. When he was questioned, he said he found it in the grove behind the school during recess. "His wing is broke," he said, "and the cats'll eat him if I don't take him home." But the teacher was mad and made him take the bird back to the grove. The teacher was new to the school. He came from Lourdes, somewhere on the west coast of the island. He once pulled Colin's ear so hard he made it bleed. "Lourdes must be out in the civilized part of Newfoundland," Molly said when she saw what had happened.

One fine summer's day when he was eleven, Colin disappeared. He didn't go only for an hour or two, in the manner of most youngsters who duck their chores. It wasn't like him to err in a conventional way; an impulse towards the extreme was in his character. And so in the evening, when the family assembled for a supper of bologna and beans, they discovered that Colin was absent and hadn't been seen since early morning. His trouting pole was in its usual place in the cellar. A search was started. First they looked into the well, then the nearby groves, gullies, and swimming holes. There was no sign of him. No neighbour had seen him all day. "He's so quiet, I hardly take notice of him," one woman said. "One minute he's there, the next he's gone." And it was true that there was a shadowy quality about him that invited overlooking; yet the future would show he was real enough, blood and bone.

Long Beach was now in an uproar. Jimmy's sisters were scared and upset, because Colin was a favourite who watched over them tenderly, keeping them away from cliffs, horses, and other dangers. A big planning session with the neighbours was in progress around the kitchen table when the oldest girl, Elizabeth, went and looked behind the porch door that had been left open all day because of the heat, and there was Colin, standing where he had been for hours, grinning, silent. "Sweet hand of Jesus," Paddy Byrne said; but he didn't give him a licking or even send him to bed without his supper because of the fright everybody got. "That little Christer'll be the death of me yet," he added. For a few years the Byrnes turned the incident into a family joke. "You going out in the porch to spend the night?" someone would ask Colin around bedtime; or, if his looks came up for comment, as they sometimes did when the family realized how little interest he had in girls, somebody might say, "His nose was flattened out behind the porch door."

While Colin may never have been chased by a bear, he spent a lot of time, often by himself, in the woods and marshlands that stretched for miles to the north and west behind Long Beach. An expert berry picker, he knew where all the best spots were, far inland on the barrens. There was something in this wild, bleak, empty stretch of barren ground, Jimmy would say later when this came up for discussion, that touched a chord in Colin's spirit; the rocky paths, rough underfoot and overgrown with nettles and alders, offered a kind of freedom. By the time they reached high school, the two explorers had a collection of quartz crystals and other minerals. They would spend evenings scrambling over tolts and glacial debris in search of specimens, taking time out to enjoy foundering cliffs, pretending they were Frank and Joe Hardy. Colin also found an abandoned ochre pit under a cliff that called for investigation. A huge chunk of granite called Peg's Rock a mile inland on the ridge behind Long Beach was a favoured spot for playing. Not everyone could climb Peg's Rock because the handholds were so small. Colin and Jimmy would sometimes stand on it on sunny days and shout things in the direction of the salt water, a wide expanse across which could be seen the blue shape of Cape St. Francis. Behind the cape, they knew, lay St. John's. "I'm getting out of that hole," Colin yelled one day from the rock as he looked towards Long Beach. "I'm going to study geology." He later quietly announced this intention at the kitchen table, where it was not encouraged. "To go to work in a bank would be nice," said their mother. Jimmy knew Colin hated adding up figures and was no good at writing things out. He couldn't even do his ovals right when he started school, and learning the McLean Method had little beneficial effect on his crabbed handwriting.

In grade nine, Tom Johnson again came first, Jimmy second, and Colin third, continuing what was now an established pattern. This was a year of growing seriousness in the school. Although the Gull Islanders, a tough crowd from the next outport down the shore, went on debating whether Hank Snow or Wilf Carter was the better singer, the pupils from Northern Bay were considering what they were going to be when they grew up. Tom Johnson decided he was cut out to be an engineer. "No sooner said than done," Molly said. "John and Mag Johnson got the cash. You can make piles of money if you own a truck." The Johnsons didn't just own a truck. They had a car too, and drove down to Long Beach to go to mass on Sunday mornings, picking up a couple of people extra along the way if it was raining. Jimmy and Colin would watch them park by the paling fence in front of the church and then stroll up to the front steps. Someone said the fence had been "painted brown to match the mud."

In grade nine, Tom Johnson also won the five dollar prize in a school essay contest on "How to make Improvements on the North Shore." The parish priest suggested the subject; he wanted to make sure his part of Conception Bay benefitted from the coming of Confederation. "If you come up with good ideas, I'll get the money to start them," he said over the altar. The priest had good contacts with the member for the district, and with the Crosbies and Pippys in St. John's. The winning entry was on "The Importance of Henneries." Jimmy entered the contest too, writing, at his mother's suggestion, on "Carrying Freight to St. John's and Other Places." His essay didn't place in the top three; nor did Colin's on "Minerals in this Area," in which he enlarged on the advantages offered by iron ore, ochre, and peat moss. Their father read the two essays when the contest was over and said it was fine and dandy to talk of carrying freight to St. John's, but what kind of freight was it going to be? The fishery was just about dead, and you didn't need many trucks for the few poor miserable berries in the fall. As for Colin's idea, he said he didn't think peat moss was a mineral. "There's nothing worth talking about underground here," he added.

In the summer after grade nine, their mother had a bad spell, and for a few weeks a woman from Gull Island came to look after the Byrne children. By September, Molly was back on her feet in time to get Alphonsus ready to go to St. Bon's, where he was to be a boarding student for a year before going off to university on the mainland. His letters home were eagerly awaited by the whole family. Jimmy and Colin got to know the names of all the students in his class and became devoted fans of the St. Bon's hockey and basketball teams. St. Bon's dominated the family discussions. When Alphonsus came back at Christmas—a grim one in which Colin got a pen and Jimmy a geometry set—he looked grown up in his blazer, blue and gold tie, and white shirt.

Their mother decided that it was to be a big year for the younger boys too. "This is the key grade, grade ten," she said. "If you do well in that, grade eleven is easy." She made a rule that Jimmy and Colin were to study at the kitchen table every weeknight for two hours, a severe discipline which they alleviated by hiding *Kidnapped* and *Lost Endeavour* inside their big geography books. She also decided that this was the year to send out application forms. "It's about time we won something in this house," she said. She herself made application only to the Sodality of the Little Flower, but Jimmy and Colin applied for Imperial Oil scholarships even though preference was given to "children of employees of Imperial Oil," and for Canadian Legion bursaries though they weren't "children or dependents of a war veteran." Molly said: "What odds? Apply anyway. They may have a bit of money left over when they get finished with their own." A form wasn't needed for the really big scholarship, the electoral, but nobody on the whole shore had ever won one of those, as far as they knew. In the meantime, at school Tom Johnson maintained his prominence, so quick was he at the two Math subjects and General Science. Jimmy and most of the other pupils were having trouble with Algebra.

Before the year ended, Jimmy came down with scarlet fever and mumps, complicated by toothache, and had to spend two weeks in bed. During exam week he had headaches and vomiting, and in the last test, Algebra, which some students finished in less than an hour, he got two problems wrong, found his mistakes with ten minutes left, and had to keep writing up to the last minute to correct them. He blotted his exam book in two places as he finished, making the blots worse by trying to rub them out. He said little to his mother when he got home.

The summer passed in gloom and anxiety. A province-wide polio scare kept all the Byrne family close to home, except Alphonsus, who had joined the army cadets in St. Bon's and was off at camp in Nova Scotia. His letters explained how hard the military life was, but he left no doubt where he preferred to be. Everybody missed him. The fishery was poor again. In August they could see that blueberries were going to be scarce, a serious matter since that was where the money came from for school books. Nevertheless, Jimmy and Colin tackled the berries as soon as the season opened, going far into the barrens with their wooden boxes strapped to their backs and returning late in the afternoon, their shoulders stiff and sore from the long haul. In late August, after a grueling, hot day, they came over the ridge near Peg's Rock with their heavy boxes and sat on the rock to take a spell. As usual, Colin had picked eight gallons, Jimmy about four and a half. Colin lingered on top of the rock, yelling and singing, watching birds circle far overhead. It was a good feeling to be almost home when your box was full.

As they headed down the hill, they spotted their sisters coming up the path towards them. What was this about? Did someone in Long Beach have polio? Had Aunt Aggie turned up? Was the baby sick? The girls were running hard. Halfway down the path, Jimmy looked over his shoulder to see if someone else, their grandmother maybe, somebody worth all the running, was coming behind them. But there wasn't. At last Elizabeth and the second oldest, Lucy, reached the two tired pickers, with Janey trailing well behind. It took a few seconds for them to catch their breath. "Scholarship!" Lucy shouted at last, "Jimmy got the electoral scholarship!" "A hundred dollars!" gasped Elizabeth. Janey now entered the picture and clung to his leg in her happiness. All three danced around him as he made the hero's walk home. "You got ninety-nine in Algebra," Lucy said.

The next day Colin didn't go in the woods and, in fact, was nowhere to be seen when Jimmy left early in the morning. When he got back, well past suppertime and with only three gallons, Colin picked a fight with him for no reason, and threatened to hit him with the hammer. Their mother and father had dressed up to the nines and gone up the shore visiting, Lucy told him, so Jimmy had to fight back. After taking a couple of hard knocks, he pinned Colin to the ground and held his arms down in the grass. This astonished him. Colin wasn't strong at all! He could be whipped. "Say uncle," Jimmy said, demanding the usual formula of surrender. No word or nod came back. This called for harder action. Jimmy drove Colin's right hand down into the grass and knelt on it in preparation for the Second Deadly Punishment, hair pulling. Colin was crying, but didn't scream when he did this, even though a piece of broken glass, unseen by Jimmy, lay hidden in the grass under his hand and cut deep into the flesh and tendons. Jimmy felt it in his knee and got up right away. As he moved, Colin struck him hard with the wounded hand, driving blood that would not easily come off all over his face and hair. "I don't care," Colin said, looking at the cut. And then, in a dreadful premonition of what would be, "I don't care if I live or die."

The Old *Royal Readers*

A. C. Hunter

> No stir in the air, no stir in the sea,
> The ship was still as she could be;
> Her sails from heaven received no motion,
> Her keel was steady in the ocean.

You all, or nearly all, know the rest of that poem, "The Inchcape Rock," familiar in your mouth as household words. You know too that in later years a lighthouse was built on the Inchcape Rock to fulfill the good abbot's purpose. But how many of you know that that lighthouse—at any rate the chief part of it—is in Newfoundland, and has been for a long time? It is at Bonavista, whither it was brought many years ago, how many I have forgotten, though we were told by the friendly lightkeeper under whose guidance we visited the place. Proud he was of his light, and well he might be, for all these years its half-dozen tiny lamps have faithfully flashed their message of warning over the ocean.

One evening not long after my visit to Bonavista I mentioned the foregoing bit of history to two friends, but though they were good Newfoundlanders—none better—their minds weren't on Bonavista; they were on Southey's poem. "Sir Ralph the Rover walked his deck," recited one: capped by the other with "Sir Ralph the Rover tore his hair," and I contributed "Down sank the bell with a gurgling sound"; and finally, in a kind of chorus, we recited the whole poem from beginning to end.

I learned that poem from the *Royal Reader*, said I—So did we! they answered gleefully. Book IV, along with "The Wreck of the Hesperus" and "The Loss of the *Royal George*:" "Toll for the Brave, the Brave that are no more!" whereupon we recited that one. And so on to "Lucy Gray" and "We are Seven" and the destruction of Sennacherib's army. We shed a tear over Little Jim in Book III—You know:

> The cottage door was opened,
> The collier's step was heard,
> The mother and the father met,
> Yet neither spoke a word!
> He knew that all was over
> He knew his child was dead,
> He took the candle in his hand
> And walked towards the bed.

Trite and old-fashioned; no doubt; but I am sorry for you if it leaves you unmoved.

So having mourned for Little Jim in Book III we laughed over John Gilpin in Book IV and rode with Young Lochlovar in Book V. Of course we recalled other parts of the books, the fables, the accounts of the entombed coal miners, the "Relief of Londonderry" and the "Death of Little Nell," and reminded each other of this or that favorite picture—Androcles' lion having the thorn removed from his paw; the elephant punishing the mean tailor with a muddy shower-bath, the death of General Wolfe; but always it was the verses we came back to. I soon became a listener only—my friends remembered so much more than I did. They were more fortunate than me. They had had the whole series as class books at school; it had been superseded as out of date in my school—out of date—sixty years ago!—and I knew it as an exciting find in a treasure chest of old books. But to all of us alike those *Royal Readers* were a treasure, over which we spent a delightful and exciting evening; a valued possession held in common by the man from the Newfoundland outport and the man from Yorkshire. There must be vast numbers of men and women, not in Newfoundland and Britain only but throughout the English-speaking world, who share and treasure this possession with us. I cannot help wondering whether the present-day school book thus captures the heart and imagination of children, entering into the enduring stuff and substance of the mind, constituting a common heritage and bond of union. It may be so, but I have yet to hear of it and I meet many young people.

It is nearly ninety years since the *Royal Readers* first appeared in print. That takes us back to 1870, the date of the great British Education Act which established universal elementary education, and we may fairly assume that the series was devised for the multitude of children brought to school by that Act. How completely out of date! You may imagine my surprise and delight therefore when quite recently, gossiping with a bookseller, I discovered that they are still in print. "Come with me," he said; and taking me over to the shelves he laid them before me, one after the other, from the little primer to Book VI. No, they were not old stock, surviving from a distant past, but brand new, though re-set and bound for cheapness' sake in limp covers. "Do you actually sell them?" I asked—"Yes indeed" was the answer. "We supply them to purchasers abroad and sell them to parents here in Newfoundland whose children are not learning to read."

Does the last remark startle you, give you a jolt, as they say vulgarly? Or, if like me you have reached what the French call a certain age, does it merely tend to confirm your impressions? Can it be that the mid-Victorians, before the art of teaching had been reduced to a science and the composition of textbooks entrusted to pedagogical experts, can it be that the mid-Victorians succeeded better than we are doing in teaching children to read and to love literature?

The six numbers of the *Royal Readers* are beside me as I compose this talk. To look at they are unattractive, at any rate unimposing, in comparison with the handsome elaborately got-up and expensive volumes of the twentieth century. When I re-opened them my first feeling was the joy of recognition. There was the *Royal George* keeling over, exactly as I remembered it; and there on the bridge was the foolish dog just about to snatch at the shadow bone and lose the real one. I went on to glance through the text, picking out the old favorites to linger and gloat over.

As I said earlier the type has been reset, but the publisher has made absolutely no concession to the passage of time. The little girl feeding the swan in Book II still wears the costume of the 1870's, her frilly laced drawers showing well below her voluminous skirt and above her neat little boots. I found a reference to photography, but there are, of course, no motor-cars, let alone airplanes, not even a bicycle; no telephones, no typewriters, no electric lights; the American Civil War is fresh in people's minds, the Suez canal has just been opened. Even the reference to doing certain exercises on slates is still there.

An anachronism: obviously, and although a curiously large number of us Victorians seem to have survived the use of slates we don't wish back again either those scratchy unwholesome things themselves or the era which they symbolize; but there are some striking things we in 1957 may well take note of. One is that in only five years from learning their letters those girls in frilly drawers who went with their brothers to school carrying slates, were expected to read, understand and appreciate the prose of Napier, the historian of the Peninsula war, of Southey, Motely, Dean Stanley, Addison, and Macaulay; the rhetoric of Burke, John Bright, and Gladstone. Listen to the following extract from Book V, and then say whether it is so anachronistic after all.

> … it became my duty, with undisguised truth to lay before the Parliament of Hungary the immense danger of our bleeding fatherland. Having made the sketch, (which, however dreadful, could be but a faint shadow of the horrible reality), I proceeded to explain the alternative which our terrible destiny left to us, after the failure of all our attempts to avert the evil: to present the neck of the realm to the stroke aimed at its very life, or to bear up against the horrors of fate and manfully to fight the battle of legitimate defence. Scarcely had I spoken the words, when the spirit of freedom moved through the hall; nearly four hundred representatives rose as one man, and lifting their right arms towards Heaven, solemnly said, We grant it—freedom or death!
>
> Pardon me my emotion—the shadows of our martyrs pass before my eyes; I hear the millions of my native land once more shouting, 'Freedom or death!' As I was then, sirs, so am I now. I would thank you, gentlemen, for the generous sympathy with which, in my undeserving person, you have honoured the bleeding, the oppressed, but not broken, Hungary. I would thank you for the ray of hope which the sympathy of the English people casts on the night of our fate. I would thank you, gentlemen, warmly as I feel, and as becomes the dignity of your glorious land. But the words fail me: they fail me, not only from want of knowledge of your language, but chiefly because my sentiments are deep, and fervent, and true. The tongue of man is powerful enough to render the ideas which the human intellect conceives; but in the realm of true and deep sentiments, it is but a weak interpreter. These are inexpressible, like the endless glory of the Omnipotent.

And the poets are there, naturally: Shakespeare, Scott, Coleridge, Tennyson, Browning, Byron, Shelley.

The literary range is indeed remarkably wide and the standard high but the scope is in point of fact much wider than is suggested even by the literature. The compilers evidently believed that what you read is even more important than learning how; that the content of a book, the moral doctrine it inculcates, the factual information which it imparts, is as important as the qualities of style. So there are generous rations of history, geography, elementary natural science under the titles of useful knowledge and great inventions; in fact everything except mathematics and religious dogma. The gospel of expressing yourself in your own words not having yet been preached there is systematic provision for growth in the command of language, correct stressing and syllabication, synonyms and homonyms, Greek, Latin and English roots, prefixes and suffixes, matters in which the university freshman of today is lamentably deficient.

The point is that the children were expected to learn a great deal: the standard of expectation, as I call it, was high. "Ask and ye shall receive" is true in more spheres than one. Ask little from school children and you will receive little: ask much and you will receive much.

A further thought is that in our anxiety to be up-to-date, to keep up with the most modern doctrines, we may exaggerate the contemporary and local, which is fleeting, at the cost of what is universal and enduring. The fundamental things which education supplies, or ought to, are timeless, and we neglect them at our peril. One reason for the decline in education which is almost universally complained of in the western world, may very well be that these timeless things, whose operations are hard to see because they are deep-rooted, have been neglected in favour of the expediencies which show immediate results. Yet it is the enduring things that make their mark with children. That is why the little ones love the ancient fables, and the parables of the New Testament, and "We Are Seven" and "The Dog at his Master's Grave"; and the reason why to thousands of Newfoundlanders who were fortunate enough to be brought up on them, the *Royal Readers* remain a classic.

Inglewood's Childhood Beach
S. R. (Bert) Cooper

Down by the landwash
Down by the beach
Sun bleached mussel shells
There a dried up leech.

    Bronzy is the bottle kelp
    White a cockle shell
    Just above the high water mark
    Growing, a blue bell.

        Pinky little crab shells
        Painted by the sun,
        In a salty puddle
        Sea lice having fun.

            Teeny weeny wrinkle shells
            Showing pearly sheen
            "Osie eggs" with stabbers gone
            Bleached to palest green.

                Years have had their way with me
                How like that dried up leech!
                But there's hunger in my heart
                For my childhood beach.

Little Orly

Bryan Hennessey

Anthony Fleming ate a loaf of toast for breakfast.

Well, Good Lord, there had to be *something* to make up for the ordeal of getting out of bed at 8 o'clock every bloody morning and going to school, right? If he absolutely *had* to get up every day of the bloody week to face hours of boredom and fear in the classroom, then at least he was entitled to a hearty breakfast, wasn't he?

Even the condemned got that. Anthony felt it wasn't so much to ask.

He chewed the last slice with care, making it last as long as possible. He wished, as always, that it was really Saturday, that he was still safe in bed, the blankets tucked around him like a shrine, snug in the womby warmth of his dreampillowed bed. He wished that there was no school today (or ever again!), that he could stay curled up like one of those little white grubs he'd found under the fallen tree in the back yard, curled into himself, safe and asleep and dreaming.

But it was Thursday, a school day.

As he licked the last buttery crumbs from the corners of his mouth, Anthony wished that he could get sick and have to stay home: a sudden flu, perhaps, or a toothache, or leprosy, like Ben-Hur's mother and sister (he knew Jesus would cure him because he was Catholic). The best time he'd had since he started school was the term he'd missed when he had hepatitis (which he called the yellow jaunders). He had been kept out of school for three months and, apart from feeling like he wanted to vomit most of the time, he'd had a ball.

He lay on the couch in the living room all day, watching TV shows like *The Friendly Giant* and *Maggie Muggins* and *Chez Hélène* (which wasn't so great, being in French and really boring) and *Razzle Dazzle* with crazy Al Hamel and Howard the Turtle and Michelle Finney (she was some cute, but he knew she was beyond his reach).

But that was two years ago and now he was in Grade Six and it was just as dull as Grade Five and Grade Four and the others: day after day of memorizing a lot of information that didn't seem to have much to do with learning. It seemed to him that most of what he wanted to learn wasn't being taught in his school. Maybe somewhere in the world there was a school that let you learn about things you were interested in, but it sure wasn't in St John's.

Most of what he was being taught didn't even make sense to him. Math was like some foreign language; it made even Latin look easy by comparison. English was okay because he spoke English, for God's sake. History and Geography were useless. The way they were taught was so stupid and boring, all lists of dates and names, facts and figures that just gave him a headache when he tried to sort them out.

It was bloody frustrating. What was the point of it all?

He left the kitchen table and went to the bathroom to brush his teeth.

"Eight-thirty!" his mother's voice called after him. Just enough time to catch today's episode of *Little Orly* before he had to go. Little Orly was a worm with a daily

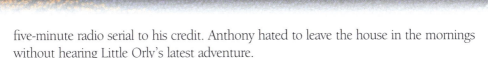

five-minute radio serial to his credit. Anthony hated to leave the house in the mornings without hearing Little Orly's latest adventure.

Today Orly was at the mercy of a remorseless robin determined to have him for breakfast.

"Wouldn't you rather have some toast?" Orly asked hopefully.

"Don't change the subject," the robin replied.

Anthony knew that worms and robins didn't talk to each other, but he still enjoyed Orly's verbal jousts with his slower-witted adversaries. Little Orly could talk his way out of any problem.

This time he convinced the robin that he wouldn't make much of a meal, being so little and puny, but if the robin would carry him over by that tree and set him down, he'd find him a *real* treat, he promised, a worm's word on it. The greedy robin fell for it (sucker!) and of course as soon as Orly was on the ground he burrowed deep into a hole and yelled wormy insults at the stupid bird.

Anthony threw on his windbreaker and, grabbing his bookbag, left the house by the back door. His mother's cheery farewell went unheard. Anthony's mind was already at work, trying to solve the dilemma that plagued him today as it had every day for the last month: would Gosling beat him up again this morning?

For weeks now, since school had started, not a morning passed that Gosling didn't corner him alone in the cloakroom before the first period and shove him around. It was always the same: Anthony would peek into the cloakroom and, if there was no sign of Gosling, he'd hurry in and hang up his jacket, only to turn and find himself face to face with the smirking bully.

Gosling would push him and shove him until the bell rang and they'd both have to race for their desks before Brother Quinlan came in for Math class. Even if Anthony waited until the last possible minute before class to hang up his coat, Gosling would somehow manage to be right behind him and pound him a few times.

Anthony could avoid him for the rest of the day in the safely crowded classroom, but there was always that awful moment of being trapped in the dark cloakroom with Gosling first thing in the morning.

At first Anthony tried to talk his way out of it, but Gosling was unmoved by verbal appeals and only punched harder. As the attacks became routine, Anthony tried dodging and squirming away, but Gosling was bigger than him and was easily able to keep him penned in. Finally Anthony, who was no fighter, was reduced to enduring the assault in stoic silence until the nine o'clock bell rang and saved him from further humiliation.

The mad part of it was that he didn't even *know* Gosling. He'd had mostly the same classmates since Grade One, but Gosling was a new boy, moved up a grade from Five-B to Six-A. Anthony guessed it probably wasn't easy for him to adjust to a class full of strangers, but why did Gosling have to take it out on him?

Anthony desperately wanted someone to help him deal with his tormentor, but he was too embarrassed to ask anyone. He didn't have any close friends among his classmates, not the kind of friends he could ask for the help he needed. He couldn't ask one of the Brothers to intervene without attracting unwelcome attention to himself.

It was best to keep out of the Brothers' way if at all possible. Nor could he go to his parents. They would only go in turn to the Brothers and Anthony would suffer the added mortification of having his Mom and Dad intercede for him in a school matter, something to be avoided at all costs.

Plainly he would have to figure this one out on his own. But there was nothing he could do!

Once, Derm Fardy from across the street made him stop playing with a bunch of the neighbourhood kids, sneering through his thick glasses: "We don't want you! Go home out of it!"

Anthony said nothing and went home. Derm didn't speak for all the kids, of course. He was just being a snot, and Anthony was playing with them again the next day as if nothing had happened.

Maybe this thing with Gosling would also wear itself out finally, but Good Lord! It was driving him cracked in the meantime.

So, what was he to do?

On the long climb up Newtown Road, Anthony passed by Belvedere Cemetery. The graves and paths were all overgrown with weeds and wild creepy bushes. There were always a lot of tombstones split or knocked over. Anthony's grandparents were buried there, somewhere among the weeds and broken headstones.

Did the worms really eat you when you were buried? How did they get inside the coffin? Anthony couldn't imagine Little Orly, for instance, feasting on decaying flesh; but then, Little Orly was only a pretend worm who cracked jokes and solved his problems with ease.

A large white statue of Jesus on the cross stood over one grave near the fence. Anthony wondered if Jesus was eaten by worms when He died. Probably not, because He was God and He rose again before the worms could get into His coffin.

Anthony had asked Jesus many times to make Gosling leave him alone, but either Jesus didn't hear him or else He wanted Anthony to suffer as He had suffered.

But I'm only twelve, Anthony thought. When Jesus was twelve He got lost in the temple but Anthony bet He didn't get the shit kicked out of Him while He was there. How could Jesus understand Anthony's problem? He'd had it good when *He* was twelve. And if Jesus couldn't or wouldn't help him, what was he supposed to do?

Was he condemned to spend the rest of the school year being beaten up by a big lout every morning? And if Gosling made it into his class next year, would it go on all through Grade Seven? What about the year after that? How long would this go on? Until Gosling got tired of it? Until they were both dead and worms ate them?

A grey autumn rain began to fall as Anthony passed by MacPherson Academy. The Protestants went to school there. Protestants were all right but they were doomed to live outside the Church so there was no point getting too friendly with them because you'd only have to turn your back on them forever at the Last Judgement.

There were boys and girls together at MacPherson. Were they in the same classrooms? He couldn't imagine what that would be like. Maybe if there were girls in his school, in his class, Gosling might be too distracted to bother him. Or maybe then some tough girl would start picking on him and he'd be worse off than he was now!

He turned down Merrymeeting Road and entered the grounds of St. Pat's under rows of dripping maple trees, part of a steady stream of boys of various sizes and ages. He kicked his way through piles of wet fallen leaves and remembered, as always, the cold winter morning in Grade One when a couple of big goons from Grade Nine tripped him and sent him sprawling on the icy driveway, then went on their way laughing like idiots. His attitude towards school changed instantly.

Until then he'd been indifferent but curious (he hadn't even cried on his first day like so many kids did). Afterwards he hated every minute of it, hated his schoolmates, his teachers, the lying school song ("Scholars, Saints and Gentlemen", indeed!), the whole bloody works. He would rather have stayed home.

Yet here he was, five years later, still in school, still hating it, still being victimized. What was the bloody point of it all?

He went down eight concrete steps to the school's basement level. The floor was wet and dirty from the tracking of hundreds of muddy shoes and rubbers. The walls were painted a drab swampy green and pissy yellow, a bargain basement parody of the school colours. Anthony hurried through the long dreary corridors and up the stairs to the main floor. Its dark polished hardwood groaned and rattled from the pressure of many leather-soled shoes.

He entered his classroom with caution. No sign of Gosling anywhere. A few boys were draped across their desks already. Tommy Hynes and Dick Nugent stood at the tall windows overlooking the basketball court that would double in winter as an outdoor hockey rink. Anthony glanced at Gosling's desk, five seats behind and two rows away from his own. No books or pencils were in evidence. So far, so good.

He peered into the dim cloakroom. It was empty except for a few coats hanging gloomily on hooks, and a couple of pairs of wet rubbers spreading small pools of water on the floor.

Anthony hung his damp windbreaker and bookbag from a protruding hook and went to the cloakroom's only window. A motley crowd of boys loitered in the courtyard, skylarking roughly with one another, pushing and shoving and shouting in their high boys' voices:

"Go on out of it, ye big gom!"

"I''ll smack the face off ye."

"Go 'way, Jackman, my son, you're full of beans."

From the direction of the gate a solitary figure entered the schoolyard, swinging his bookbag with casual insolence. Was it Gosling? Anthony couldn't make out his face, he was too far away, though it sure looked like him, the big ape. Maybe, just maybe…

I can get to my desk before he's even in the building.

The floorboards squeaked alarmingly behind him. Anthony turned around, his heart leaping, his mouth dry. Oh Good Lord, not again!

It was Gosling.

He was taller than Anthony, and heavier. The pupil of his left eye was dead white, in weird contrast to the black pupil of his right eye and the pale blue iris of each. His blond hair was cut to a brutal stubble and seemed about to jump off his head.

Catholic ears stuck out from his close-cropped skull. A long narrow nose balanced above a thin, pursed mouth.

With a rattle of phlegm, Gosling cleared his throat.

"Listen," he said. "I'm having a party tomorrow."

Anthony waited in expectant silence

"At my house. After school," he added. "Everyone's invited. You don't have to bring anything."

He seemed to be expecting an answer.

"Okay," Anthony said.

He hesitated. Then, encouraged by Goslings unthreatening demeanour, he asked, "Do you ever listen to *Little Orly*?"

The nine o'clock bell rang, changing the subject forever.

Gosling shoved him against the wall and ran out of the room with a foolish high-pitched laugh.

Anthony went to the party the next day and didn't have too bad a time. There were even some girls there. He asked a few of them if they ever listened to *Little Orly*, but they didn't seem to know what he was talking about and just made ick! faces when he told them Little Orly was a worm.

Gosling never beat him up again after the party. In fact, he became a little too friendly and Anthony eventually began to avoid him for reasons directly opposite to those he'd avoided him for in the first place.

Little Orly once said at the end of his show:

"Sometimes you just can't win."

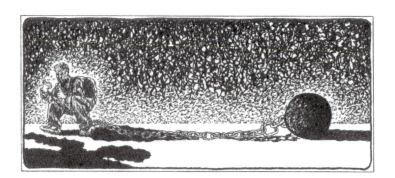

Excerpt from
Up Off Our Knees
Chris O'Neill-Yates

Chris O'Neill-Yates went to Grand Terre (Mainland) on the Port-au-Port Peninsula to produce this documentary. There, she spoke with students at École Ste. Anne and to adults in the area who recalled being a student prior to the 1970s, when a revitalization of French culture occurred on the Port-au-Port Peninsula and the first francophone association, **Les Terre-Neuviens Français***, was formed.*

Chris O'Neill-Yates, interviewer
Mary Felix, L'Anse-à-Canard resident
Joe Benoit, École Ste. Anne principal
Michael White, École Ste. Anne student

Chris O'Neill-Yates:

Mary Felix is busy at the kitchen stove. Her kitchen is a place that's as warm as she is. Mary raised a family of eight children in this house. Now, at 74, it's just Mary and her husband and the youngest son at home. Mary has always lived in Black Duck Brook– L'Anse-à-Canard in French. She remembers when children at school were punished for being French and not knowing English.

Mary Felix:

We weren't allowed to speak French; we couldn't speak English. We couldn't speak English; none of us could. There was only a family or two down here that could speak English. And when we went to school, well it was hard for us to be able to learn to read in English. But Mom could talk English a bit; like she could read English. If we had to learn our lesson, well then she could tell us the words. That helped us a bit now. So it was really hard. You know some were punished. I was punished myself. I wasn't beaten or anything like that, but I was put on my knees for half an hour because I couldn't say the words that I needed to say.

O'Neill-Yates:

And Mary remembers how she felt as a young French girl among people who spoke English.

Felix:

If you were French, if you were taught to speak French, you didn't know too much how to speak English or whatever, you were not included with them. Like you weren't as much as they were, you know. It made you feel that way. It was sad. But we made it anyway.

O'Neill-Yates:

Did it hurt?

Felix:

Oh yes, oh yes, it hurt. Of course.

O'Neill-Yates:

Joe Benoit says that the challenge is in getting across to…children that French is a language of everyday life, not just a school language.

Joe Benoit:

I just can't say that from nine to three I'm francophone, therefore I must speak French. And then outside of this, because I'm living in Newfoundland, I must speak all English. No. It depends on my situation and what I'm involved in. Where I have to speak English, I speak English out of respect for the other person. Where it's francophone, I speak French *out of total respect for me.* And that's what I want the children to understand.

[sound of accordion music]

O'Neill-Yates:

The struggle to preserve French culture on the Port-au-Port is not just about language. The culture here has survived in the music and the storytelling. Michael and his classmates have all been raised on mystical stories and the sounds of fiddles and accordions.

Michael White:

Yeah, there's a lot of music. Like I got my Uncle Emile, he played the fiddle. And Uncle Bernard, he plays the accordion. Almost everybody in my family sings and plays music….

O'Neill-Yates:

That culture was preserved under the glaring eye of the Catholic Church by Mary Felix's generation.

Felix:

We'd have dances, dances in the houses. Oh yes, on the Saturday night. I remember those nights. Well, I've seen some houses where the kitchen was not too big, [they] put the stove outdoors, take out the pipes and everything, put it all outdoors, and have our dance. And afterwards all the men bring back the stove, put it back in place, no problem.

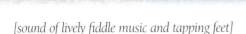

[sound of lively fiddle music and tapping feet]

White [singing]:

Il était un petit homme / Pirouette, cacahuète / Il était un petit homme / Qui avait une drôle de maison / Qui avait une drôle de maison.

Chris O'Neill-Yates:

Michael White is practicing for an upcoming concert. Michael just loves to perform. Joe Benoit wants these children to understand that French is something to be proud of, both in private and in public.

Benoit:

Even ten years ago, if we went into Stephenville, as soon as we walked into the stores we would start to speak English because we didn't want to be ridiculed. Today, no matter where we go, we will still speak our French language. I will never address my kids—no matter where it is and in front of who—I will never address my children in English. Never. I will not address another francophone in English. Not out of disrespect for anybody else, but *out of respect for us*, and that's different.

Branch by Lois Saunders.

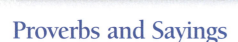

Proverbs and Sayings

P. K. Devine

[Devine's capitalization, punctuation, and sentence structure have been reproduced as in the original. Eds.]

"Either a feast or a famine" describes very well the vicissitudes of domestic life in Newfoundland. In the Autumn or Fall of the year when the season's catch of fish was sold and sent to Spain, Portugal and the West Indies, the vessels brought back wines and fruit in abundance and the people having laid in a Winter's supply of food were able to indulge in these "luxuries" also. The famine time was in March and April, extending into May if the drift ice bottled up the harbors. Another version of this proverb was: "A short feast and a long famine."

"The least said the soonest mended" was a good variant of "silence is golden."

"You can't take out of a bag what you didn't put into it."

"Sugar wouldn't melt in his mouth," said on account of the innocence, modesty and harmlessness of one reputed to possess those qualities who suddenly did something outrageous to public opinion. "I thought all along that sugar would not melt in his mouth."

"Nofty lost the pork. Nofty was forty when he lost the pork." This is a parallel proverb to "There's many a slip between the cup and lip." Nofty was a great card player at 45's and was sure of the pork.

"It is hard to tell the mind of a gull." The man in a "gaze" waiting to get a shot evidently originated this. Mr. Gull is certainly coming to its doom. The gun is raised, suddenly it takes a "wee-gee" and is off in another direction. The gun is laid down and then the gunner looks up into the sky and the gull is back again, before the trigger is pulled the bird has taken another "wee-gee."

"There's a slippery stone at a gentleman's door." In this is a reminder how difficult it is to keep in friendship with a great man and that as you have to mind your P's and Q's all the time it is better to keep clear of him.

"Not worth the candle." In the proverb last mentioned the Newfoundlander would say "The game is not worth the candle."

"Sits in one end of the Tilt and burns the other." Comment on foolish extravagances.

"Three shakes of a lamb's tail." When a man wished to tell you how speedily he would do something, he'd say, "I'll do it in three shakes of a lamb's tail."

"Out dogs and in dieters." Slogan for the first of May to get ready for fishing preparations. The dogs were useful all the Winter in hauling firewood and roomstuff and were well and regularly fed at the cookroom. Now they must go at large and forage for themselves while the Summer crews of fishermen are shipped on for the voyage and their meals supplied at the cookroom.

"A whistling woman and a crowing hen,
Is neither good for God nor men."

"When I see my own time." Asked to do a certain work a person was able to display an enviable spirit of independence when this was said.

"Praise the bridge after you have walked over it."

"Wish I had his head." Said of the schoolmaster or any other scholar in admiration of his learning.

"I'm in a hobble about you." Said with sarcastic defiance of one who tries by threat to intimidate another.

"From anchor to anchor." A good man "from anchor to anchor" was one who did his part well the whole time of the voyage.

"Cape St. Mary's will pay for all." A saying of the large number of fishermen who frequented this favourite fishing ground, including men from Conception Bay, eighty to one hundred years ago.

"A good merchant is better than a godfather."

"Always look into your flour barrel in April."

"You can get only one shot at a Shell bird." Meaning that if a Shell duck escapes your first attempt you will never see it more. Fishermen who have been stung by a merchant, and whose dealings are invited again, I have heard them say this.

"The dirt of a squid can be washed off, but the dirt of a tongue sticks and stays." Anyone who ever jigged squid will understand the wit and wisdom of this proverb.

"The sight of you is good for sore eyes." A salute to a friend one has not met for a long time.

"The fish is in eating the rocks." A saying uttered for a lazy man by his own people who want to rebuke him for his inactivity; also to pass on to the merchant who may be hesitating in issuing supplies on credit.

If the fishermen's thoughts could be expressed to the world in printer's ink the new flood of poetry would astonish mankind with its transcendental power. The idioms and obsolete words that they use still, and which were "current coin" in Chaucer's day, would grace their pages with pleasing, if startling, surprise to the reader and would by the sheer merit of their expressiveness force their way back into the English language.

Big Davey's Maxims
P. Florence Miller

Big Dave, he knows such a lot o' things
    An' tells me them ef I be's good,
Down in his stage, er by his door
    Where he's choppin' turkum timy wood.
Big Dave, he says ef you eat yer crusts
    You'll grow to be a great big man
As tall—as tall as a house is, mos'!
    So I'm eatin' all the crusts I can.

An' Big Dave says ef you screw yer face
    An' make it a shockin' sight to see,
May be, sometime the wind'll change
    An' tha's the way it'll always be!
An' Big Dave says ef you touch a bird
    Tha's new in the nest, all bill an' craw,
The mother-bird when she flies back home
    May hang it up to a bough with straw!

I whizzed a stone at a wizzel wunst,
    An' Big Dave saw me from his boat—
"Son, never do that no more," he said.
    "Er the wizzel may come an' cut yer throat.
I knows a feller as hurt one, too.
    An', though he was tucked up safe in bed,
That wizzel gnawed clear through the wall,
    An' only his grampa sove his head."

An' Big Dave says never lie an' kick
    In a rage, sometime, on yer kitchen-floor,
Cos ef somebody steps over you,
    Why, then you never'll grow no more!
There's a whole lot more that is wonderful
    That I jes' loves to be listenin' to;
Cos Big Dave knows such a heap o' things—
    Though ma says half of 'em isn't true!

Excerpt from
The Vinland Sagas: The Norse Discovery of America
Magnus Magnusson and Hermann Pálsson, eds.

Leif explores Vinland

Some time later, Bjarni Herjolfsson sailed from Greenland to Norway and visited Earl Eirik, who received him well. Bjarni told the earl about his voyage and the lands he had sighted. People thought he had shown great lack of curiosity, since he could tell them nothing about these countries, and he was criticized for this. Bjarni was made a retainer at the earl's court, and went back to Greenland the following summer.

There was now great talk of discovering new countries. Leif, the son of Eirik the Red of Brattahlid, went to see Bjarni Herjolfsson and bought his ship from him, and engaged a crew of thirty-five.

Leif asked his father Eirik to lead this expedition too, but Eirik was rather reluctant: he said he was getting old, and could endure hardships less easily than he used to. Leif replied that Eirik would still command more luck than any of his kinsmen. And in the end, Eirik let Leif have his way.

As soon as they were ready, Eirik rode off to the ship which was only a short distance away. But the horse he was riding stumbled and he was thrown, injuring his leg.

"I am not meant to discover more countries than this one we now live in," said Eirik. "This is as far as we go together."

Eirik returned to Brattahlid, but Leif went aboard the ship with his crew of thirty-five. Among them was a Southerner called Tyrkir.

They made their ship ready and put out to sea. The first landfall they made was the country that Bjarni had sighted last. They sailed right up to the shore and cast anchor, then lowered a boat and landed. There was no grass to be seen, and the hinterland was covered with great glaciers, and between glaciers and shore the land was like one great slab of rock. It seemed to them a worthless country.

Then Leif said, "Now we have done better than Bjarni where this country is concerned—we at least have set foot on it. I shall give this country a name and call it *Helluland*.

They returned to their ship and put to sea, and sighted a second land. Once again they sailed right up to it and cast anchor, lowered a boat and went ashore. This country was flat and wooded, with white sandy beaches wherever they went; and the land sloped gently down to the sea.

Leif said, "This country shall be named after its natural resources: it shall be called *Markland*."

They hurried back to their ship as quickly as possible and sailed away to sea in a north-east wind for two days until they sighted land again. They sailed towards it and came to an island which lay to the north of it.

They went ashore and looked about them. The weather was fine. There was dew on the grass, and the first thing they did was to get some of it on their hands and put it to their lips, and to them it seemed the sweetest thing they had ever tasted. Then they went back to their ship and sailed into the sound that lay between the island and the headland jutting out to the north.

They steered a westerly course round the headland. There were extensive shallows there and at low tide their ship was left high and dry, with the sea almost out of sight. But they were so impatient to land that they could not bear to wait for the rising tide to float the ship; they ran ashore to a place where a river flowed out of a lake. As soon as the tide had refloated the ship they took a boat and rowed out to it and brought it up the river into the lake, where they anchored it. They carried their hammocks ashore and put up booths. Then they decided to winter there, and built some large houses.

There was no lack of salmon in the river or the lake, bigger salmon than they had ever seen. The country seemed to them so kind that no winter fodder would be needed for livestock: there was never any frost all winter and the grass hardly withered at all.

In this country, night and day were of more even length than in either Greenland or Iceland: on the shortest day of the year, the sun was already up by 9 a.m., and did not set until after 3 p.m.

When they had finished building their houses, Leif said to his companions, "Now I want to divide our company into two parties and have the country explored; half of the company are to remain here at the homes while the other half go exploring—but they must not go so far that they cannot return the same evening, and they are not to become separated."

They carried out these instructions for a time. Leif himself took turns at going out with the exploring party and staying behind at the base.

Leif was tall and strong and very impressive in appearance. He was a shrewd man and always moderate in his behaviour.

Thorvald explores Vinland

Thorvald prepared his expedition with his brother Leif's guidance and engaged a crew of thirty. When the ship was ready they put out to sea and there are no reports of their voyage until they reached Leif's Houses in Vinland. There they laid up the ship and settled down for the winter, catching fish for their food.

In the spring Thorvald said they should get the ship ready, and that meanwhile a small party of men should take the ship's boat and sail west along the coast and explore that region during the summer.

They found the country there very attractive, with woods stretching almost down to the shore and white sandy beaches. There were numerous islands there, and extensive shallows. They found no traces of human habitation or animals except on one westerly island, where they found a wooden stack-cover. That was the only man-made thing they found; and in the autumn they returned to Leif's Houses.

Next summer Thorvald sailed east with his ship and then north along the coast. They ran into a fierce gale off a headland and were driven ashore; the keel was shattered and they had to stay there for a long time while they repaired the ship.

Thorvald said to his companions, "I want to erect the old keel here on the headland, and call the place Kjalarness."

They did this and then sailed away eastward along the coast. Soon they found themselves at the mouth of two fjords, and sailed up to the promontory that jutted out between them; it was heavily wooded. They moored the ship alongside and put out the gangway, and Thorvald went ashore with all his men.

"It is beautiful here," he said. "Here I should like to make my home."

On their way back to the ship they noticed three humps on the sandy beach just in from the headland. When they went closer they found that these were three skin-boats, with three men under each of them. Thorvald and his men divided forces and captured all of them except one, who escaped in his boat. They killed the other eight and returned to the headland, from which they scanned the surrounding country. They could make out a number of humps farther up the fjord and concluded that these were settlements.

Then they were overwhelmed by such a heavy drowsiness that they could not stay awake, and they all fell asleep—until they were awakened by a voice that shouted, "Wake up, Thorvald, and all your men, if you want to stay alive! Get to your ship with all your company and get away as fast as you can!"

A great swarm of skin-boats was then heading towards them down the fjord.

Thorvald said, "We shall set up breastworks on the gunwales and defend ourselves as best we can, but fight back as little as possible."

They did this. The Skrælings shot at them for a while, and then turned and fled as fast as they could.

Thorvald asked his men if any of them were wounded; they all replied that they were unhurt.

"I have a wound in the armpit," said Thorvald. "An arrow flew up between the gunwale and my shield, under my arm—here it is. This will lead to my death.

"I advise you now to go back as soon as you can. But first I want you to take me to the headland I thought so suitable for a home. I seem to have hit on the truth when I said that I would settle there for a while. Bury me there and put crosses at my head and feet, and let the place be called *Krossaness* for ever afterwards."

(Greenland had been converted to Christianity by this time, but Eirik the Red had died before the conversion.)

With that Thorvald died, and his men did exactly as he had asked of them. Afterwards they sailed back and joined the rest of the expedition and exchanged all the news they had to tell.

They spent the winter there and gathered grapes and vines as cargo for the ship. In the spring they set off on the voyage to Greenland; they made land at Eiriksfjord, and had plenty of news to tell Leif.

Karlsefni in Vinland

That same summer a ship arrived in Greenland from Norway. Her captain was a man called Thorfinn Karlsefni. He was a man of considerable wealth. He spent the winter with Leif Eiriksson at Brattahlid.

Karlsefni quickly fell in love with Gudrid and proposed to her, but she asked Leif to answer on her behalf. She was betrothed to Karlsefni, and the wedding took place that same winter.

There was still the same talk about Vinland voyages as before, and everyone, including Gudrid, kept urging Karlsefni to make the voyage. In the end he decided to sail and gathered a company of sixty men and five women. He made an agreement with his crew that everyone should share equally in whatever profits the expedition might yield. They took livestock of all kinds, for they intended to make a permanent settlement there if possible.

Karlsefni asked Leif if he could have the houses in Vinland: Leif said that he was willing to lend them, but not to give them away.

They put to sea and arrived safe and sound at Leif's Houses and carried their hammocks ashore. Soon they had plenty of good supplies, for a fine big rorqual was driven ashore; they went down and cut it up, and so there was no shortage of food.

The livestock were put out to grass, and soon the male beasts became very frisky and difficult to manage. They had brought a bull with them.

Karlsefni ordered timber to be felled and cut into lengths for a cargo for the ship, and it was left out on a rock to season. They made use of all the natural resources of the country that were available, grapes and game of all kinds and other produce.

The first winter passed into summer, and then they had their first encounter with Skrælings, when a great number of them came out of the wood one day. The cattle were grazing near by and the bull began to bellow and roar with great vehemence. This terrified the Skrælings and they fled, carrying their packs which contained furs and sables and pelts of all kinds. They made for Karlsefni's houses and tried to get inside, but Karlsefni had the doors barred against them. Nether side could understand the other's language.

Then the Skrælings put down their packs and opened them up and offered their contents, preferably in exchange for weapons; but Karlsefni forbade his men to sell arms. Then he hit on the idea of telling the women to carry milk out to the Skrælings, and when the Skrælings saw the milk they wanted to buy nothing else. And so the outcome of their trading expedition was that the Skrælings carried their purchases away in their bellies, and left their packs and furs with Karlsefni and his men.

After that, Karlsefni ordered a strong wooden palisade to be erected round the houses, and they settled in.

About this time Karlsefni's wife, Gudrid, gave birth to a son, and he was named Snorri.

Early next winter the Skrælings returned, in much greater numbers this time, bringing with them the same kind of wares as before. Karlsefni told the women, "You must carry out to them the same produce that was most in demand last time, and nothing else."

As soon as the Skrælings saw it they threw their packs in over the palisade.

Gudrid was sitting in the doorway beside the cradle of her son Snorri when a shadow fell across the door and a woman entered wearing a black, close-fitting tunic; she was rather short and had a band round her chestnut-coloured hair. She was pale, and had the largest eyes that have ever been seen in any human head. She walked up to Gudrid and said, "What is your name?"

"My name is Gudrid. What is yours?"

"My name is Gudrid," the woman replied.

Then Gudrid, Karlsefni's wife, motioned to the woman to come and sit beside her; but at that very moment she heard a great crash and the woman vanished, and in the same instant a Skræling was killed by one of Karlsefni's men for trying to steal some weapons. The Skrælings fled as fast as they could, leaving their clothing and wares behind. No one had seen the woman except Gudrid.

"Now we must devise a plan," said Karlsefni, "for I expect they will pay us a third visit, and this time with hostility and in greater numbers. This is what we must do: ten men are to go out on the headland here and make themselves conspicuous, and the rest of us are to go into the wood and make a clearing there, where we can keep our cattle when the Skrælings come out of the forest. We shall take our bull and keep him to the fore."

The place where they intended to have their encounter with the Skrælings had the lake on one side and the woods on the other.

Karlssefni's plan was put into effect, and the Skrælings came right to the place that Karlsefni had chosen for the battle. The fighting began, and many of the Skrælings were killed. There was one tall and handsome man among the Skrælings and Karlsefni reckoned that he must be their leader. One of the Skrælings had picked up an axe, and after examining it for a moment he swung it at a man standing beside him, who fell dead at once. The tall man then took hold of the axe, looked at it for a moment, and then threw it as far as he could out into the water. Then the Skrælings fled into the forest as fast as they could, and that was the end of the encounter.

Helge Ingstad and Anne Stine Ingstad, L'Anse aux Meadows, 1991.

Karlsefni and his men spent the whole winter there, but in the spring he announced that he had no wish to stay there any longer and wanted to return to Greenland. They made ready for the voyage and took with them much valuable produce, vines and grapes and pelts. They put to sea and reached Eiriksfjord safely and spent the winter there.

Helge Marcus Ingstad

23 May 1969

George Story

Of the Norse voyages to the New World, Mark Twain's words might, before 1960, have been fittingly cited: "the researches of many commentators have thrown much darkness on this subject, and it is probable that, if they continue, we shall soon know nothing about it." There was no reasonable doubt about the voyages themselves; but where they led was a problem canvassed with merciless prolixity, intemperate zeal, and contradictory results. The Norseman in America was a will o' the wisp, an elusive pimpernel of the North. Elusive, that is, until the middle of the present decade, when the discovery of a soap-stone spinning whorl and a small, ring-headed bronze pin at L'anse aux Meadow revealed Newfoundland as the Promontorium Winlandiae of Norse geographical tradition, and provided the final proof, the clincher, of this famous historical problem. The adventurous author and explorer who stands before you would himself be the first to share the pride and honour of that discovery with earlier students of the Norse Atlantic Voyages, with the ethnographers, the historians and the geographers who contributed to its solution; most of all, perhaps, with his archaeologist-wife, Anne Stine Ingstad. But the discovery is, nonetheless, his by virtue of the imagination and the perseverance with which, for more than seven years, he sought and then uncovered the Viking site which for generations has haunted men of the West as no other except Homer's Troy.

Helge Ingstad has, in fact, been described as one of those follow-my-nose people like Heinrich Schliemann, whose conviction, energy and imagination win triumphs where more orthodox investigators fail. Born in Norway and educated at Oslo University, he practised law as a barrister for three years before abandoning the bar in favour of the barren lands of the world. He has a small boatman's familiarity with northern waters; he has been an explorer and trapper in the Arctic; he spent several years studying the Caribou Indians of Canada; he has lived among the inland Eskimos of Alaska, as well as the Apaches of Arizona and the Indians of the Sierra Madre Mountains; he has been Governor of East Greenland, and of Spitzbergen. And he has written books about all these places and people, books which sparkle with their reflection of the singular personality of this inquisitive nomad who, in search of the historical past, has himself left his substantial mark on the history of high adventure in the New World.

I present for the Degree of Doctor of Letters, honoris causa, Helge Marcus Ingstad.

Anne Stine Ingstad
27 October 1979

George Story

> Man and woman, comely race,
> Whereof art thou sprung?
> Whence spindle whorl and needle-bone,
> In house-site F, room six?
> Whom thy finders, what their trade,
> In Lancey Meadows digging?
> Adams' hand or Adam's rib:
> Spell this riddle, prithee.

For a gloss on this, a medieval monk might refer us, if not for a literal than for a figurative explanation, to Window H in Great Malvern Priory Church, Worcestershire, panel twelve of which depicts in painted glass a scene from the Creation. Blue background (sea and sky). In a landscape, on the left Eve (red dress, white kerchief on head) is seated looking to the right, holding a distaff (yellow) and thread in her left hand and a spindle in her right. A child is seated on her lap. On the right Adam, looking downwards to the left, digs in with a wooden spade (yellow) shod with iron (white).

This audience, at least, will read both the riddle and the picture with ease in the presence of the gifted woman who stands before us: Anne Stine Ingstad who, with her intrepid husband, discovered a celebrated Viking site in 1960; directed the painstaking excavations in the seven ensuing years of a model investigation in which, characteristic of our times, she took the spade from Adam's hand, and uncovered the evidence of the earliest authenticated European settlement of America on the shores of Newfoundland; identified through spindle and needle the presence of Norse womenfolk in that pleasant room with southern exposure at house-site F; and who, clad in red like the explorer-husband who already forms part of our academic panel and Memorial fellowship, I present for the Degree of Doctor of Letters, honoris causa.

Interior of Viking longhouse, L' Anse aux Meadows.

Excerpt from
Eiriksdottir

Joan Clark

Freydis often thought about that morning. Sometimes it was a recurring dream, she was drowning in the icy sea and no one was around to help. More often it was the warnings she gave her children not to play too close to the water, the rebukes afterwards when they did. It was the stories she chose to tell her children though none of them referred to her mother. Freydis told herself her mother no longer existed, yet she continued to think her mother was lost among the stars or below the sea.

Despite its having swallowed her mother, now that Freydis was on the sea, she wasn't afraid. She was in fact so pliant and joint loose she might have been Signy's cloth doll lying in a soft hollow, bales of wool on either side. Part of the limpness was a weary letting down after months of hard work preparing for the voyage. All the wool she had spun, the provisions she had put together, the clothes she had made. Part of it was knowing that for the first time in eight years of marriage she had little work to do until she reached Leifsbudir. The food rations had long ago been neatly divided into portions and tied in sacks. True, the cow and goats would need milking but Groa would see to that. Freydis supposed she could spin. The bales of wool had been combed and spun except for one. Whether or not she spun the last bale hardly mattered. In fact it didn't matter if she did anything at all aboard this ship.

As long as she was on the water Freydis's fate was in Evyind's hands while his, in turn, was in the hands of the Three Norns. All of the Greenlanders were in the hands of three women who sat beneath the World Tree weaving the fate of others. The three sisters couldn't be bribed or browbeaten. All anyone could do was lie back and let them get on with their work. Freydis wondered how all that weaving affected the Sisters' hands, if they were rough or smooth. In the dim light of the hollow, she could see the skin of her own fingertips roughened by spinning coarse wool. The outer wool of Greenland sheep was heavy and thick, which made it long lasting and strong enough for sailcloth, but it gave little pleasure when being spun or woven. After she and Thorvard got a ship of their own, Freydis intended to buy threads of silk and linen in Norway. She would buy soft wool and make the kind of clothes the high-born wore, shifts and robes so finely woven you couldn't see the weft or warp. No doubt the Norns kept their fingers smooth by using the softest wool. Maybe not. Maybe they used fine wool only to weave the fate of the high-born, whereas coarse wool wove the fate of the poor.

The sail billowed, tugged at the rigging. The mast groaned. The ballast rocks shifted. The water hissed against the keel. The sea handled the ship firmly but gently. The crew slept. So did Freydis.

For the next three days the ship continued to follow the current Northward along the coast past icebergs and inlets, all the while enjoying fine weather and light clear skies. They passed skerries whose cliffs were white with guano from gulls and murres. Occasionally they saw great auks. The auks were good eating but the Greenlanders didn't waste time snaring sea birds when they had plenty of provisions aboard.

By now the rituals of sea travel had taken hold. Each morning the thralls who slept in the hold with the livestock shovelled the dung overboard and emptied the privy pails. The animals were given a small amount of hay. Groa left the place where she slept near Freydis and milked the cows and goats. She carried a bowl of milk to Freydis as well as Evyind, Thorvard, Ivar, Uni and the iron worker Nagli. Whatever milk was left over was taken by whichever farmer happened to be up and about. The crew woke slowly. Much of the morning was taken up with their wakening tasks, using the privy pails, dipping their cups into the water barrel. Though each man had his own spoon as well as a cup, he had little use for the spoon since the rations, served after they were all awake and then again in late afternoon, were small portions of dried fish or meat with a bit of cheese. After the first rations were eaten, the men occupied themselves in various ways. Some played board games. Others shaped bowls and cups from soapstone they had brought or made calendar sticks, uneven lengths of driftwood, grooved to mark each passing day. Only Lopt, one of the stowaways, knew runes. He refused to explain the signs he carved on wood. He said that to divulge their meaning would make them worthless. He reminded the others that the magical signs—which runes were—diminished in power if they were talked about.

After the meal was over, Groa would comb and plait Freydis's hair. The old thrall worked slowly, her fingers gnarled and clumsy by years of joint ill. Freydis's hair was thick and unruly. Whenever Groa tugged hard to get out a snarl, Freydis snatched the comb from her and finished the combing herself. Groa brought her a bowl of clean water and a cloth so that she could wash in private. When all this had been done, Freydis went round the ship and visited various members of the crew. She usually sat with Bolli, her step-brother, though after living apart for so many years, they had little to say to one another, and as always Bolli was poor at conversation. He was apt to be cast down unless Freydis was nearby. Freydis took care to nurture Bolli's attachment to her. She had never been afraid of him even when he bullied others. She had seen the helplessness in his body, the terror in his eyes when he was under a spell. Not once had she mocked him for his affliction. Bolli took this to be fondness, which it probably was.

Freydis was careful not to become over familiar with the crew. Not so Thorvard. He was well known to the hunters aboard and was regarded as one of them. But Freydis was a woman and their leader and thought she should keep herself apart, though not so far apart that she couldn't observe what was going on. Once she had sat for a time with Bolli, Thorvard, Evyind and one or two others, she usually returned to the comfort of her hollow and slept.

On the third day of the voyage Bjarney came into sight. The island, which had massive black cliffs rising above a beach, was where the hunting grounds of Northsetur began. The Greenlanders didn't attempt to hunt but anchored only long enough to take on fresh water. Then they turned West. Now there would be no coastline or landmarks to follow. During the next two days they would be travailing an empty ocean, empty except for ice. Before the land disappeared they saw whales and seals and once a white bear on an ice pan.

After a half-day sailing, Bjarney's dark forehead dropped away. There were no seals. Not even a whale was seen. The Greenlanders were alone with sea and sky. They passed several icebergs but these were easily avoided. It was mainly Ivar's task to watch for icebergs. When Ivar rested, Uni took over. These men also handled the steering oar while Evyind slept.

Though the weather held clear, the water became rougher. The Greenlanders now found the sea worked against them. As the swells increased, many of the crew began vomiting their rations into privy pails. Not Freydis; on Evyind's advice she had positioned her bed where the swell was least. Thirty years earlier when the ship had been built in Norway, the *Vinland's* knees had been tied rather than riveted to its ribs using walrus rope, replaced many times since. This made the ship pliant and allowed a friendship between water and wood.

This friendship depended on the wind. If it chose, the wind could be generous and helpful, holding the sail in a firm embrace, guiding the ship across the sea as it was now. But just as easily the wind could be spiteful, turning away abruptly, dropping the sail, abandoning the ship to useless air. Or in a fit of frenzy the wind might suddenly sweep in from the Northeast bringing punishing cold, spitting out snow and sleet, pushing up mountainous seas.

Sometimes the god Njord himself was the wind. It was difficult to say when he was inside the wind or when he had abandoned the wind to itself. Njord came and went and could never be trusted to stay in one place. Sometimes when he left the wind, he went inside the sea and became it instead. Freydis remembered her father saying that Njord was untrustworthy because he had been spurned by so many women. He was often passed over by women in favour of handsomer gods. Though ugly, Njord had beautiful feet from soaking them so long in sea water. When an exquisite maiden by the name of Skadi was deciding who among the gods would become her husband, she chose Njord because of his feet, which were the only body parts she was permitted to see. When she saw Njord's ugly face after their marriage, she was bitterly disappointed. According to Freydis's father, it was this unhappy union that made Njord shift restlessly between water and wind.

This time Freydis thought Njord might not be following the *Vinland* at all but showing his bad temper in some other part of the world. This would explain the favourable winds they were enjoying. After two days of empty ocean the Greenlanders sighted the flat stone land Leif named Helluland. They recognized this land not by its flatness which was close by the water, but by the glaciered mountains far inland. The sight of the mountains reassured the Greenlanders: once again they had landmarks to guide them, which gave them an idea of where they were in relation to where they were going. This was a map drawn with Leif Eiriksson's words which each traveller carried inside his head. Where this map placed them in relation to the rest of the world they didn't know. They knew only that Helluland was North of Markland which was North of Vinland. Leif said the southern part of Markland was only a short distance from Leifsbudir and was thickly wooded with spruce and fir. For most of the crew the world was Greenland, each field a country fenced by stone. In any case their maps were more felt than seen, the land Leif named Helluland crouched like an untamed beast on the periphery of their vision. It was now seven days since they had left Einarsfjord, which by Evyind's estimation placed them halfway to Leifsbudir. The most dangerous part of their voyage was thought to be over. For this reason Evyind agreed to anchor in Helluland for

the night so that the crew could spend a day ashore and fresh water could be taken aboard.

At Helluland the ship was picked up by a current and carried South. Once again land was on the starboard. With the sun high above and the sky so clear, Evyind said they couldn't expect fairer sailing weather. As they headed South the evenings darkened in such a way that day was more clearly divided from night. The Greenlanders enjoyed the change, for it meant they could see the moon and stars. The fine weather continued for four more days.

Late on the twelfth day, the wind shifted to the Northeast. The sky became as dark as night. Thick clouds blocked the sun. Evyind regarded the changed weather with his usual composure, saying travellers must accept foul weather and ride it out until the winds turned again in their favour. The wind blew the ship seaward and the Greenlanders lost sight of land. The swells became so massive that all Freydis could see was the bottom of the swell they were in and halfway up the next. The Greenlanders lost all sense of time, which was to say the light. Nor could they navigate. The sunstone Leif had given Evyind was useless and there was no moon or stars. Evyind ordered the men to remain in place so that the ship would be more evenly weighted. The inactivity reminded the Greenlanders how helpless they were to change their fate.

The waves steepened until they loomed above the ship like Greenland's fells. The summits were so high and the valleys so deep that the *Vinland* could no longer shape itself to the water; the ship faltered on the peaks, groaning as if it would break in two. Now even those in midship became ill. Each time the old ship was stranded on top of a wave, a sickness rose in Freydis's throat then slowly sank to her belly as the ship was plunged into a trough. Freydis gave up eating, since nothing she ate would stay down. Like the others she had stopped using the privy pails, which had been knocked over by the motion of the ship. Freydis's clothes stank of vomit and piss. The entire ship reeked with foul odours that came from the hold where a swill of piss and animal dung slopped around the legs. The livestock were neglected since the thralls who tended them were hunkered down against the bales and bundles lashed to the deck. The swill was partly sea water that had leaked through the strakes. Leif's ship was so well caulked that in good sailing weather little bailing was required. Now that the ship was being driven to the bottom of deep sea troughs, the crests of waves curled over the ship so often that Evyind ordered the thralls and as many bailers as could fit into the hold to get to work with pails and cups.

Freydis struggled out of the hollow where she had spent most of the voyage. There was nothing nearby to hold on to except bundles and bales which kept shifting themselves. Freydis crawled across the starboard stroking, reached up and held on to the rigging. An enormous wave broke over the deck. The rope that secured the water barrels snapped. One of the barrels careened across the deck, the other rolled past Freydis into the hold, knocking over bailers and smashing the pens. The ropes tethering the livestock tangled and crossed so that the animals fell over one another in bleating confusion. Two goats broke away and one of them leapt into the hollow where Freydis had been.

Evyind ordered the sail reefed. The reefing was done with difficulty since the men had to work around broken pens and animals on the loose. After the sail was reefed, some of the men tied themselves to the mast. Freydis wanted to reach the mast, but whenever she tried to crawl toward it across the slippery deck, another wave slammed against the ship and knocked her back. She saw Thorvard coming toward her on his hands and knees, a rope between his teeth. When he reached Freydis, he shouted at her to hold onto the rigging until he had the rope tied around her waist. He told her to stay where she was until he had the other end tied to the mast. When this had been done, he pulled Freydis toward the mast and tethered her beside the cow. Then he tied himself to the mast. Sometime later Freydis saw a gigantic wave wash over her sleeping hollow and carry away the goat. The next wave swept Lopt overboard.

The storm continued unabated for days. No one knew how many. It could have been four days, it could have been five, even seven. There was no sun. Grey clouds darkened into a blackness that could have been night, then into grey again. Freydis sat against the mast, her body stiff with terror, wet and cold. Clothing stuck to her like the skin of a fish; her hair hung in coils of dripping rope. She had no memories or thoughts. Fear had driven them out. Occasionally one of her children's faces floated in front of hers. She began to talk to her children, urging them to stick up for one another and for what was theirs, not to give Inga's children the advantage in a fight. She told them to help Halla and do as she said. She assured them that Leif Eiriksson would help them out of any diffculties they might have. Once this had been done, Freydis felt a peculiar thrill, a wild recklessness that came from knowing she was teetering on the edge between life and death. She heard voices around her pleading with Thor. Some pleaded with him to roll back Hafgeringar, that mightiest of waves, others begged him to save them from being swept into Ginnungagap, the hole of blackness at the bottom of the Great Abyss where the world dropped into nothingness. She ignored the voices pleading with Christ for forgiveness and salvation. She listened to a voice screaming at Thor, rising above the rest

"What kind of a god are you, that you abandon us to a storm?"

The voice filled her ears in such a way that it seemed to be part of the wind. Surely this was Njord's voice. He had disguised his voice to sound like a woman's.

"Do you want Hymir and his kind to eat us? Have you become a corpse eater yourself? If you don't help us, you are hardly worth your name or the tales they tell about you."

Freydis heard someone nearby confessing to the one called Christ.

"I took my brother's wife. I damaged my brother's reputation. Forgive me, O Lord."

Freydis knew that this new voice was the voice of a fool, though who it came from she couldn't say; the voice came out of a jumble of bodies she could barely see in the half-dark. How could anyone respect a god that had to be constantly wheedled and coaxed? She preferred gods who bullied each other as Njord was bullying Thor.

Njord's voice once again filled her ears shrieking at Thor, "Who do you want to win? You or Christ?"

"Stop screaming!" Thorvard shouted at her. Your shrieking can't save us."

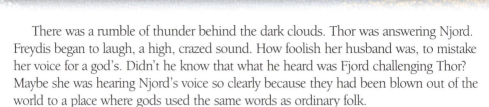

There was a rumble of thunder behind the dark clouds. Thor was answering Njord. Freydis began to laugh, a high, crazed sound. How foolish her husband was, to mistake her voice for a god's. Didn't he know that what he heard was Fjord challenging Thor? Maybe she was hearing Njord's voice so clearly because they had been blown out of the world to a place where gods used the same words as ordinary folk.

The wind finally retreated and the storm moved on. It seemed even the gods grew weary of being hectored and longed for calm. The Greenlanders untied themselves from the mast and rigging and began setting the ship to rights. The empty barrels were straightened and secured. The animal pens were repaired and the worst of the swill bailed out.

"We're lucky we lost only one man and one goat," Thorvard said.

"A lot of good Lopt's runes did him," Freydis said. "It was lucky for us that he kept their meaning to himself."

The sea became fitful in the restless way of someone who was severely disturbed and paced about until he was able to calm himself. The swells still heaved, but gradually they subsided from lack of wind.

Gaia off L'Anse aux Meadows.

River Man

Valerie Legge

"There are countries, there are rivers in your eyes."
—Pablo Neruda, "Lovely One"

It is early morning
somewhere on a river in Missouri;
first light breaks through the trees,
anoints your hands
as the ghost of last night's moon
rides over your shoulder;
you are holding the mythical fish
you've spent all your life pursuing.

You're six years old;
small and serious
you move like a minnow,
sheltered within your mother's shadow;
looming large in shoals of light,
your father leads you
to his favourite river.

At twenty-one you win
the gold in your country's lotto;
but you're too young for war,
too young to hold a gun,
too young to shoulder all that darkness home.

With family in tow you hit the road
sure that your America
must still be out there;
from Arkansas to Idaho,
from Idaho to New Mexico
you mask your sorrow,
cast out your line;
beneath a sky of exploding stars
you weep when it comes up empty.

Though weary when you reach Philadelphia,
you rescue old friends from their darkness,
you hold them oh so gently;

watching the world from the sidelines
you wonder, does anyone see their beauty?

I'm wandering the rugged shoreline
that runs to the Cape
when you rise with the mist
sweeping in from the North Atlantic.
Though I know you've never ventured
quite this far north before,
I watch you wash like daybreak on the shore;
for a brief, unbroken moment
you eclipse the stormy coast
as a cold November sun
falls in the sea.

The First Good Friday

Michael Harrington

"Now from the sixth hour there was darkness over the whole earth, until the ninth hour."

—Matthew 27:45

Over the snarling throng there came a hush,
And the loincloth's flapping just above their heads
Was all the sound for moments, till the rush
Of the hot, thickened air tore clouds in shreds;
And the last gleams of daylight glanced upon
The dying Christ, His cracking, sweating limbs,
With the blood dripping slow and sickly down
From the beams' rough ends and the nails' ugly rims.

Then in the half-light and the agony,
After interminable and inhuman hours,
He called on Eli: Why was He forsaken?
And while they fetched a sponge, the felony,
Of all the men who know this world of ours,
Was done, and Christ was dead and the earth shaken.

Didymus on Saturday
David L. Elliott

I who have trusted only certainties,
Save for a three-years dream, awake at last.
Now Jesus has his grave, Judas his gold,
Peter his praise, he of the ready sword.
I, who believed in all my disbelief,
Am left with nothing but the biting shame
That gnaws me for believing easily.
It seemed at times a thing beyond mere proof
That he was king of Judah, son of God.
His crown was made of thorns and he was nailed
Fast to a narrow cross with Roman spikes.
I saw him walk to death between two thieves,
A little man whose face was cracked with fear
And a tall man whose eyes were dull with doom.
The flesh was fixed to the complacent wood,
The crosses lifted up and downward flung,
Jolting into the jarring earth-sockets.
A triple scream splintered the quiet dawn,
And death could overtake them at his leisure,
Being so fastened.
The mob shrilled with delight to see such pain,
And that was yesterday and he is dead,
My world was ended with a hammer strike.
I might have known, I might have known, I might have known:
He was too just to be a king of Judah,
He was too kind to be a son of God
Who slew the children by the muddy Nile
And had the king of the Amalekites
Cloven to pieces in the sacred shambles.
Yet, hard is the awakening from my dream,
I must take care to guard against more dreams.
Some say he will rise and from his grave
Spring like a sleeper from a restful bed
To justify his godhead. Not for me
Subscription to these fancies. Not if he
Spoke to me in the voice that tuned my heart
To think him God; not if he broke the bread
Of love at my own table: not if he
Were seen by John, who cannot tell a lie.
And all proofs tangible and ocular
Will not convince me save I touch the wound

The Roman spear made in his dying side,
Press the torn palms, embrace the stricken feet.

Tomorrow is the first day of the week
And I shall leave this gray Jerusalem
Where he lies sleeping in the hallowed stone,
Never to come into his kingdom now.

The Listeners
Irving Fogwill

In the solid warmth of the surgery the sound of the writhing and pounding of the storm outside scarcely penetrated. There were no visiting patients sitting in the ante-room, and none in the surgery itself. Dr. Fenstein was alone there, sitting slumped behind his desk. O'Malley, when he burst in, seemed to bring the storm with him. He was covered with snow. It seemed to have been blasted into his hair and clothing. His brows, even his eyelashes, were rimmed white with it. He was somehow alien to the heavy quietness of the room.

Some frightening urgency came with him, permeating the surgery's atmosphere. Urgency and the immediacy of crisis pushed forward as his leaning and straining body pressed toward the doctor.

"Doctor!" He said it hoarsely with a thick breathless rasp. "I been phoning for over an hour. No answer. No answer from 'Central'. The line is dead. Wires must be down. And it musta took me two hours to get here." His voice petered out. He had to stop speaking so that he could inhale the air's sustenance. He was across the room, now, and he leaned forward, with his two hands, white-knuckled, gripping the edge of the desk.

"'Tis me kid, Doctor—me young-fella Joey." A spasm twisted his face, and his underjaw quivered. The click of his teeth could be heard in the savage effort of occlusion.

"It must be six hours since he was took with the pain; and when I looked in on me way back from Dr. Blair's—did you know Dr. Blair had a stroke last night?—the pain was nearly gone, but the poor little fella is half in a coma and running a temperature… an' I know his appendix is burst…Blair was going to operate Tuesday." He faltered for a moment, incoherent—his eyes widening with fear and anguish.

"He'll die, Doctor, won't he?—if he's not operated on right away…or get penicillin or something. You're the only doctor in town now. I can't get to the hospital. No cars, no buses. Nothing can move. Snow is nearly ten feet some places—in drifts. Not even a horse and slide can get through it."

Dr. Fenstein had not moved during the time O'Malley's harsh rasp grated through the room's silence, save for the strangely heavy raising of his head to look at him when he had burst in and had come toward the desk. He stared dully at O'Malley as if uncomprehending of the other's personalized terror.

As if the words were pumped out of him, O'Malley said: "You'll come, Doctor? You'll come back with me? I'll carry you on me back. You gotta come!" His voice increased in volume to a note of desperate pleading. "Me boy'll die if you don't… peritonitis…gangrene…won't he? You know Joey, don't you? He's red-headed like meself." A tiny flicker of shame passed quickly over the surface of his face at his obtruding of sentimentality, chasing quickly away a pitiful, twisted caricature of a smile that had peeped out from his tormented soul.

"How long have we got?" he continued. "How long does it take the pus to spread through him? How long, Doctor?—Doctor Fenstein! How long?"

The doctor had not answered him. He had not even moved—he only looked at O'Malley with leaden-weighted eyes.

O'Malley suddenly stopped speaking, and stared intently at the man behind the desk. Good God! what's the matter with him: drunk? God! not drunk…no! no!…not drunk…Joey! Joey! don't die! Joey. Please God, don't let little Joe die on me…"Danny Boy"—Joey, and "Macushla"—Macushla! Macushla! your sweet voice is…

"Doctor! Doctor! Do you hear me?" He leaned across the desk and shook the doctor by the arm—"Me boy is dying, Doctor."

"Yes." Dr. Fenstein pushed himself back in his chair with obvious effort. His voice was barely audible. He seemed to be fighting some kind of slowly enveloping lethargy.

"'Tis me boy, Doctor, his appendix is burst—You'll be coming over with me? Where's your coat, sir?" O'Malley moved quickly back from the desk, looking around. His movements had powerful purpose and urgency. He strode back and forth with a sort of flying imperativeness, as if he would instill in the other his own sense of driving, pressing hurry. He kicked the pool of water on the floor from the snow-melt off his clothes, hither and thither as he walked.

"No," said Dr. Fenstein. The sound of the word could barely be heard, yet it stopped O'Malley in his tracks as if it had been the sharpest whiplash of a bullet. He reached the desk as if he had flown there.

"What!" He didn't scream the word: he whispered it; but it had all the effects of a scream. It was a scream of a whisper: a sound made by the forced exhalation of shocked breath—driven out of him by the impact of the incredibility of a negative expressed in such circumstances.

"You said 'No', Dr. Fenstein?" Aghast and unbelieving, O'Malley stood bolt upright. "You said 'No'—he said 'No'!" he repeated to himself: "No! Holy Mother of God—he won't come to me little boy!—Why? Doctor, why?" His voice rose; it became vibrant, trembling with terrific feeling. "Are you refusing to come to a child that's sick—and perhaps dying, Dr. Fenstein?" His blue eyes were wide and blazing with a deadly hurt: and his teeth showed nakedly as his lips curled back, tautly creasing and rolling back the stiff white skin of his cheeks. He bent sharply and leaned over the desk. He took hold of the doctor's shoulders and shook him violently.

"Listen! Doctor, if you had a few too many today, take a straightener—seltzer or something… perhaps a coupla good shots of whiskey or brandy'll pull you together." O'Malley could feel a corrosive fury gathering inside him and beginning to mount upwards.

The violent shaking seemed to have roused Dr. Fenstein. He sat upright in his chair for the first time since O'Malley had come in. He pressed his hands against the desk's edge, thereby holding himself firmly against the back of his chair. His eyes were opened wide although, O'Malley could see, an effort was required to keep the strangely weighted eyelids up.

It was then O'Malley could fully see his face—what made it like that—bluish-white and damp looking? Christ! his eyes…they were the saddest eyes he had ever seen. All his anger slowly subsided. Only the desperate urgency of his terror for Joey remained.

"Doctor," he said quietly, and his voice had a queer sort of dignity in it, "you'll help me, won't you?"

"No!" Dr. Fenstein said, and shook his head in a halting slow-motion way that had an eerieness about it that chilled O'Malley.

"Do you mean you won't?"

"No. I mean I can't." The doctor spoke barely above a whisper; and very slowly, as if with difficulty. His heavy, strangely sleepy-looking eyes seemed to focus on O'Malley's face with blurriness, like inebriation; and they were expressionless except that they seemed to be the heart, the centre, the very core around which sorrow had built its immutable lineaments.

"Why? We can get through, sir—I'm as strong as a bull…I can—"

"No."

O'Malley stopped speaking, at the quiet interruption, and waited. For a long moment Dr. Fenstein remained silent; and O'Malley, although urgency and terror pounded him relentlessly, did not—could not—disrupt the moment of silence.

"O'Malley!" Dr. Fenstein inhaled strongly and wilfully, as for a purpose, while he spoke. "I cannot come with you…because…I am sick…I am very sick: in fact, O'Malley, I am dying; and nothing can change it…nothing!"

"Oh my God!" O'Malley said.

The low, murmuring voice of Dr. Fenstein, after the short pause, went on: "Just before you entered my surgery tonight, O'Malley, I took something." His eyes flickered toward a small tumbler which was placed on his desk near a piece of paper, that, O'Malley could see, was a cablegram.

"Poison!" O'Malley croaked, "you took poison?" It was half a question, as if he shouldn't believe it—he couldn't believe it—Oh my God! Joey…little Joey….Come on, Pop, I'll give you the old one-two; and his hair all mussed up…little carrot-top. Norah says it's not red; it is auburn. Joey trying not to holler—and screaming his head off. And drawing up his right leg…and his poor little abdomen tight as a drum. Joey! Joey! Don't let him die on me. God! please! don't let him die on me.

"Why? Doctor, in the name o' God! why?" Poison! Wait, Joey. The doctor's eyes seemed to pour out all the world's inconsolable grief on O'Malley as he spoke—"They killed too many of them for me," he said, and there was a hidden reproachfulness in the way he said it.

He means something, O'Malley thought, that got some meaning in it for me. What is it? He knew what it was. The pang of knowing what it was—of remembering—raked him with agony. He tried not to face it. He could feel himself trying to smother it under but he couldn't. He knew what Fenstein meant. He couldn't hide it from his consciousness now. He couldn't blindfold his soul from seeing it, or stuff cotton wool in the ears of his conscience. He, Joe O'Malley, had spoken those words—only he had spoken them a little differently. He had said them as a wishful inverted negative: "They can't kill too many of them for me"—that was the way he had said the words. It was in "Dutchy's" saloon he had said it…yes, and in other places too…but Dr. Fenstein had heard him saying it in "Dutchy's" saloon. He had had a few beers in when he had said it, but what difference does that make?

"They killed too many of them for me, O'Malley," Dr. Fenstein repeated. O'Malley could see that Dr. Fenstein was holding himself conscious with an obviously intense concentration. "They killed my wife and two children." He reached out with a mighty effort and took the cablegram; and holding himself erect against the chair back, with his

left hand pressed hard against the desk edge, he took up also from the desk a photograph of a small group. "My boy was named Joe too. He was about your boy's age, O'Malley. He played the violin beautifully. My daughter played the cello. They were in Poland studying under an old and famous professor. They also killed him. My son, I am sure, would have been another Heifetz; but that does not matter to the Hitlers and Himmlers and…of this world. I almost said 'and the O'Malleys', but out of respect for your grief, O'Malley, and because the O'Malleys…do not seem to understand, I will not say it."

His voice trailed off into an inaudible whisper—then silence. He breathed stertorously as if he would drag himself up and out of a creeping somnolence.

O'Malley's face was as white as parchment and his eyes were dull-stricken with pain and horror—a corroding evil pain and a deep and unshakeable horror of some terrible truth, long kept smothered, trying to struggle through the murk of his mind: some unbearable clarification of things—too late Joey, Joey, too late now Joey…Good-bye, little Joe….

Dr. Fenstein was slipping down in his chair. O'Malley went quickly around the desk and caught him before he slid forward, face-downward and across the desk. Far off he could hear the pounding and shaking of the storm's fury. He lifted the doctor and carried him to a settee and laid him down gently, putting a cushion under his head. How light he is: must be like the people in concentration camps…shouldn't be light like that…like…like a starved thing…Joey! Joey…the pain, Joey…yes, 'tis me young-fella. Joe. The man in Boston told Norah he had the grandest voice of a boy he ever heard…my Joe…me son. Auschwitz. Violin. Coma. God!

O'Malley sat on the settee's edge, waiting. Deep through his vitals a sombre anguish…his boy was dying, too, and he couldn't do anything about it. "They can't kill too many of them for me"…. I said…yes, I said it. "Oh, God forgive me!" he whispered to himself. "I was forgetting something all the time: I forgot they had children too; I forgot they were men and women, fathers and mothers, boys and girls, and kids like Joey." He stopped whispering; but the sound of whispering continued. It was not O'Malley's. Faint, very faint was the sound—a gentle sibilance like autumn leaves slowly moving and rustling across pavement before a tiny waft of wind. It was Dr. Fenstein. O'Malley bent lower to hear.

"Yes, Sol, old man," he said softly.

"O'Malley, there's something terribly wrong about things in this world."

O'Malley leaned still lower to hear. The words came in eerily spaced wisps of sound, weaving a tenuous lace of faint articulation through the ticking silence of the room.

"The—terms-of-reference-for-mankind-seem-to-be-inadequate—O'Malley. They killed my son Joe. He would have been a great artist. By killing him and all my family they killed me; and by killing me they killed your boy."

O'Malley felt as if he rose to his feet in furious strength. He seemed to see himself striding across the room and out of the doctor's house into the storm and fiercely through it to Joey. He felt the appalling straining-forward of himself to upset, in some magical way, the immutable law of death—saving Joey he would save Dr. Fenstein's children and Dr. Fenstein. But he remained sitting on the edge of the settee in the grip of a deadly inertia.

"Your boy was a singer, O'Malley; he had a beautiful voice; who knows…."

"Was!" said O'Malley, "oh my God! was!"

"…what he might have been…a McCormack or a Caruso."

"Might have been!" O'Malley whispered, "Joey might have been!" he covered his face with his hands, and rocked back and forth.

Fenstein's whispering was becoming very faint now. Soon it stopped—not abruptly—but just softly slid into a pool of silence.

O'Malley could hear the far-off thudding of the storm and the ticking of the clock; and the silence. Then, very faintly, he heard the whispering again. He noticed that the doctor seemed to be listening intently. His eyes had quivered open a little and his head had taken a position of great attentiveness. Faintly—spaced with uncanny clearness and gentleness—came the whispered words—

"Listen! O'Malley, do you not hear it? Do you not hear it? It is my son playing. It is my son playing his violin…Listen! O'Malley, is it not beautiful? Is it not…?"

The tiny spaced wisps of words ceased. The soft broom of the wind swept no more the rustling leaves gently.

O'Malley rose from the settee's edge. Without a sound he walked to the door. The tears were streaming down his face, and his head was held in a listening position. With his hand on the door knob he looked back at Dr. Fenstein. "Good-bye!" he whispered.

He stood there listening. And the dead man on the settee lay there listening.

"I'll hear it too," O'Malley said, and his words cut a lacy pattern of sibilance through the room's silence. "I'll hear it all me life now. When dawn breaks I'll hear it; always I'll hear it; at the bright blaze of noonday; and in the night's long silence."

He was listening. Listening. Listen, O Heart! And in pure, soaring sweetness of unearthly beauty he heard the boy singing:

> …That death is a dream, and that love is for aye. Then awaken, Macushla, awake from your dreaming…

"It's me boy singing, me boy, Joey," he said simply to the room's deep and abiding silence. "Is it not beautiful?"

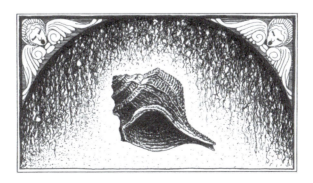

Artist's Statement
Elena Popova

I was born in 1961 in Sofia, Bulgaria. I grew up under the artistic wing of my father, who was a sculptor and my mentor. My memories of those early years are of long conversations and formative advice, coming from my father and his many artistic colleagues. Only recently have I begun to understand how the spiritual atmosphere that embraced me in my youth, has played a crucial role in my development as an artist.

I started to paint seriously when I was eleven. Two years later I began my formal artistic training; five years at the National High School of Fine Arts and six at the Academy of Fine Arts in Sofia, where I earned a Bachelor of Fine Arts and a Master of Fine Arts. By the age of twenty-four I was becoming a successful young painter in my native land and was honoured by having my work included in the collection of the Bulgarian National Gallery.

In 1990 I came to Canada with my husband Luben Boykov and our infant daughter, Anal. As fate would have it we landed in Newfoundland, the Easternmost province of Canada. Now after eight years, we are still living on this foggy and rugged coastline, which we have made our home and spiritual shelter. Acclimatizing to a new country was a time filled with hopes, fears, uncertainty, tears of joy and sorrow, caring for my two children and helping Luben in his career as a sculptor.

The last eight years profoundly changed my sensitivity as an artist. When I started to paint again in 1997, a river of long accumulated ideas, passions and emotions overflowed its banks. Now, one year later, I am still painting with the passion and impatience of a person that has been muted for years.

During the first years in Canada, the delicate threads connecting the roots of my past with my new homeland were sometimes broken. It took a long time before I could fuse the song of the one with the distant thunder of the other. This fusion gives me the sense of harmony and balance that I need to exist through painting.

The technique of Monotype was, for me, a fortunate discovery. I am charmed by it, because it allows me to express spontaneously and intuitively my visions. When I am painting I hold my breath, my body vibrates and time disappears. All of time becomes one moment which I try to capture by becoming one with it. Sometimes I am made out of pain, I see myself crying over the human drama, other times, harmony, hope and faith fill my heart. These states make me paint, vibrate and sense life to the fullest.

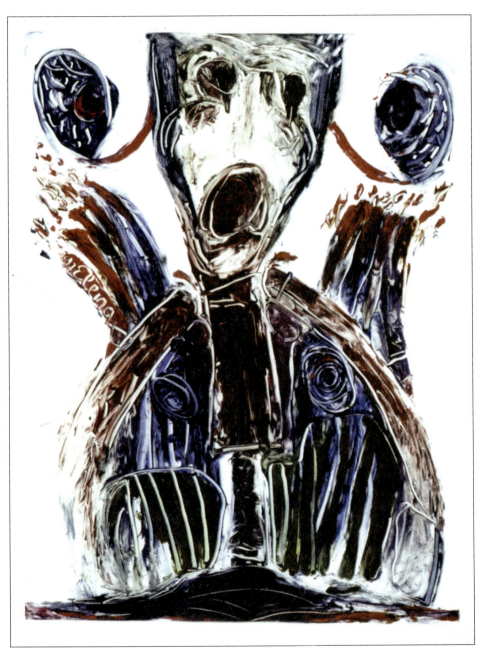

Cry, My Chest Hurts, monotype, 20" x 26" by Elena Popova.

The Oyster
Peter Walsh

Wears a cold grey suit
Locked in a slimy office.
Life is easy for the oyster
Until a problem—a grain of sand
Forces past his pinching door.

He hopes it goes away—
It doesn't. The problem is real.
So he smooths it with a layer
Of creamy sweet-nothings.
But now the problem is bigger.

Brainless, he tries again.
Bigger still.
He hates the sand, curses and spits
More of the same—
The problem grows.

Then, employing all the oyster-wisdom
Of past generations
He assaults the problem
In a blizzard of silky lip-service…
And speaks a pearl.

The problem is smothered,
We have been tricked—
He is rich.
So it is for all oysters
Snug in their crusty beds.

But crack his skull
Or slide a knife
Through his crooked smile—
There's only a grain of sand
Drowned in years of vicious sweet talk.

Black Coral

Clyde Rose

Part I

Come dive with me
into the deep blue Cuban sea
and follow me down
into undersea coral gardens
where the fish are velvet
black, blue and gold
and pinnacles of coral growth
in mossy brown
stand out like the antlers
of a seasoned bull moose.

You have just one breath
to glide you to this garden
under the surface
where you must carefully sway
with the current
avoiding the jagged razor
edged reefs
alert to unexpected movement
as fish dart in and out
from the murky, shadowy
grottos on the rocky bottom.

The light that comes from the sun
one hundred and forty four billion
kilometres away
transforms the scene
into a virtual kingdom
under the sea.

It was in this primal soup
that life began
and may yet end.

Part II

Follow me down deep with Luis
master diver of the Carribean.

In the evolutionary process
Luis is a marvel—
genetic development allows him
to live underwater for four minutes.

I watch him now as I glide
behind him in this coral haven
on a steady line of descent
his left arm around his back,
his hand gracefully placed flat,
as if he were about to do a cotillion.
He pirouettes his body
through the coral ballroom
filled with magic and light
and schools of fish
doing orchestral movement
swaying in harmony
to a silent waltz
in this Vienna ballroom under the sea.

Luis reaches the ledge
beyond which is a
dark blue darkness
he looks back
over his shoulder
with a thumbs up
to his partner
this is the signal:
I'm ok—
carry on independently.

He tumbles over
into the darkness
in search of the black coral
twenty-five metres down
at another sunlit level.
I head back up
leaving a trail of pearly bubbles behind
as I exhaust my way
to the surface
lungs burning
shooting for the sunlight—

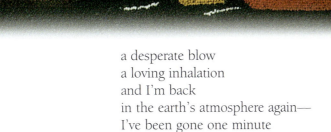

a desperate blow
a loving inhalation
and I'm back
in the earth's atmosphere again—
I've been gone one minute
it will be three more before
Luis returns.

Part III

I bob around waiting
on an empty ocean—
down there somewhere
Luis seeks his quest
the elusive black coral
man the challenger of nature
nature the nurturer of man—
putting him to his test
one minute, two minutes,
three minutes, four minutes
how much longer and how much further can the species go?
perhaps a great gene
will click and clone with
Luis' and our species will once again survive
under the water.

Part IV

A fierce spout grabs my attention
a jet of spume shoots
sunward—
a mask, a head
then a hand brandishing
black coral in the sunlight
Luis has risen
I thrash my mortal way
to him in the water
to grasp his godly hand.

Canadien Cultural Games
Tim Ronan

Peter:

Hello everyone and welcome to the first annual Canadien Cultural games. I'm Peter Mallam and it's a fine day of competition today. So far today, we've had some wonderful downhill sculpting during which the competitor from Alberta wowed the judges and spectators alike by carving a 150 ft. ski slope into a life-like representation of an elk fight.

And, in speed writing, the competitor from NWT took gold with his trilogy concerning the rise and fall of communion written in just 14 hours. BC's Freddy Sanchez was thought to have won this event until it was discovered his twelve book epic was nothing more than the words "Once upon a time" followed by the letter 'E' 80,724,693 times. On a sad note, the Yukon writer had to leave competition early due to a severe case of writer's cramp. But, now we move over to Jonathan Trask who's been covering the acting match.

Jonathan:

Hello everyone, and welcome to the Humber Gardens. We're just getting set for the acting match and what a match it will be. We have two very fine competitors involved here today. In the red corner, representing Ontario, we have Shane Williams. He's a tough opponent, very much into the method style of acting and enjoys using Shakespeare a lot in these matches. But his competition is the home town favorite. In the blue corner, representing Newfoundland, is Donnie Squires. Donnie is a feisty young actor, full of a number of surprises. You could see anything from ancient Greek to Quentin Terrantino if he's involved So, it's lookin' to be a very exciting match with a possible Oscar nomination. Back to you in the studio, Peter.

Peter:

Thank you Jonathan, we'll be sure to check in on that match in a moment, but first we'll go to Chet Short who's been covering the Freestyle Poetry. Chet…

Chet:

Hello Peter.

Peter:

Chet, how has the competition been looking?

Chet:

Well, Peter, it has been a great competition for the most part. We've seen rhyming and free verse, some sonnets and even a ballad. But in the latter half of the competition, some injuries took some of the more skilled poets.

Peter:

How so?

Chet:

Well, Peter, the competitor from New Brunswick sprained his wrist while trying a particularly difficult rhyming couplet, and, while attempting to prove black is white, the competitor from Prince Edward Island promptly went mad. But, in spite of these injuries, the competitor from Quebec managed to stun the judges win a brilliant poem laced with imagery, alliteration and deep metaphors like "war is peace" and "death is life." Using such powerful poetic devices such as these, it was no surprise that he took home the gold. Back to you in the studio, Peter.

Peter:

Thank you very much, Chet. Now, before we go to the acting match, a quick update on the art tournament. Nova Scotia beat Saskatchewan four sculptures to two landscapes. Ontario edged out Quebec two still lifes to a wood carving and British Columbia tied with Alberta one water color to three thousand stick men cartoons. And now, back to Jonathan Trask for the acting match.

Jonathan:

Hello and welcome back, the acting match is just about to start. The players are just having a final look at their scripts. Shane, the rep from Ontario is just getting into costume and Donnie, the rep from Newfoundland is checking over his props. Okay, they're going to the center, they touch prop swords and there's the bell. Whoa, Shane explodes with a "To be or not to be" and catches Donnie wide open. Now Donnie is reeling, what a blow. And Shane isn't letting up. There's an "A Horse, a horse! My kingdom for a horse!" followed by a "Now is the winter of our discontent." Oh! And a "Is this a dagger I see before me?" Donnie is getting pummeled. But wait! Shane needs to check his script. This may give Donnie a chance to mount some offence. He's launching some Euripides. There's an "Air, Zeus's mansion" and a "It was my tongue that promised, not my brain." But this is countered by Shane with a chorus from Sophocles's *Antigone*. And now Shane is lacing into Donnie with some brutal Shakespearean prologue. Iambic pentameter is flying fast and furious. Oh, and a "Wherefore art thou, Romeo?" right in the kidneys. And there's the bell.

Oh, what a bad round for Donnie. He really needs to start some offense…He's really getting hammered out there. But Shane is on fire! Those quotes were being thrown with timing and precision that's hard to find outside of a theatre. Okay, Shane is tightening his prop belt, Donnie is checking his stage directions and his drama coach is drilling him with a focus speech Now the bell and they're back in the ring. Shane is reciting some Oscar Wilde but Donnie is resisting. He seems to be doing something. What is…Oh my God! It's the "Royale with Cheese" scene from "Pulp Fiction." And Shane is feeling that. He's trying to break Donnie's rhythm with some Neil Simon, but it's not working. Donnie keeps pumping out that Tarrantino. But wait! Shane's stopped moving. He's stopped talking, too! He's being totally still and completely silent. What is he think....Oh! It's a dramatic pause! It's a dramatic pause mixed with a powerful silence and Donnie is staggering back. And Shane is holding it. But Donnie is miming! Donnie is matching Shane's pause with the old invisible box routine. He may make some headway with this. But oh! Shane is singing the score of the HMS Pinafore. Donnie looks dazed. He could be in trouble. But he shakes it off. He starts to sing the score of Jesus Christ Superstar and the crowd is going wild! Oh, the bell sounds. They return to their corners. What a great round. Wait, I'm just getting this. Apparently something has happened at the freestyle poetry competition. We'll go there now with Chet Short.

Chet:

Hello, and yes, there is indeed some big news from here. The Quebec competitor has failed his drug test. Yes, he has tested positive for a performance enhancing drug. Cough syrup. Officials say it was because of a medicine induced high that he was able to produce such bizarre metaphors and surreal imagery. The gold will now go to the Manitoba competitor for his poem about puddles. It is a sad, sad day. Back to you, Jon.

Jon:

Thanks, Chet. Well, round three is just about to get underway. Shane is calmly sipping bottled water while Donnie's drama coach is finishing up the last of the "Speak the Speech" monologue from Hamlet, in the hopes of boosting his morale. And, now they're up again and the bell sounds. Wow, Shane starts this round with some Shakespearean insults. We have a "Shag eared villain" and a "Young fry of treachery" and these are followed by an "Et tu, Brute." But Donnie is unaffected. This kid isn't budging. Oh and Shane just delivered a brutal Christopher Marlow/Ben Jonson combination but Donnie is holding his ground. He's, he's stopped suspending his disbelief! Donnie Squires has stopped suspending his disbelief and Shane is at a loss. And Donnie is preparing an offence. Oh, he's unleashing some pretty powerful performance art. I'm seeing bad poetry and black stretch pants galore. He's got Shane on the ropes. But Shane pulls a reversal and blasts Donnie with a "Get thee to a nunnery!" And Hamlet is pouring out of Shane. This looks like it could be over for Donnie. But wait! Donnie, he's, he's, he's improvising! Ladies and gentlemen, we have improv! He's telling an extremely funny joke about a banana in a cow farm. Shane doesn't know what to do. He's looking around, trying to get some sort of a....Oh! the punch line gets him, right in the side of the head. And he's down. The ref counts, but it doesn't look like Shane will be getting up after that one. And it's official. Newfoundland's Donnie Squires has beaten Ontario's Shane Williams for the gold medal. Well I can tell you, the movie deals will start pouring in for Donnie. Well, that's it for this great acting match here at Humber Gardens. What a great match. Back to you in the studio, Peter.

Peter:

Thank you, Jonathan. Well, that's it for today, be sure to tune in tomorrow for the synchronized songwriting. I'm Peter Mallam and this has been the Canadien Cultural Games. Good night, everyone.

Hockey Night in Canada

Vernon Mooers

It's Hockey Night in Canada
    a half hour later in Newfoundland
at the Mariner's Lodge
    down Fortune Bay
    the scallop boats are in
the Leafs score
the Leafs are at St. Louis.
Quite an upset last night, I say
the Flames beat Edmonton
    a beer spills into my lap
We don't see much of 'em down here Buddy
    the boys are getting pissed.
Have a brew they yell
    bottles slide across a slippery table
Ya in from Town Buddy?
    New York—it's Hey Mac
    in London, Love
    Toronto—Hey Charlie
    In Newfoundland, it's always Buddy.

You from the mainland?
Pull up a chair, si'down
Fer T.O. Buddy?

The Leafs score
the lodge erupts
four guys slap my shoulder
one does a jig on the table
suddenly,
I've got a room full of friends.

December hockey
Ian Wiseman

We scatter and gather on a smooth miracle
the work of a windless night.

                        When the puck
rolls near the unlocked end where the brook
circulates a small child full of misplaced trust
retrieves it

                 The ice is clear, revealing waist-
deep water with white air trapped in places,
and moves in waves, a boom and grumble
under the burden of too many skaters.

I can see my house, my mother's heartache
at the window watching me make my own choices.

St. John's by Lois Saunders.

Should Pro Athletes Be Unionized?

Don Power

When you think of unionized workers, what picture do you see? For me it's a long line of men wearing hard hats, faces full of grime from a long day's work, lunch pail in hand, waiting to punch the time clock and begin the trek home.

For some reason the picture is in black and white and it's dull, but there it is. Union workers.

And while that may be over-stereotyping unionized employees with one stroke of a keyboard, I think it's safe to say the term blue collar is an apt description. Granted, there are teachers and nurses unions, too, which may not be described as blue collar, but when you get to the bones of it, they really are just labourers.

Over the course of the past decade, however, the picture of union members has changed dramatically—at least on the sports pages.

With "labour" disputes in baseball, football, hockey and now basketball this season, all four of the major sports have had "work stoppages" where games were canceled or postponed. Negotiators for both sides sat down to bargaining tables to hammer out agreements, much like unions in this province sit down with government to sign collective bargaining deals.

The usefulness of unions can be debated forever. Some people are staunch supporters, while others are strong detractors.

Who's to say who's right? Unions have won gains for many employees over the decades, such as paid holidays, sick leave, these types of things.

But do professional athletes need these benefits? In fact, why do professional athletes have unions?

Surely they can't argue about the wages or working conditions. That'll look good, Shaquille O' Neal filing a grievance over his $110-million contract.

Pro athlete unions came into full force in hockey when Alan Eagleson helped organize players to get a larger piece of the owners' pie more than two decades ago, while Curt Flood's refusal to accept a trade led to the formation of the baseball players' union.

And in decades past, pro athletes were virtual slaves to their club owners, being forced to accept whatever the owner felt was a reasonable salary, even if it was unreasonable.

For sure, the owners were the ones making the big money. But times have changed. The average salary of a pro athlete today must be more than a million dollars.

So where is the hardship? Yes, pro careers are short, and not everybody makes $1 million a year. But nobody said becoming a professional ball or hockey player guaranteed you'd never work another day in your life.

Teams have insurance policies in case an athlete receives an injury, and any athlete who can't survive on the couple of hundred of thousand dollars he receives annually doesn't deserve it anyway.

But should they be in a union? (I realize most athletes are in player associations but that's just semantics: They're unionized.)

Unions, after all, are about seniority and keeping jobs, retirement benefits and holidays with pay.

Pro sports are about athleticism and talent. Survival of the fittest, strongest and fastest.

Unions fight to keep an employee's job because of "seniority." Pro athletes lose jobs to younger and better—and often times, cheaper—athletes all the time. When a more talented hockey player comes along, whether he's twenty, thirty or forty, he takes the place of another player. Loyalty doesn't have anything to do with it. Nor should it.

It's all about talent, that's the name of the game.

And as most people know, talent has no place in a unionized environment. There are dozens of examples of that, where a more talented, but junior, employee is laid off, fired, whatever, in order for the senior, but slower, less gifted, dinosaur to retain his or her position.

You tell me that's fair?

Life is about competition. There are no free rides (unless you're a twenty-year union man with plenty of job security), especially in the world of professional athletics.

Perhaps it's time to rid the sports world of unions, and leave them to the working class.

Hockey Then…And Now… by Kevin Tobin.

Pictures
Bernice Morgan

For the last twenty miles they hadn't seen another person, another car—or a house that was lived in. Sara wet a Kleenex in the bottle of water and wiped the dust from around the baby's mouth. The old car hit another rock, the water sloshed over her already damp slacks, the boys in the back seat woke and began at once to argue.

"This is not the way I pictured our vacation," she said.

Her husband didn't take his eyes off the narrow road.

"How did you picture it, Sara? Paved highways, eternal sunshine and clothes dryers? In the far reaches of Bonavista North?"

The answer, of course, was yes. She had not thought about roads of rock and dust, of cold rain that turned sleeping bags soggy, of sun too weak to dry them, of a crying baby, of fighting children, of herself and David bickering. Those few precious days David could take away from work she had thought of as a series of lovely pictures—like those in TV ads—her laughing family running across a sea-smooth beach—singing by moonlight outside the tent—roasting potatoes over a camp fire. She had even dared to picture herself having long, long conversations with some relatives, unknown—but surely still living along this shore where her mother, long dead, had grown up. She sighed.

"This is an absolute waste of time," her husband said. "We're never going to find Cape Freels, much less Cape Island. Anyway, what would you find in a place that was abandoned before you were born? We should have stayed in St. John's. At least we should not have taken those two," he made an ineffectual swing towards the back seat, the children ducked and giggled. "They can't sit next to each other for five minutes without fighting, much less five hours. Mom said she'd take care of them. I don't know why we didn't at least leave them in town."

I will count the finger-marks on the dashboard, I will remember all the kings of England, in order—I will not say a word! Sara resolved.

She took a deep breath. "Your mother," she said, "gives those children whatever they ask for—the last time we left them with her for a day they were sick for four days afterwards. She refuses to believe that any grandson of hers could be allergic to chocolate, and it took fifteen dollars worth of drugs—fifteen—to get Jay over the garbage she let him stuff himself with. I'm never going to leave the children with her again. Your mother has a way of spoiling men rotten!" Too late she clamped her lips shut.

There was silence, even in the back seat. They drove up and down through the pale dust and paler sunlight. She turned her head away, trying not to cry and stared at this place she had insisted upon coming to. The deserted houses, two-storey, box-like, had been built helter-skelter in little hollows or atop stony hills, wherever there was a small flat space. There were no trees but tangles of dust-choked bushes that even in the July sun looked starved. The sea rolled in against black rock and rotting wharves. What must the place be like in winter—when wind slashed in from a freezing sea and pushed snow down against the unprotected walls of the houses?

The road widened where a lane cut down a steep hill. David pulled the car over, got out and walked forward, looking out to the sea. The boys seemed to have settled down with their comic books and after a few minutes Sara, with the baby on her shoulder, climbed stiffly out to join him.

"You're right, it is awful," she said, and immediately felt guilt, for it was awful—awful and beautiful almost beyond bearing. They leaned against the car and looked out at the endless sea. Far off they could hear the roar. After a time Sara could feel the lines around her mouth and the muscles across her shoulders begin to relax.

The sharp, hopeful sound of a hammer, so out of place in all that desolation, startled them. They swung around, and looking down the path, saw below the house, and the people.

The roof of the two-storey house was almost level with the road; it had a one-storey back porch, and on the porch roof two men worked. The man hammering was round shouldered, he had dun-coloured hair, wore a buttoned sweater of the same colour and the trousers of a serge suit. He was carefully replacing boards across staring, empty windows blotting out the last glimpse of limp lace and stained wallpaper. The other man on the roof was younger, in his twenties probably—it was hard to tell—his face, with protruding eyes and lolling tongue, wore that blank innocence that misses age. This boy-man was sweeping glass into little piles on the black felt roof. He held the broom awkwardly in both hands and with concentration carefully manoeuvred each piece of glass into position, smiling as the piles of glitter grew.

The scene had the quality of a dream. Sara and David had been watching the two men for some time before they realized that they were being watched—by a woman in the garden of the house—a woman who held her hand shading her eyes and looked up at them without moving. A big woman, in her early sixties probably, her print dress was almost covered with a faded blue apron. She had a green knitted sweater on under the dress, the sleeves barely covered her wrists. Her legs were very white, she wore men's dark blue socks and white shoes.

Sara passed the baby to her husband. "I'm going down to ask them if this is Cape Freels." Before David could speak she had started down the path to the grey gate.

The man saw her coming and climbed slowly down the ladder. He and the woman came over to the gate: only the boy on the roof continued to work, smiling at his piles of jagged glass.

The path was so steep that Sara had to run the last few yards and arrived at the gate breathless. "I wonder if you could help me?"

"Yes?" the man's voice was soft, almost a whisper. The woman, although she stood a few feet back, gave the impression of protecting him.

"We were wondering if we could get out to Cape Island this way—or is this it?"

"No...no, this is Cape Freels South. I s'pose you could get out to the Cape. You'd have to walk, though..."

"It's not really an island, then?" Sara asked, although she knew the answer.

"No, no, more of a little sand arm, a peninsula. You'd go up around the curve of the beach—see where the herd of horses are? You'd have to walk around the point there, and on about a mile—you would probably get your feet wet." The man's voice was so mild, so colourless, that it seemed part of the silent houses and overgrown paths.

The woman stepped forward, she had pulled her apron off. "What would you want to go out there for—there's nothing out there—nothing except a few horses that are left loose for the summer."

Sara had the sudden illusion that these three people were not real, they were the guardians of this place and would surely disappear when she and David got back into the car. The woman was really asking, "What right have you got to go out there?" Sara tried to answer.

"My mother grew up there, and her father was buried there."

"Who might you be, then?" the woman bent towards Sara, studying her face. "What was your mother's name?"

"Sadie—Sadie Vincent," Sara said.

The man and woman looked at each other, then back to Sara.

"Poor Sadie's girl."

How strange the long gone title sounded, Sadie's girl, like slipping on a glove you'd forgotten, and finding all the curves of your own hand. In this place she was Sadie's girl.

Unexpectedly, the man smiled. He had a nice smile.

"Oh, I remember you, many's the time I stopped at your poor mother's house in St. John's. I remember you when you were no bigger than the little one there," he nodded at the baby David had brought down.

The woman looked at the baby a long time. "The baby is Sadie's granddaughter—just think! And poor Charlie's great-granddaughter."

The man spoke to David: "You won't find anything out on Cape Island. The graveyard just slipped into the sea, they floated the church over—and some of the houses, too. The rest just rotted and blew away. There's nothing there, just a few hollows where the houses and cellars were. We moved grandfather's house here," he nodded to the house behind him, "but it were a mistake. Twelve years later they moved almost everyone out of this place. Of course grandfather was dead by then—a good thing, too, because it almost killed him to leave the Cape. Father and Mother kept on here though, until five years ago when she died, then Father come to live with us over in Lumsden…," he hesitated, "…I teach school there…I used to…"

His voice dribbled out, but his wife spoke up quickly over the doubt that moved across her husband's face.

"He hasn't been well the past few years. The children are gone now. Ted is living in Toronto, he sells business machines, and Greta teaches school in St. John's—so no one is interested in this old place. But we try to get down here every summer and keep the place respectable—the boys up the shore make sport of breaking the windows—it looks so bad…like poverty."

Her husband nodded.

Glass tinkled as the boy on the roof tried to sweep all the little piles into one big pile, tripped and fell to his knees.

"I had better go back up with Sammy—his mother would break her heart if we let anything happen to him." The man nodded to the young couple with grave courtesy—"I'm certainly pleased to meet you both."

He turned and re-climbed the ladder to the roof. David nodded goodbye to the woman and turned also, to climb the path to the car where the two boys were calling.

"We take Sammy with us, it's a treat for him," the woman said. Then she noticed the ravelled cuff of her sweater and became self-conscious. "What you must think of us—like a bunch of gypsies…."

Sara shook her head—there seemed nothing she could say. She suddenly remembered the man—had placed him in the distant assortment of relatives who had visited during her childhood. His name had been…was…Ray, and he used to come in to St. John's for summer school. In her mother's old album there was a brown snapshot; it showed Ray and her mother in the backyard, two smiling young people, her mother already painfully thin. A lovely summer's day it had been; her mother had moved the old footpedalled sewing machine out into the garden and was making lace curtains. In that picture her mother, one frilly white curtain draped bride-like around her face, stood with an arm linked into her cousin's ("He's going to be a teacher," her mother had told the children reverently). Ray was standing tall and tanned, his lips pressed together to restrain the loud laugh that would any second burst forth.

"Do you ever see Greta in St. John's?" the woman asked.

"No—no, I suppose I wouldn't even know her if we met—it seems terrible, doesn't it?"

There was a long, uncomfortable pause.

"I wish I could give you a cup of tea, but we don't keep anything over here now." The woman shifted uncomfortably, wanting to end the meeting. "I don't know what you must think of us," she said again.

"That's alright," Sara reached out but did not quite dare touch the woman's hand, "we have to get back—the baby, you know."

"You're not going out to Cape Island, then," it was not a question.

"No—no, I don't really think we will, now."

She turns and starts climbing the path towards the car. At the top of the hill David, holding the baby, leans against the fender. The boys stand on each side of him. Their eyes screwed against the sun, they all watch her with grave anxiousness. The dusty car, the two little boys, the sour-looking baby, the tired, thin young father—caught forever in the pale light of a fading picture.

Excerpt from

Waiting for Time

Bernice Morgan

Lav finds her way easily, as she'd known she would. The last four or five miles are over a brown mud path across marsh and bog. There is not a house in sight. The only sign of civilization, in the general sense—not in the way Philip would have used the word—is a power line strung between poles set down into cages that are filled with rocks. She cannot see the ocean, just sky and bogland.

The road ends in a torn up patch of mud that is littered with beer bottles, Kentucky Fried Chicken packages, condoms and a large roll of filthy carpet. Packing bread, fruit, cheese and the remaining coffee into her knapsack, Lav locks everything else into the trunk of the car and slings the army parka, knapsack and tent bag over her shoulder. She starts down a footpath that is hollowed deep into the bog but a few hundred yards along stops, turns and goes back to the car.

There is something unpleasant about the parking spot. It reeks of mindless vandalism, a kind of casual evil. She cannot leave the journal there. Telling herself that what she is doing is stupid, Lav unlocks the trunk and removes the journal. Wrapping her sweater around the heavy book, she slides it into her knapsack, gathers up her belongings and starts off again.

It is enjoyable walking on the spongy peat path between low marsh plants. Lav fancies she can catch an elusive minty smell—the white winter-shrivelled berries perhaps, or the tiny yellow blossoms growing near the path. Or maybe it's just the brown leaved bushes percolating in the heat. The sun warms her hair and the back of her shoulders. She wonders why she brought the bulky parka.

The path becomes wetter as it meanders towards the sea. It skirts outcroppings of rock and perfectly round ponds of bog water shining like melted chocolate in the sun. She can feel the water, pleasantly warm, seeping into her running shoes, oozing between her toes. Each time she lifts a foot she hears a small plopping sound and when she looks behind sees brown water filling her footprints. Who would have thought that walking through a bog could be a sensual experience? She walks slowly, knowing, despite Alf Andrews' warning, there are still two or three hours of daylight.

She comes to the neck more quickly than she had expected. The strip of land that anchors Cape Random to the shore is today cut by a deeply flowing river. It is not, of course, a river but two arms of the sea. A narrow bridge over the water looks as if it has been deliberately hacked apart and crudely repaired. However, she crosses without difficulty—and is on the Cape.

The expected rush of excitement does not come. According to the journal the church should be nearby—but she sees no building of any kind. The path rises a little, curves around a giant lump of speckled marble, smoothed by wind, snow and ice until it looks like a huge egg resting in a nest of bushes. Lav climbs the gentle curve to the top of the rock—and there is the ocean!

She sees it, hears it, smells it! Around her stretches the long sweep of beach where the sea rolls in and out—its soft swish belied by the ominous roar that rumbles up

after each receding wave. Overwhelmed by the combination of sight, sound and smell, Lav drops her belongings, runs toward the wet sand.

Here, along the landwash, the beach is covered in small shells, cream, peach and pale mauve, blue mollusk, purple starfish, amber kelp, long strings of seaweed from which green translucent grapes hang, algae, white corallina and black mermaids' purses, ivory sand dollars and scarlet jellyfish shining like glass bowls. There are broken lobster pots, driftwood carved into abstract sculptures, bits of worn glass that resemble sugared candy and garish plastic containers not even the sea can make beautiful. Lav walks back and forth, gathering things until her pockets are full and her hands smell of kelp and seaweed.

She sits on the sand, watching gulls and seabirds swoop and dive, watching the sea roll up the beach. She tries to imagine a city, but cannot.

Intoxicated by light and air and salt water, she climbs the bank, returns to the speckled rock and tries to orient herself. She picks up her belongings and clambers through thick brush up towards a rock ledge where she guesses the potato garden would have been. But on the brow of the hill there is no sign of cleared land—just alder and wind-stunted evergreens, their bare roots clutching at rocks.

Then, towards the edge of the hill, she sees the mound of stones, grey surfaces half covered with mustard lichen. The stones have been piled in a great heap, carried one by one to this spot to make a kind of rough wind-break for the vanished garden. They are the only sign that anyone has ever lived here. She picks her way over the thistle and dandelion that ring the stones and steps gingerly onto the rock pile. The rocks appear loose but time, weed and lichen have bound them together. It is easy to reach the top where she spreads out the parka and sits down. Scraping back the threadlike tentacles of some subterranean plant, Lav eases a large grey rock out of its place.

She sits, holding the rock, giving herself up to which of the women—Jennie, Meg, Sarah or Mary—last touched it? Surely one of them had pried it up out of the ground and carried it, perhaps in her apron, to toss onto this pile. Lav rubs her fingertips over the hard surface. The top of the rock is smooth but its underside has a rough wave-like pattern, incised eons ago by the great ice cap as it retreated, pressing silt and sand down to make the hills, bays and islands along this coast.

Wishing for clairvoyance, Lav closes her eyes, holds the cool rock against her forehead. Nothing happens. No face, no voice, no presence appears before her mind's eye.

"A good thing, too—supposing it worked both ways—suppose they could see me," Lav looks ruefully at her well-manicured hands, her tapered varnished nails.

Feeling foolish, she puts the rock back in its place, stands, searches for a flat spot to pitch her tent. Down where the houses must have been there is only rock and low bush, no cellar, fence or barn, no lilac tree or wharf. It looks like Tennyson's land, Lav thinks, staring out over a landscape where nothing but the sea moves—a land where no one comes or has come since the making of the world.

Excerpts from
Playing Around With Time
An Interview With Bernice Morgan — by Bruce Porter

I have so much admiration for young people who begin writing now in their teens and identify themselves immediately as writers. I think that's wonderful, to say, "I'm a writer." I dared to say that after *Random Passage* came out, never before. A group of us got together when we were in our early twenties, a spinoff from a group that took a night course in creative writing. Many of us had day jobs and many of us were mothers and we would certainly have identified ourselves as a teacher or a mother and never a writer. Part of it was we had grown up in a place where there weren't writers. I didn't know anyone who did it. None of the books I had read had been written by Newfoundlanders. I must have been in my twenties before I heard about Margaret Duley. The writers I was reading then with such admiration were people like John Updike. And he is, of course, a wonderful writer. It wasn't until I started reading Margaret Laurence that I started to think about things nearer home.

There was money available in International Women's Year so Helen [Porter], Gerri [Rubia] and I decided to put together a collection of writings (*From This Place*) by Newfoundland women. While we were looking for things, I came across Lydia Campbell's material. Somehow her voice clicked with Margaret Laurence's for me. Margaret Laurence was a polished, crafted writer; Lydia Campbell was barely literate, but there was some common bond. There was a thread there of honesty and a voice that spoke from the insides of houses, from where families and women lived instead of from battlefields and businesses. It took me a long time to make that connection and to start thinking: this is something you can do. I think it was because I really wanted to write honestly that I started thinking about who I was. It wasn't the other way around.

It was both. I had been reading Margaret Laurence before I encountered Lydia Campbell. Remember there's a line in Lydia Campbell's work: "I am what I am, Praise the Lord." That sentence! I sat in the library and started to cry, and I can hardly read those words now without crying. To think that somebody, out of what she'd come through, had that much strength to write that down. It's such a statement, and so honest and straightforward.

I don't know if I've found it yet. I wrote many short stories before that, one in particular about a trip we took. I wrote it about thirteen years before it was printed. It's called "Pictures." We took the kids down camping in Windmill Bight (at Cape

Freels). It was the first time I had been back there. My mother was from Cape Island. She died when I was nine. Once, before she died, we had gone down there. There were still people there at that time, three or four houses, still out there on the sand. And I never forgot that. I went back and I said, "We're going to find them," but we couldn't, and I really had this sense of a place that was being kept almost deliberately from me. Anyway, I wrote that story, and I think that story is really the beginning of *Random Passage*.

Oh yes, almost word for word, and that strange incident happened. The picture I described exists in a book in this house now of that man standing behind my mother with a sewing machine in the back yard sewing curtains. And this same man I encounter twenty, thirty years later! It's exactly what happened. I think I really wanted to read the story of how people could settle in a place like that. What made them go there and how did they stay? People have been writing it about other places and I kept wanting to read it. (I say this to students now. I'm always telling them how important it is to write about their own place.) Somehow, in almost every story I wrote, there's something about that place—not deliberately, it just happened.

I think it must have been over three years from the time I started writing until I had this mass of about seven hundred pages. I didn't know what to do with it, so I went to the library and looked up agents. I sent letters of inquiry to six and heard from one, Jack McClelland. He said he'd look at it so I bundled this mass up and sent it off. It was gone for a month and then it was back. I'm not a weepy person, but I bawled before I opened it. Anyway, he said he was sympathetic to Newfoundland work, but no publisher would think of publishing that big a book from an unknown writer. He suggested I break it into three books. He also suggested, later, that I consider whether I really wanted to set it in Newfoundland. He said that with even a well-known writer like Farley Mowat books about Newfoundland were poor sellers.

The way I had conceived the book first was to have it begin with the story of a Beothuck woman looking at a place where her family has come for hundreds of years and feeling that something has changed. She has this terrible sense of unease, because there are fewer people coming. The book was to end in 2024 with another woman looking at the empty Cape with the same feeling—that her people were disappearing. So I had fish disappearing in 2024. We hadn't heard the word moratorium then (although in Newfoundland anyone who had eyes in their head knew they were

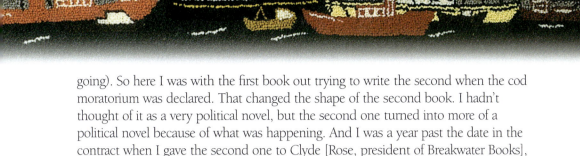

going). So here I was with the first book out trying to write the second when the cod moratorium was declared. That changed the shape of the second book. I hadn't thought of it as a very political novel, but the second one turned into more of a political novel because of what was happening. And I was a year past the date in the contract when I gave the second one to Clyde [Rose, president of Breakwater Books], because, to tell you the truth, I threw away more than I saved. Like most of us in Newfoundland I was in a rage, so I was writing sermons. I think the two books are less of a piece than if they'd been produced as one. There are jarring things there.

Sometimes I see something and say, "That's it, that's the thread that runs through it all." And then I see something completely contrary. It seems to me—and this almost sounds racist—that we do have an anti-bureaucratic trait in us. We're hard to regiment. My father would never go on a picnic at a picnic site. In the last years of his life these beautiful picnic sites appeared along the highway with tables and chairs. He hated sitting on the ground so he used to carry a folding chair in the car and our family would have picnics in gravel pits—that trait of working underground, taking rules that are imposed on you and twisting them round to your advantage is the only thing that has let us survive.

No, it was not conscious in that way. I have often thought of how easily we are moved by words and how sometimes in many Newfoundland communities there's somebody who has that power. One time it was the power of the storyteller; in more modern times it's more likely to be the power of political persuasion. Words define us in ways that are so important. It's frightening to see young people who accept that they live nowhere because they haven't seen their place reflected in words. They have no sense of their own myths. I think it's such an obvious thing in Canada now. There's no Canadian curriculum. We have no vision of ourselves, not just as a people but as a unit of different people with any kind of unifying myths or background. I really think that you can destroy a people with words. You can make them or you can destroy them and we don't have a sense of that now because the TV image has wiped out our sense of the power of words.

Yes. It's an attachment to place, I think. Although Newfoundlanders feel themselves insecure, in some respects we're the most secure people in Canada. I got this sense in Vancouver. On at least two occasions Newfoundland young people came up to talk to me after readings. They've been working in B.C. for years, and they all have this sense

that there's a place they could go back to if they had to. Two of them said, "And I've got a piece of land there." I said to one young fellow, from Random Island as it turned out, "That piece of land is rocky and it goes straight up the side of a hill, doesn't it?" And he said, "Yes." But it's there. I think it gives us the feeling of continuity. A lot of the dispossessed of the world can't go back to the land they've run away from or had to leave to get work. If this is a preoccupation of Newfoundlanders, maybe it stems from some need to articulate that it's there, it has been there and that we've come through other times worse than this and we're here and will be here.

I'd like to think of them as being positive. These people had a really deep sense that they were working for something worthwhile, and that the next generation would have it better. They didn't have any sense of futility.

My mother's dying gave me two things: it made me think there's no fairness in the world; and it gave me the need to impose some kind of artificial order on things, to make one event flow out of another, which it doesn't. Most things are random. The big things that shape our lives are often things we have no control over. And maybe what a writer tries to do is to impose control. I realized recently maybe that's what I've been trying to do ever since. I can't imagine anything that would be more devastating to a child. How little adults know of what is happening to children, of what they think! As I remember those times—I was the oldest of four—our grief was not manifested in any outward way; it was very much covered and it was almost as though our mother had disappeared and we weren't supposed to talk about it.

Sesame and Lilies: Tattered Treasure
James Wade

hemotherapy. After twenty-five months it's come down to this in a square hospital ward with three others. The room is in various shades of industrial green—mint, avocado, and dinosaur. Not a smidgin of art to be seen. And except for the corner of a window, where the evening clouds are pinking in, not a smidgin of life either. The place is drained dry of soul-food. Why?

I've thought of eventually changing the name of this column to "Life Lines"—how it might be infinitely more engaging to be grappling with the nuances of endless vitality than going on endlessly about art. It might be a good idea. This could be the first official edition.

Tonight I'm sitting up alert, Celtic harp on low on my tape-machine. Tomorrow the supposed horror of the treatment begins. But they tell me it's not that bad; that I'll be home again on Saturday. Thing is, today is my usual day for writing up my column. In the rush of this morning's short notice—a hospital call at 9 a.m.—I took a handful of tapes—mostly masses—and four books. This is my only art.

Late evening, with all hands asleep, I wander down the corridor and chance upon a workroom. Tables and chairs—ideal for my purpose.

But what can I say about it? My art?—*The Penguin Book of Irish Verse*, a pocket Bible (NIV), Knut Hamsun's *Pan*, and an old edition of John Ruskin's *Sesame and Lilies* (lectures delivered in 1868, on the treasures to be found in books). They all happened to be in my line of vision on my bookshelves as I packed.

The Bible pulsates for me in great, fiery wings; everything it touches it burns. It could be said of it, as Kafka said of Christ, "He is an abyss filled with light; we must close our eyes if we are not to fall into it." It rests on my table, secure. I pick it up and read it; and no one can ever take it away from me. That's a fact. And I believe that ultimately all art stems from it.

The lesser books reflect a noble beauty nonetheless. Knut Hamsun, awarded the Nobel Prize for Literature in 1920, once fished off the Grand Banks of Newfoundland. His work shines with his startlingly subjective style, containing a harmony found only in the highest types of poetry.

I leaf through the decades-old edition, sampling prose that brings tears:

> A few days passed as best they might; my only friend was the forest and the great solitude. Dear God, I had never known such solitude as on the first of these days. It was full spring; I found wintergreen and yarrow in the fields; I knew all the birds. Sometimes I took a couple of coins from my pocket and chinked them together to break the solitude.

The Irish verse remains my life-long study—it cannot be matched. It belongs in that twilight world of intransience and impermanence that speaks to the heart of humanity. This is its special mission. There's no more to say.

Sesame and Lilies fell into my hands from a towering bookshelf in a cluttered Halifax shop last spring. It's ancient (inscribed in 1911), tattered, and its pages smell of cinnamon and musk. The essays seem quaint and dated today. But they're worth the effort; they obviously cost Ruskin much thought and much strong emotion.

In the concluding lecture, "Of the Mystery of Life and its Arts," he urges us to dream of fullness in harvest, of wisdom in counsel and of providence in law.

"Although your days are numbered," he writes," and the following darkness sure; is it necessary to share the degradation of the brute, because you are condemned to its mortality?…Not so; we may have a few thousand days to spend, perhaps hundreds only, perhaps tens; nay, the longest of our time and when looked back on, will be but a moment, as the twinkling of an eye; still, we are men, not in we are living spirits, not passing clouds. "He maketh the wind His messengers; the momentary…His minister; and shall we…than these."

It's been a profitable evening.

Good night.

Old Bonaventure by Lois Saunders.

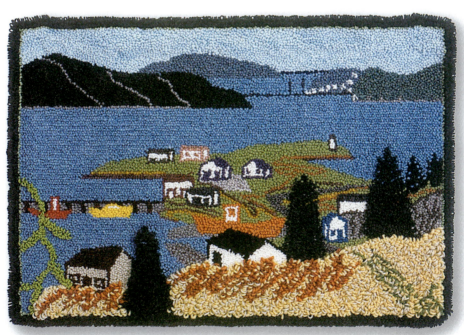

Dunville by Lois Saunders.

Artist's Statement
Cary S. James

Cultivating a childhood interest in minerals and gemstones I became an avid mineral collector and prospector. I am primarily involved in original and custom-work metalsmithing using a variety of precious metals, diamonds and gemstones. I sometimes use a technique called Mokume-Gane, which dates back to the seventeenth century in Japan. Metalsmith Denbai Shoami invented this process to adorn the handles of Samurai swords, attempting to match patterns formed by the Damascus steel of the sword blades. Layers of metals of contrasting colour are fused or soldered together into a solid stack, or billet. The billet is then reduced to approximately half of its original thickness by forging the metal. The billet is then folded and fused again. This process is repeated a number of times and produces a billet of many layers. Once the layering process is completed, unique patterns can be created in a number of ways. For instance, drilling and hand carving the billet as it is being reduced will achieve the flowing patterns of a wave, while hammering the metal with round punches will create a more random "wood-knot" pattern. The myriad of different techniques which can be applied at this stage of the process, ensures that no two pieces are ever identical. I design and manufacture my jewelry as one-of-a-kind pieces of art, which I hope to see last for generations.

Sterling silver ring by Cary S. James

Chrome tourmaline brooch by Cary S. James.

Sterling silver brooch by Cary S. James.

Will of Peter Weston, Ferryland, 1775
Collected by Ronald J. Fitzpatrick

In the Name of God Amen. I Peter Weston Esqr. of the Kingdom of Great Britain but now Residing in Ferryland in N.f.Land Merchant Being sick & weak in Body, but of sound mind, memory, & understanding, Do make this my last Will and Testament in manner and form following (that is to say) I recommend my soul to God hoping his Gracious Acceptance of it thro' the merit of Jesus Christ the Saviour fallen, And my Body to the Earth to be Decently Buried.—And as touching such worldly Estate with which I am Intrusted I dispose thereof as follows.

I Will that just payment and Discharge of all my lawfull Debts as soon as Conveniently may be after my Death—

I give and bequeath unto my well Beloved Wife Catherine Weston the One third of my whole Estate whether Real, Personal or Mixed, and where so ever Situated,—

I give and bequeath unto my Daughter Catherine Weston the One third of my whole Estate, whether Real, Personal or Mixed, & where so ever Situated

And it is my Will and desire that the One third of my whole Estate to Bequeathed unto my Beloved Wife Catherine Weston, the One third of my whole Estate Bequeathed unto my Daughter Catherine Weston, And the One third of my whole Estate Bequeathed unto my Daughter Sarah Weston is to be held by them in Severality & to Hold the name to them their Heirs and assigns for Ever,—

And it is my Express Will and order, that should my Beloved Wife Catherine Weston, die before my two Daughters, Catherine & Sarah then the One third of my whole Estate, Real Personal or Mix'd & where so ever Situated, which I have now bequeathed her, be Equally divided between my two said Daughters, Catherine & Sarah, And in Case Either of them should die without issue, then the Survivor shall have the whole, together with the One third of my Real, Personal or Mix'd Estate, and where so ever Situated that was bequeathed by me unto the said Deceased—

I Give and Bequeath unto my Nephew William Ludwig One Shilling Sterling to be paid him by Executors, when Demanded, or shall be convenient for them to do so,—

Which Sum is to be taken from my whole Estate,—

And it is my desire that my Estate be settled as soon as Possible after my Decease, and that my Beloved Wife Catherine Weston may have her One third in her own Possesion as soon as my Executors hereafter—

Mention'd shall be able to settle & adjust her said part of my Estate,—

And it is my desire that my Daughter Catherine be put in possesion of her One third of my Real, Perrsonal, or Mix'd Estate, as Bequeathed her, upon the Day of her Mariage, Provided my Estate is Settled by my Executors, who I hereby appoint to be her Guardians, or as soon as my sd. Estate is Settled—

And it is my desire that my Daughter Sarah be put in possession of her One third, of my Real, Personal, or Mix'd Estate, as Bequeathed her when she shall Arrive to the Age of Eighteen Years, Provided my Estate is settled by my Execr. at said time, if not, as soon as my sd. Estate is Settled,—

And lastly I do hereby Constitute and appoint my Beloved Wife Catherine Weston, and my Friend Mr. Edmund Gomond of Bristol, in Great Britain Merchant Executors of this my last Will and Testament and Guardians to my Daughters Catherine and Sarah, hereby Revokeing all others,—

In Testimony whereof I thereunto sett my Name and Seal this fourteenth day of June in the Fifteenth year of his Majestys Reign, Signed, Sealed, Published & Declared, by the said Peter Weston Esqr. the Testator

Peter Weston
as & for his last Will and Testament.

In Presence of us
William Dobel
Peter Dobel
Walter Butler

I here Certify the above is a true Copey of the Last will and Testament of Peter Weston Esqr. Ferryland Newfoundland Compared by me—

In Testimony hereof I have hereunto set my hand. Ferryland, Newfoundland, September 28th, 1775.
Robert Carter, Justice [of the] Peace.

Winter scene, western Newfoundland

Commentary on
The Will of Sir James Pearl
Ronald J. Fitzpatrick

A copy of the Last Will and Testament and Probate papers of Sir James Pearl can be found at the Provincial Archives, 1000-2000 Series, Box 2, #1012. He died 13 February 1840, with his Estate sworn at 500. It is a true example of how a document such as this can portray the personality of an individual.

In his will he stipulates that his Estate of Mount Cocharane in the District of St. John's was "granted in perpetuity to me as a small reward for my naval services." The word small was underlined in the original document, and possibly shows with his dissatisfaction with the amount of land given him.

He goes on to say that "… it is my positive desire and will that the aforesaid estate shall have its name immediately changed to Mount Pearl and that it shall ever after be so called and that no parts of the lands composing the said estate shall ever be sold, but that my dearest beloved wife shall enjoy whatever may accure there from during her life, and that should she again marry the person to whom she may unite herself in wedlock shall not have any control over the aforesaid estate or its proceeds but that the whole shall be at her individual disposal, should my beloved wife have any children by such marriage the eldest if a boy and he takes the name of James Pearl (should his conduct be such as she approves) shall inherit the estate of Mount Pearl, if a girl and there should be no boy she shall be Anne Eunice Pearl and shall inherit the aforesaid estate after her mother's death … but she shall not change her name on marriage as it is my will that the estate shall never be enjoyed by any one but a person bearing the name of Pearl."

As this will was dated a few years before his death, it is likely that Pearl went ahead and changed the name from Mount Cochrane to Mount Pearl before his death.

He goes on the say that if there are no children by his wife's marriage, a nephew would inherit, providing he has the name of Pearl. It also states that this inheritor must retain the name of Pearl throughout the generations. The will also refers to property at Singapore, and that his wife would inherit this as well.

The will is dated 29 January 1835 at 11 Aston Street, Liverpool.

(His wife's will is also contained in this file.)

Will of John James, Trinity

Transcribed by Shannon M. Lewis

The Probate

In The Probate Office Of The Supreme Court Of Newfoundland.
> By the Honourable John Gervase Hutchinson Bourne, Esquire, Chief Judge,
> and the Honourables Augustus Mallet des Barres
> and George Lilly, Esquires, Assistant Judges of the
> Supreme Court of Newfoundland.

We do, by these Presents make known to all Men, that on the sixth day of July One Thousand Eight Hundred and Forty-two and in the sixth year of the Reign of Our Sovereign Lady Victoria, before Benjamin Sweetant, Esq., a Commissionaire of Affidavits of the Supreme Court of Newfoundland, the last Will and Testament of John James Cake of Trinity in the Northern District deceased, hereunto annexed, was proved, approved, and ordered to be registered; the said deceased having whilst living, and at the same time of his death, divers Goods, Chattels, Credits and Effects in the said Island, and within the Jurisdiction of the Supreme Court of Newfoundland: —By reason whereof the proving and registering the said Will, and granting Letters of Administration of all and singular the Rights, Goods, Chattels, Credits and Effects of the said deceased, and also the auditing, allowing and final discharging the accounts thereof, are well known to appertain to only and wholly to the said Supreme Court: And that Administration of all and singular the Rights, Goods, Chattels, Credits and Effects of the said deceased, and any way concerning his last Will and Testament, was granted to Mary James of Trinity, aforesaid widow and David James of the same place the Executors named in the said Will; they having sworn well and faithfully to administer the same, and to make a true and perfect Inventory of all and singular the Rights, Goods, Chattels, Credits and Effects of the said deceased; and to exhibit the same into the Registry of the said Supreme Court of Newfoundland, at St. John's, in the Island aforesaid, on or before the last day of June next; and also to render a just and true account thereof, when thereto lawfully required.

> In testimony whereof, we have caused the Seal of the said Supreme Court to be hereunto affixed, at St. John's aforesaid, the eleventh day of July One Thousand Eight Hundred and Forty-two, AD 1842.

> By Order,

> [signature]
> Chief Clerk Registrar

The Will

In the name of God Amen-The 4th day of March one thousand eight hundred and forty-one. I, John James of Winbourne in England being of perfect mind and memory, thanks be given unto God: therefore calling unto mind the mortality of the body, knowing that it is appointed unto all men once to die to make and ordain this my last Will and Testament; that is to say principally and first of all I give and recommend my soul into the hands of Almighty God that gave it and my body I recommend to the Earth to be buried in decent Christian burial at the discretion of my Executors (David James and Mary James) nothing doubting but at the general resurrection I shall receive the same by the Almighty power of God. And as touching such worldly estate where with it hath pleased God to bless me in this life I give demise and dispose of the same in the following manner and form: First I give and bequeath to Mary my dearly and beloved wife my house and household goods for her widowhood if she survives me, in care and trust for our son William Henry James who I now constitute and make my heir forever under the proviso that it never shall be sold or let out of the family name of James. Secondly I give and bequeath what money I have in England (if any at the time of my decease) half to my wife and child and half to my brother if living, if not my wife shall have it and must erect over my tomb a head stone with the following inscription—Sacred to the memory of John James a native of Winbourne in Dorsetshire who departed this life in the 6th day of September 1841. Aged forty-two years—

    Beneath this stone lies a man
    Let those say he was honest that can
    John James signed sealed and delivered in presence of David James Humphrey Logan.

Her Mark
Michael Crummey

I, Ellen Rose of Western Bay in the Dominion of Newfoundland. Married woman, mother, stranger to my grandchildren. In consideration of natural love and affection, hereby give and make over unto my daughter Minnie Jane Crummey of Western Bay, a meadow garden situated at Riverhead, bounded to the north and east by Loveys Estate, to the south by John Lynch's land, to the west by the local road leading countrywards. Bounded above by the sky, by the blue song of angels and God's stars. Below by the bones of those who made me.

I leave nothing else. Every word I have spoken the wind has taken, as it will take me. As it will take my grandchildren's children, their heads full of fragments and my face not among those. The day will come when we are not remembered, I have wasted no part of my life in trying to make it otherwise.

In witness thereof I have set my hand and seal this thirteenth day of December, One thousand Nine hundred and Thirty Three.

Her
Ellen X Rose
Mark

"*Bounded above by the sky...*"

Artist's Statement
Anne Meredith Barry

As an artist, I take a field trip of discovery every summer. In my backpack are notebooks, pens and watercolours because the reason for my adventure is to gather new drawings and notes as a source of winter paintings and prints in my studio. Each trip, I discover new places and people, hear new stories and learn new histories which is very important because artists make images about ideas, not about "things." A few years ago I took a two-week trip along the coast of Labrador on the *Northern Ranger*. Captain French allowed me to draw from the wheelhouse, which was the highest part of the ship, with windows all around. One day as I watched the navigator plot our daily journey on his coastal chart, I realized that I was similarly recording my life's journey every day through my drawings and writings. After that I wrote every chart's code number in my books. Back home, I bought all of the charts from a chandlery in St. John's, started selecting images to be screenprinted directly on to the charts instead of on to paper and got permission from the Canadian Cartographic Department in Ottawa to use them. In this way I felt my images would be more related to the places and times where I saw them. I wanted the viewer to be on my trip with me. When looking at my print, COASTAL JOURNEY #1 – CROSSING THE STRAIT, the viewer can read from Chart #4731 all of the places and waters where the *Northern Ranger* travelled that day, see some of the things I saw, and perhaps feel some of the things that I felt while sailing the beautiful and dangerous Labrador Sea.

Coastal Journey #2: Past the Dog Islands, 1994 by Anne Meredith Barry.

The Ghostly Yarns of Ishmael Drake
Tom Dawe

You can call me Ishmael….Though the people back where I used to live always called me Uncle Ishmael. My family, the Drakes, used to live in Hemlock Cove. And I was one of the last ones to leave that place when everyone moved away back a few years ago.

I'll never forget our little cove out in the bay. 'Tis sad in the wintertime to think of the empty houses with the doors and the windows gone and the snow coverin' the flowers on the wallpaper. And in the spring, to think of junipers growin' up through the old cellar floors. And summer comin' with warm southwesters goin' mad down through the long rat-tails in poor father's garden. And the fences all gone. And the fall of the year comin' back again with no trawl lines in the water and the loon bawlin' somewhere in the dark tide. 'Tis sad, indeed, to call it all back now.

How we enjoyed the long hours around the stoves when the yarns were told. I can still see seven or eight men in Grandfather's kitchen on a winter's night, tellin' ghost stories.

Over and over again, as the years passed, I heard some wonderful tales! Many the night I was afraid to go to bed by myself because of those ghostly yarns. In dread, I expected the ghost of poor Neddy Gaunt, the merchant who drowned himself off his stage-head one dark November night, to be waitin' for me drippin' wet at the top of the stairs. Or I feared bumpin' into the demon dog that haunted the woods back of Rampike Arm.

Night after night when I found it hard to get to sleep, I would lie there listenin' to the wind in the walls and the old peaked roof creakin' in the long dark hours. In those times, after everyone was gone to bed, I would even hear somebody down in the kitchen rattlin' the dishes and the kettle on the stove. And a phantom would be choppin' away out in the yard until the dawn showed in the sky and the rooster crowed. When rain was heavy on the roof and the window panes rattled in the wind, I used to burrow far down under the bed sheets and dream of ghost ships comin' around the point….Lost sailors would be cryin' out in the cold fog, and broken bodies pitched in the dark waves that clawed at the headlands.

When I look back at those story-tellin' days, I see that we told all kinds of weird stuff. There were tales of souls comin' back from the grave to get even with those who had tormented them in life. Old women, for example, came back to frighten those boys who used to call them names and steal their crab-apples: horrible, witchy ghosts in clothes that waved across the moon-light as they waited in the narrow lanes snakin' in from the landwash.

I remember one story about an old woman who could still be heard singin', night after night, long after she was buried, singin' those ballads that praised the men of a bygone age. And 'twas said that her song was always heard by men with guilty consciences who ran by that boarded-up house if they were ever caught on the road alone after dark.

I remember another yarn about an old man who loved his grandson, a little baby, so much that he didn't want anybody else in the house to touch the baby at all. Day after day, he complained that the baby wasn't bein' treated right. He said that only he could care properly for the child. One day the baby got very sick. The old man was also sick in bed at the same time. So the doctor came to attend to both. One dark night when October winds moaned in the chimney stones, the old man said that he was goin' away. And he was takin' the baby with him. Nobody paid much attention to what the old feller said; he was almost dead anyway and his mind was wanderin'. So when the old man died and was out under the sod, the people forgot what he had said. But the baby didn't get any better. And one night in the middle of a rainy November, the child died. When they were gettin' him ready for the coffin, the women noticed strange marks on the baby's sides…dark marks like long fingers. So the women who were dressin' the corpse said that the old man had come back from his grave to take the child.

Of course we had a number of tales about ghastly birds, evil spirits in the form of loons; they feared no mortal guns, their great wings swishin' in the nighttime, and their lonesome cries on the air when the sun was sinkin' in the western waves. Sometimes 'twas even said the Devil himself took the shape of a great bird and made sport with men who went gunnin' in small boats.

It was also said that, when people died, the spirit was sometimes seen movin' out of the house in the shape of a wing or some strange, flyin' creature. I remember Polly Simms, a mid-wife, tellin' me about the night she minded the youngsters of a woman who was dyin'. The woman was far away somewhere in a hospital. And when she died at ten past three in the mornin', a big ghostly bird flew through the house. Polly remembers noticin' the hands of the clock when the thing flew through the children's room and vanished. She found out afterwards that this was the exact time the poor woman had died.

We had our fairy tales too; those of the strange little folk who stole sweet children from their cribs and led people astray in the deep woods. Sometimes the fairies would even change the landscape to deceive poor mortals. I heard a story one time about a woman who had a very cross baby; and the poor woman was up night after night with it.…So she finally concluded that the child wasn't hers. The fairies had taken her own sweet child and left the cross one in its place. 'Twas shockin' stuff to hear a mother say to her cross baby: "I guarantee, you won't be around here much longer!" I heard such talk myself years ago in Hemlock Cove. To protect against such evil, folks used to put a coin, tied on a string, around the necks of new-born infants.

We had ghost stories too, to warn people of their sins. People who were afraid to work on Sunday told yarns about the Devil comin' in some form to frighten wrong-doers back to their senses. I remember a couple of those. One was about a hall where a crowd were havin' a dance on Sunday night. But they needed somebody to play the fiddle because the regular player was delayed somewhere. So they were all standin' around not knowin' what to do, when in comes a handsome stranger who offers to play for them. His music was not of this world! Later in the dance, somebody looked down at the stranger's feet and saw that he had a cloven hoof. Then he quickly

vanished from the hall leavin' people screamin'. 'Twas said the Devil could take any shape he wished, but the one thing he couldn't do was change his cloven hoof.

Once I heard about a woman who was scrubbin' her floors early one Sunday mornin'. She was by herself; her family were all upstairs asleep in bed. Suddenly she heard a thump over in the corner by the porch door. She looked over but could see nothin'. So she kept scrubbin' away…. But after she heard the sound a couple of more times she went over to the door. And there, right in front of her, was the print of a hoof in the floorboards, the devil's cloven hoof marked out in her kitchen. The poor woman had a hard time gettin' over that experience.

Of course, we always had omens to warn us of what was to come. Like, if there was goin' to be a death, somebody in the place might see the ghost of the one who was goin' to die. And in houses where death was soon to visit, there would be knockin' in the walls. Just before my poor uncle died, his wife heard a commotion in the walls for nine nights in a row. Knockin' as if there was little people in there in the dark partitions.

We also got warnin' of storms when ghost ships were sighted goin' up the bay. I remember one time hearin' poor Grandfather talkin' to a man at duckish when they were unloadin' caplin from a skiff. 'Twas a calm evenin', and Grandfather was sayin' they couldn't expect a fine day tomorrow because they had just seen the lights of a schooner, a boat lost in a storm years ago, headin' up to the west. Grandfather said such lights always meant a comin' storm of rain from the southwest and a big gale.

We also used to hear some frightenin' tales about spirits from tragedies of shipwrecks. There used to be a place not far from home where just a few families lived. 'Twas a very rough piece of coast, and over the years, a number of vessels were wrecked there. In all those years, many bodies washed ashore in that cove, and the livyers had to bury them: though some people in our place used to accuse these same livyers of lurin' the boats in on the rocks with false lights so they could be wrecked and their cargoes taken.

I saw a letter one time that a livyer in that cove wrote to her relatives. In her letter, the poor woman described how terrible it was to be livin' in such a spot…where, sometimes, arms and legs and heads and other pieces of human bodies washed up on the beach day after day. Anyway, 'twas said the people finally had to leave that little cove because, in the dead of the night, they could hear the ghosts of the poor foreign sailors strugglin' far out in the icy water or down in the clefts of the big rocks where only the gannets could sail.

There were many unmarked graves on that coast. I remember one river in a cove where we used to go to catch salmon. On the banks of this river alone, from just one wreck, there were over one hundred corpses buried.

And there were always tales of pirate treasure around our place. Some of the islands off our cove were said to have treasure hidden in pirate graves. It was said the pirates always murdered somebody and buried the poor soul with the treasure chest.

A number of stories were told about some unlucky people in our place who tried to dig up that gold. A curse always followed them after they disturbed the grave. One man in particular saw a ghost so terrible guardin' one of the graves that the poor man

had trouble with his speech for the rest of his days. And he heard footsteps in his house night after night goin' through his upstairs bedrooms as if they were searchin' for something.

In another story, a man searched for pirate gold for days and days. One night his wife was alone in the house when she heard voices out in the yard. 'Twas quite dark outside so she pressed her face to the windowpane to see what was out there. Then, in a flash, she had a feelin' like a hand had slapped her across the mouth. And 'twas said that her face was twisted to one side for days after that. Indeed, her face was never the same again. The poor woman carried this deformity to her grave.

Some terrible tales were told havin' to do with spirits that an animal could sense. Once, my grandfather couldn't get his horse to cross a particular spot on a turn in the road. 'Twas the darkest time of day, just before dawn showed in the sky. The frightened horse refused to budge; she just stiffened and threw her head back. Then Grandfather saw something the size of a sheep by the fence on the bank above him. But 'twas no sheep…Grandfather always said 'twas a spirit, and the horse could sense this. The only way Grandfather could get the horse to cross this spot was to cover her eyes with his cap, grab her by the winkers and pull her along.

Yes, there were many yarns like that. And other stories about something chasin' a person but stoppin' on the edge of a brook, or a bridge, or any place there was water flowin'. Once I heard a story of a man whose house was haunted by the spirit of his dead son, a poor young feller who got drowned while workin' on the Great Lakes up in Canada. So the man sent for the priest, but the priest couldn't get the spirit to leave. Several times the man noticed a figure followin' him, and the priest said that if he could only get it across the bridge by the house, 'twould never return. But they couldn't get that ghost to cross water. So the poor man had to leave his house to the ghost and build a new one for himself….

Like I said before, we heard lots of ghost stories when we were young and the winter nights were long. To tell the truth, sometimes I wouldn't mind bein' back there now listenin' to the birch hissin' in the grate with Grandfather, Uncle, and all the others alive and well again. 'Twould be some nice to be cosy in the walls of that kitchen again with poor Mother singin' as she greased the bread-pans with fresh-butter and cocked her head to listen yet again to another one of Grandfather's yarns about the dark creatures that howled out in the cliffs on stormy nights, or the screamin' sailors that floundered in the landwash when the moon was full, cryin' in strange tongues that none of us could understand. But I can't go back there anymore. All I can do now is tell others those stories my people used to tell so often, and so well.

Afraid in the Dark!
Ron Pollett

I don't mean I'm afraid in the dark everywhere. It's the dark outdoors where I was reared in a salt-water village in Trinity Bay. Though it hasn't been my home since I was a tomcod many years back, on occasional summer visits I only bum around on the roads nights when I have to, for fear I'll see something.

This timid feeling stems from the ghost yarns I digested as a sprout. Hardly a day in those storied times but some imaginative oldster uncorked a hair raiser that happened last night. Sometimes it was a new spirit in a new spot, but most often it was an old one hashed over. All the lonely places were haunted, to hear people talk.

To my credulous young ears this was gospel. Every item stuck in my memory. I have overgrown a lot of things, but not that. Trying to be logical is no good; the more I say spooks are not so, the more I get to thinking about it. I'd just as soon stay home after dark, if you don't mind, as traipse around without company.

Spooky yarns dogged us

We villagers started getting the scary works early in life, as mere knee-bobblers, beginning with tales of red-nosed fairies who tolled strayed children off into the woods to be lost forever. There was purpose behind that as it kept us near the house yard, where fairies never ventured. Later, stories of sea monsters that reared ugly heads out of the deep stopped us from swimming out too far—that and the threat of sharks which never materialized either. These and like simple things we outgrew, just as we learned to spoof the threats of our elders to tell Constable Bishop and Magistrate Thompson on us when we got out of hand. These kindly gentlemen were the Law from Brigus who paid our place one-day visits monthly in my time and found little to do. But the spooky yarns we couldn't fight at all, and they dogged us like bucksaws all through the years.

Maybe not everybody's hair stuck up like mine. Some there were who would snap their galluses and spit in the eye of the Old Boy himself. These, in my opinion, were lunkheads, lacking imagination. The bright ones sponged up all the ghost lore and quavered.

So I was a bright one—and I've been paying the piper ever since. For instance, take that oldtime sawpit a short piece from our house. In daylight it's as nice a secluded holler as you could find, where a fellow could sit and count the emmets in peace. But at night—no, thank you. It's the one spot I never pass without cricking my neck trying not to look. According to the yarns, the place has been haunted since a hanging there in olden times, so long ago the ghost is bearded to the knees. It's no good to tell me, as some do, that this spectre is nothing more than a long-tailed white horse standing rear on, or a patch of windblown paper or rag snagged on a bush. Legend has it there's a spirit in that pit and that's enough pencil for me to draw a picture.

Five cemeteries in a mile

True, many of the storied crannies have been built over in recent times and now have lights aglow till a decent hour, scaring off the spooks. But there still are enough jumpy sections left to keep me from falling asleep on my feet. Especially is this true of the lonely mile of road to a neighbouring settlement, which stretch is now lined with five cemeteries instead of the three in my early days. Now as everyone knows, cemeteries are harmless places no more to be feared than the cabbage garden. But that wasn't the way I heard it. In our village lore they were the home of spirits.

At any rate, for the lonesome wayfarer sensitive to ghost yarns the passage here continues to be as stormy as they come. No dark seems able to hide the gaunt white headstones smack by the roadside fence. Eyes front is no good either; things seem to sneak up from behind. You hear strange footsteps which you hope are only sheep crossing the gravel, and cracking sounds which may be trees snapping in the frost or wind. Whistling is slight comfort despite its reputation as a nerve tonic; it only confesses fear when you know you are brave. And spare the moonlight, please; that is worse than dark because it livens the shadows, making long, dangling arms out of tree limbs—arms with bony fingers that reach out over the fence as if to skiver you up. When some boy boosted he covered that mile in ten minutes, you could bet it was at night and alone.

As if that weren't enough, this road also boasts the only haunted culvert reported in our section. The footbridge hugs a deeply wooded spot dark as pitch after sundown. But you don't have to see to feel. The culvert is so shallow that only a you-know-what can hide there. As a boy I sprang across the narrow bridge to avoid the reputed unearthly bump from below; today, sagged and weary, I'd have to holler for a handbarrow if silly enough to be trapped there alone.

And it's a darn good thing my courting days are over and I don't ever again have to suffer cold sweats beating the path all hours of the night several times a week conquering the "haunted" knobs, gravelpits, cavernous coves, lonely beaches, and dark holes underneath fish flakes—all of which figured in the yarns. A year or two of such hazardous trails is enough for one lifetime, and I've had it. Indeed, looking back, I can only think it was the nerviness of adolescence plus an overwhelming devotion to Cupid that carried me through this supreme test.

Ghosts clanked their chains

Anyway, it took courage to visit a girl in the next village or far out on the Point, or to squire her anywhere on the back roads where you knew you had to return alone in the 'fraid-of-my-life dark. In any direction there seemed no end to the spectral hurdles. If it wasn't a deserted house with eerie lights pricking the gloom upstairs, there was bound to be an echoey cove resounding madman screams above the drone of seawash— screams of a tortured soul out of the past who as a murderer had been left here to drown tied to a stake at ebb-tide. Almost any rockbound cove was good for that story, just as every gravelpit housed menacing phantoms, mostly headless men. The decapitated spectres, you gathered from the yarns, were ghosts of executed pirates, and

on stormy nights they clanked chains. It took little imagination to at least hear the chains where there was junk metal, such as barrel hoops of wire or steel, among the loose rocks and pebbles.

Of course, the farther you had to travel the oftener you were beset by the seeming supernatural phenomena, whatever that is. Among the most dreaded places to navigate were the oldtime burial grounds—cemeteries, again—now fenceless and overrun by sheep, goats, cows and horses that stabled in the ruins all night in fine weather. Ghostly silhouettes the animals made, and odd noises too, such as scratching themselves on creaky stumps and chomping on cuds, and in the otherwise stilly night a mere snap was gunfire to your cocked ears and the faintest baa a dismal moan. But bad as that was, the real skinner was the crash of a temperamental yoked goat splitting the bushes in sudden fright at your footsteps. That is, you hoped it was a goat. Things not of this world were constantly being reported from such places. And you knew the old grounds also to be the reputed rookery of spectral night birds that fanned your face as they flew past. Bats were never that big!

Old soldiers are dead already

Nor was the stretch of open road along a beach entirely safe. True, there was only a remote chance of a phantom ship bearing toward shore since our harbour was so shallow that only one was ever reported and that 'way back when my grandfather was cutting his teeth on a sparhoop. Still, there were ghostlights—well offshore, granted, but who could tell what direction these erratic balls of fire would take! Of course, the phlopping of washtub waves among the searocks, like a thousand dogs lapping water, had nothing to it. But not so the final, desperate whistle-wheeze of a standard fat squid. That could well be, instead, the ghostly remnant of a fatal shipwreck. Our spook yarns were well punctuated with groans, whistles and cries coming over the water.

As to the dark recesses underneath flakes, stages and stores along the lonely route, these held tapping, rapping and knocking terrors along with firebrand eyes which popped to life in the reflected light from the sky or from windows if there were any houses still awake at the late hour you returned from courting. Since such hideaways usually nested dogs, cats, sheep and goats—well and good. Even the giant oblong orbs of a seeming monster peering in slit-eye fury from the pitch dark could be explained as a couple of old soldiers in all their phosphorescent glory. But when you considered a pair of such eyes might very well disembody themselves and stalk you à la the ghost tales—well, this dark-hole business was no fun either. Incidentally, the kind of old soldiers we have in our place never die—they're dead already. Let the outlanders who may read this ponder that one!

Neither were you out of the woods yet on reaching your own friendly lane. A house lane was the acknowledged habitat of apparitions. Apparitions, in our ken, are familiar people you meet when they are not there. These appeared at midnight if there was light enough to be recognized. It was no one from your family, though the subject could be paying your house a call. He or she passed the time of night and moved on, you supposedly in a hurry to get home. It was when you discovered the truth later your hair started to curl. A person whose apparition appeared was in grave danger at the moment, usually dying before dawn. Although a fellow knew from the yarns that this vision was reserved for old women mostly—now, who's that coming down the lane?

Now the ghosts are scared

On such lonely trails any kind of companionship was a straw to grasp, even that of a dog at your heels or a stray horse cropping on ahead. "Faint heart ne'er won fair lady" could well have been said of us brave swains of other days.

Of other days, yes, because all this scary stuff seems fast becoming history. Such clammy fears as I "enjoyed" on the back roads appear to have faded in the new generation. Today's youths mostly scoot about nonchalantly in motor cars whose dragon eyes bite into the creepy nooks and crannies. Now it's the ghosts' turn to be scared. So, like their city cousins whose scant spectre lore comes in film cans from Hollywood, the new crop treads mundane ways. As for me, I'm still afire, even when sheathed in a car. Alone at night on an isolated homestead stretch, I step on it passing the scene of a recent drowning, and I fly past the Big Rock from behind which unseen hands pelt pebbles. In the house where I was cradled I send my city-reared children to fetch bedtime snacks from the "icebox" out in the yard—the underground cellar where my grandmother saw a spook. Cityites, of course, "don't know from nuthin'". It's a fact I have never seen or heard anything in all my days—nights, rather—that couldn't be answered. But I can't be lucky all the time.

Dark woods and winter gales

The Ghost of the Murdered Cook

Alice Lannon and Mike McCarthy

On June 15, 1915, the banking schooner *Marion*, owned and operated by Burke Brothers sailed from her home port of St. Jacques, Fortune Bay, for the Grand Banks. The skipper of the banker was Ike Jones and his crew hailed mostly from Boxey, but the cook was a young lad, Jimmy Evans, from St. Jacques. Jim's mother didn't want her son to go to sea, but he was determined, and after a few trips as "cagey," or cook's helper and jack-of-all-trades he was promoted to cook and was part of the *Marion*'s crew when she sailed on what was to be her last voyage.

Ike Jones, as tradition has it, was a good skipper, a fish killer who always made a good voyage, but a hard man when "in liquor." After leaving St. Jacques the banker's compass gave trouble and to get it fixed Jones put into St. Pierre. This also gave him and his crew the opportunity of settling an old score with the captain and crew of a French steel beam trawler undergoing repairs in St. Pierre.

The quarrel with the French crew went back a couple of weeks earlier. On their way in from the Banks, Captain Ike had put into St. Pierre to get a little liquid refreshment. At the Café Midi, a popular sailor's bar near the waterfront, the captain and crew of the *Marion* had tangled with the men from the French beam trawler. In the brawl that ensued the Newfoundlanders claimed victory, for Ike Jones was a fearsome fighter. The Frenchmen vowed vengeance if they met up with the *Marion*'s crew again.

When the *Marion* arrived at St. Pierre, they had to berth next to that very same French trawler. When sailing into the quay, the *Marion* brushed against the trawler's sides and the trawler captain called Ike Jones a drunken lout who couldn't pilot his own vessel. Jones replied with certain vulgar remarks on the French Skipper's ancestry. Some of the crew of the *Marion* were a bit uneasy for they knew what was going to happen if the two skippers met.

They did meet again that night at the Café de France, and Ike Jones gave the French skipper another good trouncing. The next morning when the crew of the *Marion* were getting ready to sail, the French captain stood on his quarter deck and uttered threats of vengeance and vowed he would settle the matter at sea. Ike Jones told the Frenchman he would meet him at any time and place, and teach him respect for his betters.

The *Marion*, with all sails set, slipped out of St. Pierre harbour and then seemed to simply disappear. The French trawler left shortly afterwards, but returned to her berth at the quay a couple of hours later. There were suspicions of foul play on the part of the French captain, but for thirty-one years the disappearance of the *Marion* remained an unsolved mystery of the sea. Only one person ever saw a member of the *Marion*'s crew again after she sailed out of St. Pierre Harbour, and that was Jimmy Evans' mother. She claimed to have seen her son's ghost on the very morning the *Marion* sailed from St. Pierre.

It was around eleven in the morning and Mrs. Evans was working away in her kitchen preparing dinner. She happened to look out of her kitchen window towards Burke's Cove on the other side of the harbour and saw a dory coming from the cove. When it got nearer, she was very surprised to see her son, Jimmy, who had sailed a couple of days earlier on the *Marion*.

Her first thought was that something must have happened to him. She watched him anxiously, but was a little reassured when she saw that he was pulling away at the oars.

Whatever was the matter it couldn't be too serious. He rowed in towards their stagehead and as he came into the wharf she saw he was wearing something like a red collar around his neck. "Ah," she thought to herself, "the quinsy throat most likely." She knew that the seaman's cure for this was to tie a red flannel collar around the throat.

Jimmy came into the stagehead, got out, tied on the boat and then disappeared into the stage. Mrs. Evans turned back to her cooking impatiently waiting for Jimmy to come in and tell her what had happened. She waited and waited, but Jimmy didn't come up the path from the stage. Finally she went to the back door and shouted out to him. She got no answer except the screams of the gulls and kittyhawks. This puzzled her and she decided to investigate. Throwing a shawl over her shoulders she ran quickly down the path to the stage door.

"Jimmy," she called out, "are you in there?" She called again, but still there was no answer. Then, she opened the stage door and gasped in horror. The stage was empty, but a set of wet footprints went from the stagehead to the middle of the stage and then ended. Immediately she knew that some disaster had overtaken her son and her screams brought several neighbours to her assistance. At first she was too overcome to speak and could only point to the wet footprints. The neighbours got her up to her own house and after a small tot of brandy she was able to tell them what she saw.

Some of them agreed that it must be Jimmy's death token, others just laughed and said she must have dozed off for a minute and imagined she'd seen him rowing across the harbour. She would see that they were right when the *Marion* returned. When the days passed into weeks and the weeks into months and there was still no sign of the *Marion*, Mrs. Evans knew for sure that Jimmy had come to say good-bye. The only thing that puzzled her was the red collar around his neck, why was he wearing it?

The years passed slowly away, and the mystery of the *Marion's* disappearance faded from people's memories, but it was generally felt in Boxey and St. Jacques that Ike Jones and his crew had met with foul play. Then, in the early spring of 1945, word came to the clergyman at St. Jacques that an Italian sea captain who had recently died in a seaman's home in Boston had confessed before he died to sinking the *Marion*. He had been the captain of the French beam trawler that Ike Jones had tangled with and who had vowed vengeance. He had put to sea after the *Marion* and rammed her, cutting the ship in two. The stern section sank immediately and Ike Jones and most of his crew drowned. However, the forepart of the banker floated away with young Jimmy Evans on it. The trawler captain knew that young Evans must be silenced and the forepart of the *Marion* sunk before another ship came along.

The captain ordered a dory launched, and he and the mate went after young Evans. They persuaded the terrified young man to get down into the dory, but as soon as he did the captain and mate seized him and cut his throat, and, with the blood still welling up from the wounds, threw the body overboard. Seeing that it would take some time for the forepart of the *Marion* to sink on its own, the Captain went back to his ship and rammed it until it sank. The steam trawler, with all its crew sworn to secrecy then returned to St. Pierre.

The crime had not weighed heavily on the captain's conscience, until he knew he was dying and he wished to confess to his crime. As the war was still on with thousands dying every day on the battlefield, the final chapter of the *Marion* story went unnoticed. However, in St. Jacques people remembered Jimmy's mother's story of seeing Jimmy's ghost, and at last the mystery of the red scarf was explained.

The Loss of the *Marion*

Bud Davidge

The wind from the northwest a fine summer breeze
As Ike Jones from St. Jacques he steered
And the boys in the fo'c'sle made plans for that night
When they'd all go ashore in St. Pierre

Some were uneasy there'd be trouble they said
'Cause Ike Jones was noted to fight
And at the Café de France on the last trip he made
A Frenchman had threatened his life

The challenge to fight was issued that night
While the cheap French liquor ran free
The French captain then warned the *Marion*'s men
He would answer the challenge at sea

Next day the *Marion* set sail again
And so too the story relates
The French beam trawler weighed anchor as well
And followed close by in her wake

Chorus: She's a Fortune Bay schooner heading out for the banks
With fine hardy Fortune Bay men
But some on the quay were rumoured to say
She'd never be heard from again

The fate that befell the *Marion's* crew
And their schooner will never be known
Not a trace and no tidings were ever again
To be heard by those waiting at home

Some say the Frenchman was true to his word
Some say he confessed 'fore he died
That he scuttled the *Marion* and settled the debt
Not taking one man o'er the side

Families of Skinners and Vallis and Miles
Grieve for their loved ones on shore
And the Newfoundland story of loss to the sea
Was told as so often before

She's a Fortune Bay schooner sailing out from St. Jacques
With a fine crew of Fortune Bay men
But never no more will she pass by the light
With her jig flapping into the wind

No never no more will she pass by the light
With her jib flapping into the wind

The Savage Cove Devil

Account of Ellen Learning

Just about everyone around the Paradise River, Cartwright area who have ever been up around Savage Cove have heard the Savage Cove Devil. It's been heard for years and years. The sounds are still the same. There been people who even went as far as to search for whatever was making the noises but they couldn't get close to the noises even. You can't get close because the sounds are always the same distance away.

I was out on the rocks in front of the house at Calloway's Cove when I heard it. 'Twas a real pretty evening, right calm. You could hear for miles. 'Twas so hot that evening that there wasn't even any flies. Most evenings when there's no wind the flies are thick enough to carry you away.

The sounds I heard was like someone callin' out for help. 'Twas so human sounding that my step-mother told Bob to go up around the shore and see if there was someone drove ashore with engine trouble. Bob told her that was only the Savage Cove Devil.

The sounds started like someone callin' for help, then it changed. Sometimes it was like people fightin', then people cryin' and babies cryin'. 'Tis all kinds of sounds, people sounds. 'Twould be a bad thing to have to listen to if you was up there alone in the night. Awful scary. After we heard it I couldn't get to sleep all night. I kept my brother Bob awake for company, I was so nervous…

Daddy been there lots of times, years ago, cuttin' wood for the Hudson's Bay Company. He said it used to be so bad it would keep the dogs howlin' all night. He'd have to get out of it.

Some people believes 'tis something in the rocks. P'raps the way the wind blows among the trees and the rocks. It can't be that though because we heard it on a flat calm day. Others believes that years and years ago there was white people there and the natives killed them all. Where the bodies fell was where they rotted and their souls haunt the place now.

When someone tells you a story like that, you don't pay much attention to it. You thinks they're puttin' you on. You got to experience it yourself before you believe it. All the years I was growing up I heard about the Savage Cove Devil and I just took it to be another ghost story. Not anymore. I heard it and it's real. Whatever it is, it is real.

Account of Neil Lethbridge

There's always been a Savage Cove Devil ever since I can remember.

Don Martin and Roll McDonald and, I think, Butler Martin was camped in there one summer, or spring, or something, and they heard this noise. Don feared nothing on earth, eh. He went on in lookin' for it, by the side of the hill somewhere. It must have been late spring, I s'pose 'cause they had dogs. Anyway, he was goin' about the woods lookin' for this 'thing' and all of a sudden he heard it comin'. It ripped— whipped right between his legs. You know most men would have fainted with the fright. Don never batted an eye. He never feared nothing, that man. 'Twas one of the dogs got clear and chased him.

One dark night in the fall, early fall, September, I think it was, me and Burton was up to Savage Cove. We had a house-cabin boat. I woke up in the night, thirsty, and we had no water. Burton was still asleep. I got up, got the boat and went ashore to Eagle River Harbour. Samse Learning got a little cabin there now, I think. Dark as the devil. I rowed ashore. Not a breath of wind, just flat calm. I was just takin' my paddles in when I heard this god-awful noise. I don't mind admittin' to anyone…that I could feel the hairs movin' on my head.

I was nervous and I nearly went back, but there was no water and I said, "If I do go back, Burton will laugh at me." So I went ashore. I had no flashlight or anything. I did have matches. So I was lightin' matches and goin' to find this little small stream that was there; this little spot of water, you know, you could hear trickle. Just before I got to get the water, those noises came again. You'd get this creepy old feeling, you know. I can't explain it. Sometimes it's like an infant cryin', or wolves howlin' in the distance, you know, mournful, and then those bitter screeches.

I nearly went back to the boat without my water but I felt sure Burton would laugh at me. 'Twas only nonsense, only a bird or an animal. Got to be, eh?

Lots of people, people my age, have heard the Savage Cove Devil, you know, like Max Pardy and Horace and George. Max was Jud Pardy's brother, Uncle Arch Pardy's son. They was camped on Saddle Island down there, right in the mouth of Savage Cove one time, gettin' a load of wood. They had it cut there for Pack's Harbour or something. They was lyin' in camp when they heard this noise. The younger guys wouldn't go and get water. Max went and got the water and when he left, they left camp with him. They wouldn't stay in camp alone. That was the kind of noise it was, 'twould nearly scare you. I don't know; no one knows, what the hell it is for sure. Must be a bird or animals or something, maybe water pressure, air pinned up. 'Tis hard to know what it is, but it's been heard now for many, many years.

Account of Samson Learning

The Savage Cove Devil was a very interesting thing. You wouldn't notice this in the middle of the summer, you had to be there in the fall of the year when 'twas icy. Sounds funny but, I mean, that's the way it was, eh.

Me and Forward was camped out on Saddle Island, a little island there in Savage Cove not far from the brook. We had a flashlight each, of course, and like I say, I was a devil myself, not afraid of anything and game for anything. So we took our flashlights and followed the little brook up through the hill, zig-zagged through willows and grass. We could hear this noise up there.

There was a wee bit of snow on the ground and 'twas icy. There was water streamin' down and, of course there was the tide from the current comin' down. There was a big tree with bare roots out on to the rocks and the sod was liftin' where the root was growed on. When the tree would rock, 'twould choke the water, see, and 'twould bubble and then when the tree would lift, 'twould squeak and grind, make a very mournful sound. Me and Uncle Far shined our lights in and this was what it was, just the tree, water, turf and woods that was makin' all this fuss. We went back in the morning and cut down the tree so there's be no more noises to bother the hunter in the fall.

St. Mary's Keys: A Story of the Supernatural
Captain George C. Whiteley, C. B. E.

> How far that little candle throws his beams! / So shines a good deed in a naughty world.
>
> —*The Merchant of Venice*, Act 5

Tom Fewer, of Harbour Main, was my mate and friend for thirty years. A warm-hearted Irishman, fearless and good in all the years we were together up to the day he was fatally injured hauling a load of wood with a spirited horse by the load of wood tipping over on him, almost crushing his life out. I never knew him to utter a falsehood.

Sitting by the bed in the hospital where they brought him, there was no hope from the first. We both knew it was the end.

We were talking of the many narrow escapes we had passed through on the seas, and now to be dying as a result of hauling a load of wood.

"The nearest time to death I remember," said Tom, "was when I was about eighteen years of age, before I came with you. I was shipped to a man from St. Mary's Bay named Con Sullivan. He owned a western boat of fifty tons. I was engaged for two summers and one winter and lived in his house when we were on shore between trips to the banks. We were five in crew: skipper and four men, two dories. The skipper did the cooking, sometimes we all took turns at it. Sometimes we anchored on the banks. Sometimes we had a trawl set and the skipper would sail the boat and pick us up.

"We passed the summer and at the end of the voyage we had a poor catch. Fish was scarce that year on the St. Mary's Bank and it looked as if there would be hungry people before winter passed. The same conditions were all over the Bay. People were poor and even the game (rabbits, partridge and such) seemed to have deserted the woods.

"It was Ash Wednesday, the beginning of Lent, and the family were sitting before the fire at the close of the day, when the door opened and a man slipped into the kitchen with the words,'God save all here!' The skipper knew the man. His name was Mat Colloney, from one of the little coves within a few miles. The poor chap had a tale of woe; a family and no food. The fishery, after the merchant had taken his share, had left very little for the winter. There was not a dollar to be earned. He asked Skipper Con if he would spare a pan of flour as he had not a crumb left.

"Con stood up and said,'Well, Mat b'y, I am on the last barrel of flour, but half of it is yours.' A sack was found and the barrel of flour divided, and the man went his way.

"May first, the boat was made ready for the summer's work and three men shipped, making four, and the skipper, five, and she sailed for the banks.

"A look at the map showed a very dangerous breaker off the mouth of St. Mary's Bay. Many ships have been wrecked on that breaker. It is called on the map, The Keys. Two of the last ships to end their days there were the *S.S. Bloodhound* in 1918, total loss, crew saved, and the *S.S. Sam Blandford*. The *S.S. Newfoundland* was reclassed and made into a new ship in New York, at great expense, and her name changed to *Sam Blandford*.

"I do not think Newfoundland seamen are any more superstitious than other

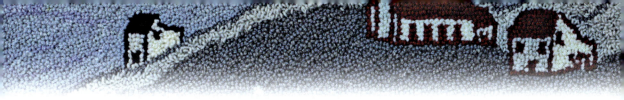

seamen. But one thing we have in common, and that is, it is courting disaster to change a ship's name—coming from New York for St. John's running near the land in dense fog, she ran over The Keys and that was the end of the *Sam Blandford*. Pass the bottle"—Tom continued his story.

"We fished on the banks and found fish plentiful. In three weeks we had a full load and bore up for home. With a light south west wind, during the day it closed in, dense fog, with a fresh breeze. Skipper Con felt confident of his position and ran on, setting his course for Cape St. Mary's. As night came on with the darkness and dense fog, the boat made a big bow wave, a regular bone in her mouth.

"I took the wheel at twelve midnight. The other two men turned in and the fourth man on watch with me stood in the bow on look out. The skipper was busy below, boiling a pot of tea.

"It was pitch dark. We were running wing and wing and it took me all my time to keep her on the course. I thought of that French song I had somewhere read—'The night was dark, like one black cat—The sea run high and fast,' I tried to sing—but somehow I could not overcome the feeling of dread that came over me, and I was glad when I saw the Skipper coming aft—it was 2:30 a.m. 'Give me the wheel, Tom, and you go forward and get yourself a mug up —the kettle is boiling, and pass a mug up to Murphy who is on the look out forward!'

"I went forward, poured myself a cup of tea, passed a mug up to Murphy—and, taking my mug, sat down. I felt very uneasy. After a while, I stood up and went to the hatchway and, half up and half down, I stood and looked aft.

"As I looked, I saw the form of another man standing by the Skipper. I could feel the hair rise on the back of my neck. What man was that? Turning around, I felt in the berth and touched the two sleeping men, counting to myself: one, two, myself three, Murphy, on look out, four, the skipper at the wheel, five. Where or what was that misty form standing beside the Skipper? As I looked, I heard a shout. 'The Keys! The Keys! Hard down, for God's sake, hard down!' Skipper spun the wheel. The boat gave a lurch. The mainsail came over from the starboard to port with a bang, and there on the beam rose the white, roaring breaker. She passed by a hair's breadth. When it was over, only the Skipper had the wheel; no sign of the form I had seen standing by the Skipper.

"Half afraid to go on deck, I waited a few minutes and then groped my way aft. As soon as I reached the wheel the Skipper burst out, 'Well, boy! I was well paid for the half barrel of flour I gave the poor man last Ash Wednesday. Did you see the breaker rear up? My son! It was touch and go.' He came and stood by me and let a screech out of him. 'Hard down Con! You are running on The Keys!' I spun the wheel. The mainsail came across with a bank and she shot clear. A narrow shave, Tom! Not a soul of us would have escaped!

"It was too thick to make the light, but after a bit we heard the horn on the cape, and knew we would make the port. As daylight came, we entered the harbour and anchored. The light was burning in the house window and as the anchor splashed over, two girls came down to the beach and launched a dory. They came alongside and Con and I went ashore.

"The women had been up all night. The boat was expected and the night so dark with the fog, the wife and girls had spent most of it on their knees praying for us.

"At breakfast a knock came and a man entered. 'Welcome home Skipper Con, with a good trip,' said the man. He added, 'I have been with poor Mat Colloney. He died in the night.' 'What time did he die?' asked Con. 'Well do you know it,' said the man. 'I was sitting by the bed when he sat up and let a screech out of him, "The Keys! The Keys!" Then lay back. When I looked he was dead. God have mercy on him.'' What time was it?' asked Con again. 'Time?' said the man. 'It was top high water. I know, as I went out to the beach and when I came in I looked at the clock; twenty minutes past three.'' Just the hour I saw him,' said the Skipper."

Lobster pots

Fair Marjorie's Ghost
Collected by Kenneth Peacock

Fair Marjorie was sitting in her bower chamber window, A-combing back her hair, it was there she saw young Willie and his bride A-climbing the upper church stair.

She drew the ivory comb out of her hair
And flashed it across the floor,
It was out of the bower chamber window she jumped,
She was never to be seen any more.

About the middle part of the night
When all were fast asleep
Fair Marjorie appeared in Willie's bedroom
And stood there at his feet.

"Oh how do you like your blanket," she said,
"And how do you like your sheet,
And how do you like your new married bride
Who lies in your arms asleep?"

"Very well I like my blanket," he said,
"Very well I like my sheet,
But better do I like fair Marjorie
As she stands there at my feet."

She took the ivory comb out of her hair
And smote him across the breast
Saying, "Be prepared and come along with me
To find your final rest."

He kissed her once and he kissed her twice,
And he kissed her three times o'er,
And then he fell there at her feet
To kiss a woman never more.

Excerpt from
The Miners of Wabana
Gail Weir

This story and the next show that some parts of the mines were spooky and creepy. The main areas were well lit but, in a lot of places, the only light was the one you had with you. If you had anything on your mind, travailing alone through these unlit areas did not help matters, as Clayton found out.

When he was still living at home, Clayton's grandmother was with the family. She had been with them ever since he was a small child. As young children, he and his siblings used to play tricks on her, such as making the alarm clock ring so that she would think it was the telephone and get out of bed to answer it. Then they would crawl under her bedclothes, lie still until she got back into bed and then tap her on the back to make her scream with fright. His grandmother had been bedridden for quite a while by the time he was working in the mines. One Saturday night, he was sitting at home with his mother when they heard a thump upstairs. They found his grandmother on the floor in the bathroom with her hand clasped around the chrome supporting leg of the wash bash She was still alive, but they could not get her hand from around this leg. His mother called this the "death hold." Clayton had to unscrew the leg and slip it out of her hand that way. At the time, he was working on the continuous operations, and he had to go to work the next morning, even though it was a Sunday. And, of course, he was worried about his grandmother. No sooner was he down in the mines then he got the call saying she had died and he had to go back up again:

> Where I was working at that time, you could go from No. 3 up to No. 4. This is where we were working at. Now to get from No. 3 to No. 4 you had to go through a place called 'Dogs Hole Hill.' This was a place where you had to duck down, you wouldn't have to crawl This was in the mines, to get from one mine to the other. No. 4 then had no deckhead. The ore from No. 4 used to come down to No. 3 and go on up that way. So, to get back to the surface, I had to come back to No. 3 and come down over this Dogs Hole Hill. And coming down the Dogs Hole Hill all this was coming in my mind. It was only foolish; it was only stuff running through your mind. I figured she was going to come and get me for all this old foolish stuff that we'd be doing. I couldn't wait until I saw the first light. The next lighted area you'd see was the warehouse. And when I saw the first light, I was right relieved.

These stories show that when a man was alone underground, he was really alone. Eric puts it this way:

> Everything was silence. You never know what silence is until you get underground and it's quiet, dead silence, grave silence, fearful.

There were even some miners who got to the point where they had to quit mining because working in that silence bothered them so much. Eric tells the reason a relative of his decided that mining was not the work for him:

> He was down in the nighttime, quiet, deadly quiet, loading away. No one there, perhaps by himself, and he heard the sand, the sea, rolling above him No. 6 only had two hundred feet above, between the roof of the mine and the ocean floor And he was loading away, and he heard the beach rocks rolling.

With this kind of loneliness and stories being told of ghosts of dead miners, it can be expected that there would be some practical jokers who would take advantage of this situation to set the scene for their pranks. One such prank caused another nervous man to give up mining:

> This story is true and concerns a miner who was easily agitated. On this particular occasion, a fellow workman stripped himself of his clothes and hid in an area where a workman had previously been lulled, knowing that his intended victim would pass nearby on his return from the mines. When he heard the victim approaching, he began to moan and make peculiar noises, giving the victim the impression that he was seeing the ghost of the departed one in anguish. The unfortunate man got such a fright that he became mentally disturbed and gave up his job, never to work underground another day.

Ghosts were not the only supernatural beings observed by Wabana mine workers. Many of these men believed in the existence of fairies. A man who worked at No. 4 compressor claimed that one night, when he was on duty, the fairies visited him. He described them as little men about three feet tall, all wearing red stocking caps on their heads. When he began cursing, they went away. And, at a certain time each year in an area near the mines, people were said to have observed a fairy celebration with dancing and merry making.

One miner gives the following vivid account of something that happened while he was working on the surface around 1918:

> Meself and me buddy were working on the buckets one day, you know. We had to wait for the ore to come up and dump it. It's getting on in the morning, and he says to me at about eleven o'clock, "Will you cover for me for ten minutes. I gotta go down in the woods for a while." I said, "Okay, Jim." So he goes on down in the woods. Time goes by. Half an hour, hour. Still no Jim. I says to meself, "That son of a bitch is down there sleeping." So I rounded up a couple of me buddies and we went down for him, but we couldn't find him So we came back and told the foreman on the job, and he goes and tells the big boss. I can't, remember his name now. Anyway, this is something big now, you know, cause Jim was never one to run away from work The boss comes and forms a search party of about fifty men and we still couldn't find him. Then he sent someone to get the police. It wasn't the RCMP then. It was

the local fellers. My son, we searched high and low. Had people come from town and everything but, you know, we couldn't find Jim.

This kept up for two or three days. Then one day when I was back to work, up walked Jim outta the woods, beaming like an electric bulb. I says, "Where have you been?" He says, "Where have I been? I been down in the woods. That's where I been. Sorry to be so long but, Jesus, no need to be mad. I was only gone an hour. I just met the nicest little people. You go on to lunch now and I'll take over." "Take over," says I. "You son of a….where have you been this past three days? We was all worried to death over you." "What are you talking about?' says Jim "Tis only twelve o'clock. Listen. There goes the whistle." And so it was twelve o'clock, but three days later.

Jim was telling me later that he met a whole pile of little people, and they had food and beer and danced and played the accordion. Real friendly, he said. Well, it was some going on when everyone found out he was back, cause we all thought he was dead, you see. After falling off the back of the Island or something. Yes sir, he was the only one that was ever treated that good by the fairies. But people always thought him a little queer after that. And you know, he swore that was the truth right up until he died. And you know something else? I believe him.

The Miner, Bell Island, Newfoundland

Save Our Ghosts
For David Elliot

John Steffler

they used to be all around when
I was young
ghosts of the French, the Basques
the Beothuks
    not to mention our families' ghosts
they didn't seem dead at all
by comparison

at first when I'd noticed
they'd gone,
I thought it was the electric lights
had scared them away

but now I figure it's
electricity itself they don't like
radio and t.v. waves
cut them up
crowd them out

they can't compete with
our loud factory-made ghosts
Archie and Edith, the Flintstones
Hockey Night in Canada
bellering and knocking them about
a hell of a lot more frightening
than the old kind

and now they're driven away
to the bogs and barrens
and God knows where
standing around in gloomy groups
lonely and cold

how it must hurt
to be replaced by this noisy yammering!

how despicable
we must seem—
to have rejected all the fields
and riches of their ancient laughter
their gripping love
their dying

we've got to organize,
      those of us who see what's happening,
campaign to let the old ones back

or soon enough
we'll all be out there with them
in the cold

"and now they're driven away"

Our New Flag

In this flag, the primary colours of red, gold, and blue are placed against a background of white to allow the design to stand out clearly. White is representative of snow and ice; blue represents the sea; red represents human effort and gold our confidence in ourselves.

The blue section, most reminiscent of the Union Jack, represents our Commonwealth heritage which has so decisively shaped our present. The red and gold section, larger than the other, represents our future. The two triangles outlined in red portray the mainland and island parts of our province reaching forward together. A golden arrow points the way to what we believe will be a bright future.

But the design of the flag encompasses much more symbolism than this. For example, the Christian Cross, the Beothuck and Naskaupi ornamentation, the outline of the maple leaf in the centre of the flag, a triumphant figure and our place in the space age. The image of a trident stands out. This is to emphasize our continued dependence on the fishery and the resources of the sea.

Hung as a banner, the arrow assumes the aspect of a sword which is to remind us of the sacrifice of our war veterans.

Since the whole flag resembles a Beothuck pendant as well as all of the above, the design takes us from our earliest beginnings and points us confidently forward. It therefore, mirrors our pasts, present and future.

Newfoundland flag.

Labrador Flag

This flag is meant to be a permanent declaration of the unique identity of the people of Labrador and their common heritage. The top white bar represents the snows, the one element which, more than any other, coloured our culture and dictated our lifestyles. The bottom blue bar represents the waters of our rivers, lakes and oceans. The waters have been our highways, like the snows, and nurtured our fish and wildlife. The centre green bar represents the land. The green and bountiful land is the connecting element that unites our three diverse cultures.

The symbolic spruce twig was chosen because the spruce tree is the one thing that is common to all geographic areas of Labrador. It has provided our shelter, transport, fuel, and, in an indirect way, our food and clothing since the spruce forests became the environment for the wildlife which gave us meat for our tables, skins for our clothing and trade. It was from the spruce that we sawed our planks and timber for our boats, komatiks and houses.

The three branches of the spruce twig represent the three races, the Inuit, the Indian and the European settlers. The twig growing from one stalk represents the common origin of the people regardless of race. The twig is in two sections, or year's growths. The outer growth is longer than the inner growth. This occurs because in the good growing years the twig grows longer than in the poor years. Thus, the inner and shorter sprig reminds us of times past, while the longer sprig represents our hope for the future. This is our flag and symbol of faith in ourselves and the future, our pride of our heritage and our respect for the land and the dignity of people.

Labrador flag.

Ode to Newfoundland
Sir Cavendish Boyle

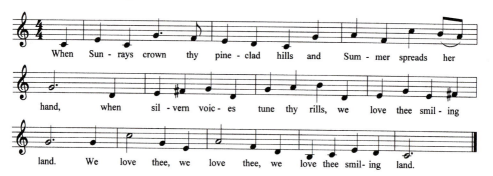

When spreads thy cloak of shimm'ring white,
At Winter's stern command,
Thro' shortened days and starlit nights,
We love thee frozen land,
We love thee, we love thee,
We love thee frozen land.

When blinding storm gusts fret thy shore,
And wild waves lash thy strand,
Thro' sprindrift swirl and tempest roar,
We love thee wind-swept land,
We love thee, we love thee,
We love thee wind-swept land.

As loved our fathers so we love,
Where once they stood we stand,
Their prayer we raise to heav'n above,
God guard thee, Newfoundland,
God guard thee, God guard thee,
God guard thee, Newfoundland.

Ode to Labrador

Lyrics: Dr. H. L. Paddon
Music: Shirley Montague

Dear land of mountains, woods and snow, Our Labrador; God's noble gifts to us we know, Our Labrador. Thy proud resources waiting still, their splendid task will soon fulfill, Obedient to thy maker's will. Our Labrador.

Thy stately forests soon shall ring,
Labrador our Labrador.
Responsive to the woodsman's swing,
Labrador our Labrador.
And mighty floods that long remained, their
raging fury unrestrained
Shall serve the purpose God ordained,
Labrador our Labrador.

We love to climb thy mountains steep,
Labrador our Labrador.
Or paddle on thy waters deep,
Labrador our Labrador.
Our snowshoes scar the trackless plains, we seek
no city streets nor lanes.
We are thy sons while life remains,
Labrador our Labrador.

Author Index

Barker, A. 113
Barry, Anne Meredith 264, 265
Bell Island Murals Assoc. 287
Benson, David 122
Boland, Grant 149
Boyle, Cavendish 292
BBL Archives 57, 66, 96, 105, 135, 211, 214, 220, 259, 263, 273, 282, 289
Brookes, Chris 52
Brown, Cassie 156
Buddy Wasisname 59
Byrne, Joe 24
Byrne, Pat 24
Campbell, Lydia 23
Cartwright, George 12
Chaulk, Byron 13
Chaulk, Wayne 56
Chaulk-Murray, Hilda 131
Chubbs, Boyd 10, 11, 33, 44, 51, 52, 53, 54, 79, 82, 125, 129, 156, 160, 196, 200, 224, 225, 229, 243, 246, 253
Churchill Falls LC, Ltd. 20
Clark, Joan 215
Cooper, S. R. (Bert) 195
Crummey, Michael 55, 263
Davidge, Bud 276
Dawe, Tom 266
Devine, John V. 112
Devine, P. K. 204
Duncan, Norman 44
Editors 42
Elliott, David L. 223
English, Anastasia 138
Evans, Jerry 68, 69
Evening Telegram, The 172
Fitzpatrick, R. J. coll. 258, 260
Fogwill, Irving 121, 225
Fowler, Adrian 119
Fox, Matthew 178
Gale, Donald 108
Goodridge, Edythe Ryan 176
Government of Nf. & Lab. 290, 291
Grenfell Handicrafts 21
Guy, Ray 102, 105
Harrington, Michael 222
Hayashida, David 62
Hennessey, Bryan 196

House, Douglas 166
Hunter, A. C. 191
Igloliorte, Susie 21
James, Cary S. 256, 257
Joe, Michael 70
King's Point Pottery 62, 63
Lannon, Alice 274
Lawrence, Ruth 137
Learning, Ellen 278
Learning, Samson 279
LeDrew, Lisa 168
Legge, Valerie 221
Lehr, Genevieve 170
Lethbridge, Neil 278
Lewis, Shannon L. 148, 261
Loder, Millicent (Blake) 25
Lynch, Gilbert 173
McCarthy, Mike 274
Magnusson, Magnus 207
Massie, Mike 179, 183
McGrath, Carmelita 64
Miller, Elizabeth Russell 85
Miller, Florence P. 206
Minty, Dennis 33
Mitchell, Gerald 13
Montague, Shirley 293
Montgomerie, Stuart 168
Mooers, Vernon 239
Moorehouse, Shirley 22
Morgan, Bernice 243, 247
Moss, Bruce 171
O'Flaherty, Patrick 186
O'Neill-Yates, Chris 73, 201
Paddon, H. L. 293
Pálsson, Hermann 207
Paterson, Mike 116
Peacock, Kenneth 283
Peddle, Walter 114
Pittman, Al 118
Pollett, Ron 270
Poole, Cyril 34
Popova, Elena 230, 231
Porter, Bruce 249
Pottle, Herbert Lench 77
Power, Don 241
Power, Gregory 152, 175
Pratt, Christopher 60, 124
Pretty, Lloyd 109

Provincial Archives   157
Ricks, Brian   115, 116, 117
Rodgers, Gordon   111
Ronan, Tim   236
Rose, Clyde   24, 233
Roy, Jean-Claude   43
Russell, Ted   90, 91
Saunders, Lois   28, 29, 30, 31, 61, 67, 123, 203, 240, 255
Scammell, Arthur   95
Smith, Ed   106
Soper-Cook, JoAnne   125
Squires, Gerald   28
Squires, Harold   161
Stagg, Bruce   97
Steffler, John   32, 288
Story, George   93, 212, 213
Strong, Joan   163
Strong, Scott   33
Strowbridge, Nellie   120
Them Days   17
Tobin, Kevin   94, 242
Traditional   136
Vaughan-Jackson, Mark   58
Wade, James   253
Walsh, Agnes   130
Walsh, Peter   232
Watts, Enos   165
Weir, Gail   284
White, Winston   14
Whiteley, George C.   280
Winter, Kathleen   65, 70
Winter, Nellie   22
Wiseman, Ian   240
Yates, Linda   62

Title Index

Above the Harbour 64
Address to Convocation 176
Afraid in the Dark! 270
An Interview with Mike Massie 178
An old fishing stage 66
"and now they're driven away" 289
Anne Stine Ingstad 213
Appeal to Parnassus 121
Aquaforte 67
Away to the North 10
Away to the North: A Landscape
    is Singing 10
The Badger Drive 112
Barry (Artist's Statement) 264
Battle Harbour 31
Beaumont Hamel 43
Big Davey's Maxims 206
Black Coral 233
Boarding School in Muddy Bay 25
Bogwood 175
Bottle Cove 31
"Bounded above by the sky..." 263
Branch 203
Brigus 30
Bucket, Grub box / Lunch bucket,
    piggin 117
Buddy and the Other Fellers 58
But Who Cares Now? (Excerpt) 166
Call Me an Indian: The Calvin White Story 73
Canadien Cultural Games 236
Captain Kirk Surveys the Seal Hunt 163
The *Caribou* Disaster 156
Cartoon 94
Carved washstand 117
Child's duffle coat 22
Chimney Cove 105
Chrome tourmaline brooch 257
Coastal Journey #2: Past the Dog Islands 265
Commentary on the Will of
    Sir James Pearl 260
Cry, My Chest Hurts 231
d'Lard Liftin' 59
Dark woods and winter gales 273
December hockey 240
Detail from Grenfell parka 21
Didymus on Saturday 223
Dunville 255
Edward Russell 93

Eiriksdottir (Excerpt) 215
Evans (Artist's Statement) 68
Exploits 30
Fair Marjorie's Ghost 283
A Fairy Tale 106
Final remnant of the *Ocean Ranger* 172
The First Good Friday 222
Fog, This Time 33
François 29
French's Cove, Bay Roberts 43
The Fruits of Toil 44
Gaia off L'Anse aux Meadows 220
George Cartwright - circa 1790 12
The Ghost of the Murdered Cook 274
Ghostly Yarns of Ishmael Drake 266
Harbour Le Cou 136
A Harmless Deception 138
"Hauled up and rotting..." 96
Hebron 29
Helge & Anne Stine Ingstad 211
Helge Marcus Ingstad 212
Her Mark 263
High on the Mountain of Old Mokami 13
Hockey Night in Canada 239
Hockey Then…And Now… 242
Humour: Forms and Functions 77
Iceberg 120
Illustrations by Boyd Chubbs 51, 129, 160,
    200, 224, 229, 246
In My Dream, We were Together as One 183
Inglewood's Childhood Beach 195
Interior Viking Longhouse 214
Interview with Grant Boland 148
Inuit woman with toddler 17
Inukuluk Designs 21
James (Artist's Statement) 256
Jeremiah the Bandmaster 17
Jethro Noddy 90
Journals "Sixth Voyage" (Excerpts) 12
Keels dish dresser 115
King David 91
King's Point Pottery 62
Know Me, Know You 69
Labrador Flag 291
Labrador Flag 291
Labrador Footprints (Excerpts) 14
Labrador travelling box 115
The Land God Gave to Cain 24

The Life and Times of Ted Russell
   (Excerpts) 85
The Listeners 225
Little Orly 196
Lobster pots 282
The Loss of the *Marion* 276
Marriage 131
Middle Son 186
The Miner, Bell Island Newfoundland 287
Miners 55
The Miners of Wabana (Excerpt) 284
Mining 124
The Money Crowd 125
Mosey 108
Mosey 109
My ancestor was a shaman 22
Newfoundland Flag 290
Newfoundland Outport Furniture 114
Newfoundland Sealing Disaster 165
Ocean Ranger monument and plaque 168
Ode to Newfoundland 292
Ode to Labrador 293
Old Bonaventure 255
The Old *Royal Readers* 191
Our New Flag 290
The Outdoor Motor 95
The Oyster 232
Paterson Woodworking
   (Artist's Statement) 116
Paterson Woodworking showroom 116
The Phantom Iceberg 119
Pictures 243
Playing Around With Time (Excerpt) 249
The Poor We Have With Us Always 102
Powerhouse – Churchill Falls (Labrador) 20
The Price of Bread 152
Profile: Jean-Claude Roy 42
Proverbs and Sayings 204
Popova (Artist's Statement) 230
Recipe 111
Required Reading 122
River Man 221
A River Runs Through Her 118
Rodway's Point 61
Rocking chair 117
S. S. *Caribou* and Captain Ben Tavenor 157
S. S. *Eagle*: The Secret Mission
   1944-45 161

St. John's 240
St. John's shrouded in fog 33
St. Mary's Keys 280
Saltwater Joys 56
The Savage Cove Devil 278
The Savage Cove Devil 278
The Savage Cove Devil 279
Save Our Ghosts 288
September 149
Sesame and Lilies: Tattered Treasure 253
Sharpening a traditional bucksaw 113
Shell plate 63
Should Pro Athletes Be Unionized? 241
Snowy Owl 179
The Soul of a Newfoundlander 34
Special DADication 94
Sterling silver ring 256
Sterling silver brooch 257
Strip-mined 60
This Dear and Fine Country 105
The Time That Passes 130
Those Thirsty Critters 173
To See Things and to Understand 23
Towers and Monuments 32
Traditional Spiritualism 70
Trouty 123
Two Dresses from St. Pierre 137
Uncle Mark White's Rat 97
Untitled by Kathleen Winter 70
Up Off Our Knees (Excerpt) 201
The Vinland Sagas (Excerpts) 207
The Voice of Dinah 65
Waiting for Time (Excerpt) 247
Wedding photo, 1940 135
Whale and wave bowl 62
Whale and waves tableware 63
What Happened Was….(Excerpts) 52
When Orchards Green 170
Where They Built Their Lives 28
Will of Peter Weston 258
Will of John James, Trinity 261
Winter scene, western Newfoundland 259
Winter view of Bonne Bay 57
Wise to Who From Within 183
Your Last Goodbye 171

Text Credits

ABOVE THE HARBOUR by Carmelita McGrath. Reprinted by permission of Killick Press. Originally published in *Poems on Land and on Water.*

ADDRESS TO CONVOCATION by Edythe Ryan Goodridge. Reprinted by permission of the author.

AFRAID IN THE DARK by Ron Pollett. Reprinted by permission of Flanker Press. Originally published in *The Outport Millionaire.*

AN INTERVIEW WITH MIKE MASSIE by Matthew Fox. Reprinted by permission of *Inuit Art Quarterly.*

ANNE STINE INGSTAD by George Story. Reprinted by permission of the Estate of George Story.

APPEAL TO PARNASSUS by Iriving Fogwill. Reprinted by permission of Sylvia Thomas, for the Estate of the late Irving Fogwill.

AWAY TO THE NORTH: A LANDSCAPE IS SINGING. by Boyd Warren Chubbs. Reprinted by permission of the author.

ARTIST'S STATEMENT by Anne Meredith Barry. Reprinted by permission of the author.

ARTIST'S STATEMENT by Jerry Evans. Reprinted by permission of the author.

ARTIST'S STATEMENT by Cary S. James. Reprinted by permission of the author.

ARTIST'S STATEMENT by Mike Paterson. Reprinted by permission of the author.

ARTIST'S STATEMENT by Elena Popova. Reprinted by permission of the author.

BIG DAVEY'S MAXIMS by Florence P. Miller. Reprinted by permission of Doug Strong.

BLACK CORAL by Clyde Rose. Reprinted by permission of the author. Originally published in *Christ in the Pizza Place.*

BOARDING SCHOOL IN MUDDY BAY by Millicent (Blake) Loder. Reprinted by permission of *Them Days Magazine.*

BOGWOOD by Gregory Power. Reprinted by permission of Gregory Power Jr. Originally published in *Choice Poems from the Newfoundland Quarterly.*

BUDDY AND THE OTHER FELLERS by Mark Vaughan Jackson. Reprinted courtesy of *The Telegram.*

BUT WHO CARES NOW? by Douglas House. Reprinted by permission of the author.

CALL ME AN INDIAN: THE CALVIN WHITE STORY by Chris O'Neill-Yates. Reprinted by permission of the Canadian Broadcasting Corporation.

CANADIEN CULTURAL GAMES by Tim Ronan. Reprinted by permission of the author.

CAPTAIN KIRK SURVEYS THE SEAL HUNT by Joan Strong. Reprinted by permission of the author.

THE CARIBOU DISASTER by Cassie Brown. Reprinted by permission of Flanker Press.

COMMENTARY ON THE WILL OF SIR JAMES PEARL by R.J. Fitzpatrick. Reprinted by permission of the author.

DECEMBER HOCKEY by Ian Wiseman. Reprinted by permission of the author.

DIDYMUS ON SATURDAY by David L. Elliott. Reprinted by permission of the author.

EDWARD RUSSELL by George Story. Reprinted by permission of the Estate of George Story.

EIRIKSDOTTIR by Joan Clark. Reprinted by permission of the author.

A FAIRY TALE by Ed Smith. Reprinted by permission of the author.

THE FIRST GOOD FRIDAY by Michael Harrington. Reprinted by permission of Michael Harrington Q.C.

FOG, THIS TIME by Scott Strong. Reprinted by permission of Colin Scott Strong.

THE GHOST OF THE MURDERED COOK by Alice Lannon and Mike McCarthy. Reprinted by permission of Mike McCarthy.

GHOSTLY YARNS OF ISHMAEL DRAKE by Tom Dawe. Reprinted by permission of the author.

HELGE MARCUS INGSTAD by George Story. Reprinted by permission of the Estate of George Story.

HER MARK by Michael Crummey. Reprinted by permission of Brick Books. Originally published in *Hard Light* ©Brick Books, 1998.

HIGH ON THE MOUNTAIN OF OLD MOKAMI by Byron Chaulk and Gerald Mitchell. Reprinted by permission of Gerald Mitchell.

HOCKEY NIGHT IN CANADA by Vernon Mooers. Reprinted by permission of Killick Press. Originally published in *Gypsy Hymns* ©Killick Press, 1993.

HUMOUR: FORMS AND FUNCTIONS by Herbert Lench Pottle. Reprinted by permission of Helen L Wesanko.

ICEBERG by Nellie Strowbridge. Reprinted by permission of the author. Originally published in *Shadows of the Heart* ©Jesperson Publishing, ©1995.

INGLEWOOD'S CHILDHOOD BEACH by S.R. (Bert) Cooper. Reprinted by permission of Harry Cuff Publications.

INTERVIEW WITH GRANT BOLAND by Shannon Lewis. Reprinted by permission of the author.

INUKULUK DESIGNS by Susan Igloliorte. Reprinted by permission of *Them Days Magazine*.

JETHRO NODDY by Ted Russell. Reprinted by permission of Elizabeth Miller.

KING DAVID by Ted Russell. Reprinted by permission of Elizabeth Miller.

KING'S POINT POTTERY by Linda Yates and David Hayashida. Reprinted by permission of David Hayashida.

LABRADOR FOOTPRINTS (EXCERPTS) by Winston White. Reprinted by permission of the author.

THE LAND GOD GAVE TO CAIN by Byrne, Byrne and Rose. Reprinted by permission of the authors.

THE LIFE AND TIMES OF TED RUSSELL (EXCERPTS) by Elizabeth Miller. Reprinted by permission of the author.

THE LISTENERS by Irving Fogwill. Reprinted by permission of Sylvia Thomas, for the Estate of the late Irving Fogwill.

LITTLE ORLY by Bryan Hennessey. Reprinted by permission of Killick Press. Originally published in *Waking Up in the City of Dreams* ©Killick Press, 1993.

THE LOSS OF THE *MARION* by Bud Davidge. Reprinted by permission of the author.

MARRIAGE by Hilda Chaulk-Murray. Reprinted by permission of the author.

MIDDLE SON by Patrick O'Flaherty. Reprinted by permission of the author.

MINERS by Michael Crummey. Reprinted by permission of Brick Books. Originally published in *Hard Light* ©Brick Books, 1998.

THE MINERS OF WABANA (EXCERPT) by Gail Weir. Reprinted by permission of the author.

MINING by Christopher Pratt. Reprinted by permission of the author.

THE MONEY CROWD by JoAnne Soper-Cook. Reprinted by permission of the author.

MOSEY by Donald Gale. Reprinted by permission of The Southwest Cabot 500 Committee.

NEWFOUNDLAND OUTPORT FURNITURE by Walter Peddle. Reprinted by permission of Walter Peddle - Curator Emeritus, Newfoundland Museum.

NEWFOUNDLAND SEALING DISASTER by Enos Watts. Reprinted by permission of the author.

THE OLD *ROYAL READERS* by A.C. Hunter. Reprinted by permission of Breakwater Books.

THE OUTDOOR MOTOR by Arthur Scammell. Reprinted by permission of Carrie Scammell.

THE OYSTER by Peter Walsh. Reprinted by permission of the author.

THE PHANTOM ICEBERG by Adrian Fowler. Reprinted by permission of the author.

PICTURES by Bernice Morgan. Reprinted by permission of the author.

PLAYING AROUND WITH TIME (EXCERPT) by Bruce Porter. Reprinted by permission of the author.

THE POOR WE HAVE WITH US ALWAYS by Ray Guy. Reprinted by permission of the author.

THE PRICE OF BREAD by Gregory Power. Reprinted by permission of Gregory Power Jr.

PROFILE: JEAN CLAUDE ROY by the Editors. Reprinted by permission of the authors.

RECIPE by Gordon Rodgers. Reprinted by permission of the author.

REQUIRED READING by David Benson. Reprinted by permission of the author.

RIVER MAN by Valerie Legge. Reprinted by permission of the author.

A RIVER RUNS THROUGH HER by Al Pittman. Reprinted by permission of Breakwater Books.

S. S. EAGLE: *THE SECRET MISSION 1944 - 45* by Harold Squires. Reprinted by permission of the author.

ST. MARY'S KEYS: A STORY OF THE SUPERNATURAL by Capt. George Whiteley. Reprinted by permission of Stark Whiteley.

SALTWATER JOYS by Wayne Chaulk. Reprinted by permission of the author.

THE SAVAGE COVE DEVIL by Ellen Learning. Reprinted by permission of *Them Days Magazine*.

THE SAVAGE COVE DEVIL by Neil Lethbridge. Reprinted by permission of *Them Days Magazine*.

THE SAVAGE COVE DEVIL by Samson Learning. Reprinted by permission of *Them Days Magazine*.

SAVE OUR GHOSTS by John Steffler. Reprinted by permission of the author.

SESAME AND LILIES: TATTERED TREASURE by James Wade. Reprinted by permission of Kathleen Winter.

SHOULD PRO ATHLETES BE UNIONIZED? by Don Power. Reprinted by permission of *The Express*/Robinson Blackmore Printing and Publishing.

THE SOUL OF A NEWFOUNDLANDER by Cyril Poole. Reprinted by permission of Harry Cuff Publications.

SPECIAL *DADICATION* by Kevin Tobin. Reprinted by permission of the author.

STRIP-MINED by Christopher Pratt. Reprinted by permission of the author.

THIS DEAR AND FINE COUNTRY by Ray Guy. Reprinted by permission of the author.

THE TIME THAT PASSES by Agnes Walsh. Reprinted by permission of the author.

THOSE THIRSTY CRITTERS by Gilbert Lynch. Reprinted by permission of Violet Lynch. Originally published in *Changing Scenes* ©Cuff Publications, 1987.

TO SEE THINGS AND TO UNDERSTAND by Lydia Campbell. Reprinted by permission of *Them Days Magazine*.

TOWERS AND MONUMENTS by John Steffler. Reprinted by permission of McClelland and Stewart Ltd. Originally published in *The Wreckage of Play* ©1988.

TRADITIONAL SPIRITUALISM by Michael Joe. Reprinted by permission of Newfoundland and Labrador Human Rights Association.

TWO DRESSES FROM ST. PIERRE by Ruth Lawrence. Reprinted by permission of the author.

UNCLE MARK WHITE'S RAT by Bruce Stagg. Reprinted by permission of the author. Originally published in *The Crowd From Roaring Cove* ©Creative Book Publishers, 1997.

UP OFF OUR KNEES (EXCERPT) by Chris O'Neill-Yates. Reprinted by permission of the Canadian Broadcasting Corporation.

THE VINLAND SAGAS (EXCERPTS) by Magnus Magnusson. Reprinted by permission of Penguin Books, UK.

THE VOICE OF DINAH by Kathleen Winter. Reprinted by permission of the Newfoundland and Labrador Human Rights Association.

WAITING FOR TIME (EXCERPT) by Bernice Morgan. Reprinted by permission of Breakwater Books.

WHAT HAPPENED WAS... (EXCERPTS) by Chris Brookes. Reprinted by permission of the author.

WHEN ORCHARDS GREEN by Genevieve Lehr. Reprinted by permission of the author.

WHERE THEY BUILT THEIR LIVES by Lois Saunders. Reprinted by permission of the author.

WILL OF PETER WESTON collected by R. J. Fitzpatrick. Reprinted by permission of the Newfoundland and Labrador Genealogical Society.

WILL OF JOHN JAMES, TRINITY collected by R. J. Fitzpatrick. Reprinted by permission of the Newfoundland and Labrador Genealogical Society.

YOUR LAST GOODBYE by Bruce Moss. Reprinted by permission of the author..

Visual Credits

Music prepared by Fergus O'Byrne

All page bars and mats on the following pages created by Lois Saunders: 28, 29, 30, 31, 61, 67, 123, 203, 240, 255

Illustrations on the following pages custom created by Boyd Warren Chubbs: 10, 11, 33, 44, 51, 52, 53, 54, 79, 82, 125, 129, 156, 160, 196, 200, 224, 225, 229, 243, 246, 253

17: Courtesy of *Them Days Magazine*; **20**: CFLC Ltd.; **21**: Contributed by Grenfell Handicrafts (1984) Ltd.; **22**: (top) Courtesy of Nellie Winter; (bottom) Courtesy of Shirley Moorehouse; **33**: A Dennis Minty photo; **43**: Courtesy of Jean-Claude Roy; **57**: Breakwater Archives; **59**: Wayne Chaulk (Buddy Wasisname and the Other Fellers); **62-63**: Courtesy of King's Point Pottery; **66**: Breakwater Archives; **69**: Courtesy of Christina Parker Gallery. Photography by Terry Upshall; **70**: Reprinted by permission of the Newfoundland and Labrador Human Rights Association; **94**: Courtesy of Kevin Tobin; **96**: Breakwater Archives; **105**: Breakwater Archives; **109**: From original work by NFLD artist Lloyd Pretty; **113**: A. Barker/Breakwater Archives; **115-117**: Photography by Brian Ricks; **135**: Breakwater Archives; **149**: Kind permission of the artist and Christina Parker Gallery. Photo by Ned Pratt; **157**: Courtesy of Provincial Archives of Newfoundland and Labrador; **168** Photos by Lisa LeDrew; **172**: Courtesy of *The Evening Telegram*; **179**: Courtesy of Mike Massie; **183**: Courtesy of Mike Massie; **211**: Breakwater Archives; **214**: Courtesy of the Government of NF, Department of Tourism; **220**: Breakwater Archives; **231**: Courtesy of Elena Popova; **242**: Courtesy of Kevin Tobin; **254**: Breakwater Archives; **256-257**: Photos by Mary James; **259**: Breakwater Archives; **263**: Breakwater Archives; **265**: Courtesy of the artist and the Emma Butler Gallery; **273**: Breakwater Archives; **282**: Breakwater Archives; **287**: Courtesy of the Bell Island Murals Association; **289**: Breakwater Archives; **291**: Photo by Ray Fennelly;